Lifetime

Encyclopedia of

Letters

REVISED
— AND —
EXPANDED

HAROLD E. MEYER

PRENTICE HALL

Library of Congress Cataloging-in-Publication Data

Meyer, Harold E.
      Lifetime encyclopedia of letters / Harold E. Meyer. — Rev. & expanded.
         p. cm.
      Includes index.
      ISBN 0-13-921065-2. — ISBN 0-7352-0034-3
      1. Letter writing. 2. Commercial correspondence. .I. Title.
PE1483.M43   1998
    808.6—dc21   98-27538
                                              CIP

Acquisitions Editor: *Tom Power*
Production Editor: *Eve Mossman*
Formatting/Interior Design: *Robyn Beckerman*

© *1998 by Prentice Hall, Inc.*

All rights reserved. No part of this book may be reproduced in any form or by any means, without permission in writing from the publisher.

Printed in the United States of America

10 9 8 7 6 5 4 3 2 1

ISBN 0-7352-0034-3

ATTENTION: CORPORATIONS AND SCHOOLS

Prentice Hall books are available at quantity discounts with bulk purchase for educational, business, or sales promotional use. For information, please write to: Prentice Hall Special Sales, 240 Frisch Court, Paramus, New Jersey 07652. Please supply: title of book, ISBN, quantity, how the book will be used, date needed.

PRENTICE HALL PRESS
Paramus, NJ 07652

A Simon & Schuster Company

On the World Wide Web at http://www.phdirect.com

Prentice Hall International (UK) Limited, *London*
Prentice Hall of Australia Pty. Limited, *Sydney*
Prentice Hall Canada, Inc., *Toronto*
Prentice Hall Hispanoamericana, S.A., *Mexico*
Prentice Hall of India Private Limited, *New Delhi*
Prentice Hall of Japan, Inc., *Tokyo*
Simon & Schuster Asia Pte. Ltd., *Singapore*
Editora Prentice Hall do Brasil, Ltda., *Rio de Janeiro*

TO IRMA

About the Author

Harold E. Meyer is an industrial accountant with a lifelong passion for words and the shades of meaning they convey. For over thirty years in business, Mr. Meyer collected, analyzed, and rewrote scores of fuzzily written letters and directives that crossed his desk. He is also a former newsletter editor. Now to assist letter writers who wish to write clearly, gracefully, and effectively, he has assembled his years of research into this lifetime volume.

How You Will Benefit from This Book

Do you sit down to write a letter and wonder, "Just what is it I'm trying to say, and how should I say it?"

Is your letter clear enough that you can confidently omit the popular last sentence that reads, "If you have any questions, please call me?"

How do you reprimand an employee, to "put him in his place," and still inspire him to improve?

When you have to terminate an employee, how do you write a letter that does the job and still remains a model of fairness?

Can you apologize appropriately to your boss after demeaning her at the company party?

If your lifelong friend were to die, what would you write to his or her spouse?

When your church asked you to write a fund-raising letter did you panic?

Complete Range of Categories

These and many other questions are answered in the *Lifetime Encyclopedia of Letters*, which covers 625 separate categories of letters, including:

Thanking a person
- For being our customer
- For helping my career
- For doing a job well
- For accounting help

Congratulating a person
- Upon graduating
- Upon receiving a promotion
- Upon exceeding a sales goal
- Upon marrying

Selling

- A sales-promotion book
- A loaf of bread
- An executive-search service

Raising funds

- For churches
- For hospitals
- For schools
- For mentally retarded
- For runaway children

Hunting for a job

- Using résumés
- Using application letters
- Using interviews
- Using references
- Using help-wanted ads

Collecting accounts

- By reminding gently
- By appealing to fear
- By taking legal action

Requesting favors

- To alleviate fear
- To find a job for my relative

Requesting information

- About a warranty
- About a claim
- About an investigation
- About a chemical hazard

Providing information

- For claims against the city
- For instructions not followed
- For a price increase

Answering complaints
- About a misunderstanding
- About a faulty product
- About a foreign object in food

Making complaints
- About transit damage
- About billing errors
- About misrepresentation

Reprimanding an employee
- For uncleanliness
- For misconduct

Refusing
- A request for credit
- A job applicant
- A donation or gift
- A volunteer's help

Apologizing
- For ignoring a customer
- For failure to complete a project
- For behaving indiscreetly

Expressing sympathy
- To the spouse of the deceased
- To a relative upon the death of an employee
- To a mother of a defective child

If you need help with your writing in these or in any other areas, this encyclopedia gives you that help.

We Can All Use Help

Many writers of business letters and reports need direction because their compositions are too often disorganized, wordy, and unclear.

Note the lack of clarity in the following true example written by a college graduate employed by a manufacturer:

Subject: Special instructions regarding order No. 98227.

In order to complete orders 99411 and 99412, please ship 98727 as close to equal amounts of A, B, and C as possible.

What was the shipping clerk to do? Obviously, call the writer of the instructions—valuable production time spent clarifying a written communication. The growing emphasis on speed in communication requires letters the reader can understand clearly the first time.

Among the many aids to easier and better writing, the *Lifetime Encyclopedia of Letters* shows you how to write an interest-arousing first sentence, to write a persuasive closing sentence, to be polite yet positive, to solve the problem of saying "no," to be encouraging, to complain, to make a sales letter sell, to open the pocketbook of a potential contributor, to collect money, to organize your thoughts, to retain the reader's goodwill, to fire an employee, to express true sympathy, to take your guilt out of an apology, and to get action from your request. Just locate your topic, read the lead-in comments, and follow the model letter.

Easy-to-Follow Models

All the model letters in this encyclopedia are written in current, up-to-date language. Letters of long ago that were once considered standards of good writing but contain outdated expressions do not appear.

Many of the examples can be nearly copied. Only the change of a name or a few words is required to turn a sample into your own personal letter. You may want to take a sentence or two from one letter and additional sentences from others, creating a letter you prefer to any of the models.

But what can you do if you want to create your own letter? For each type of letter there is a basic outline called "How to Do It."

How-to-Do-It Outline

One special feature of this encyclopedia that helps you organize your thoughts is the "How to Do It" section preceding each group of model letters. This feature is a step-by-step outline for your letters. Using these steps, you will be able to include all the essential parts of your message and eliminate any unnecessary digressions.

For example, the "How to Do It" section for a letter of encouragement lists these four steps:

1. Admit that an adverse condition exists.
2. Name the condition or problem.
3. Indicate your conviction that the condition can be overcome.
4. Suggest how to overcome the condition.

Note how smoothly the following letter fits the outline, without sounding as if it were chopped into four separate pieces.

> Teaching at P.S. 24 is a difficult assignment for any teacher, and even the most seasoned instructors often find the integration process takes time. Thus, it comes as no surprise that you have spoken of submitting your resignation at the end of the school year.
>
> Discipline remains a problem for many new teachers here, as you have discovered. Students tend to "test" a teacher. Once the test is passed, however, teachers often find themselves responding with enthusiasm to the challenge.
>
> Please take a little time to reconsider your decision, then see me to discuss the matter at your earliest convenience.

If you can't find a model letter or topic outline for the subject of your letter, this book still helps you.

How to Use This Book When You Can't Find Your Topic

The first step is to determine exactly what your subject is. Are you confusing a thank you with a congratulation or providing information with sales? On the other hand, letters can be categorized many ways, and the letter you are looking for may be found in a related topic. For example, goodwill letters may be combined with a thank you, appreciation, request, apology, or reports. An adjustment letter may be a letter of information, apology, or complaint. Read the introduction and the "How to Do It" section to a related or similar topic. Then, after reading a few model letters, you will have a clear understanding of how to write *your* letter.

When writing to a politician, public-office holder or high-ranking company officer, ask yourself which topic in the table of contents most nearly covers the *subject matter* of your letter.

A common question at this point is, how do I start? This book suggests many beginning and ending sentences.

Beginning and Ending Sentences

A special feature of *Lifetime Encyclopedia of Letters* is the 331 suggested beginning and ending sentences for letters. Often, suggested beginning sentences can give you the necessary impetus to start your letter writing.

Chapter 2, "Declining Requests," suggests that one way to decline a request is to start with a thank you, for example:

Thank you for your recent request for a charge account at Fordham's.

Thank you for your invitation to join the Delta Cost Accountants group.

We appreciate receiving your order for 50,000 boxes.

This chapter offers statements of refusal, and the last step in the "How to Do It" section suggests offering help or encouragement to the reader. Some encouraging statements are listed:

We are interested in your business venture.

Best wishes for success in your campaign.

I wish you well in your program to help these children.

In many letters, the last paragraph or sentence is a summary of the letter, an expression of appreciation, or a call for action, as illustrated by these sales-letter endings:

Your credit is good. Just tell us what you want.

We cut all the red tape—simply mail the card.

If for any reason you're dissatisfied, simply return it . . . and owe nothing.

Our supply is limited. Act now!

Hard-hitting sentences such as these, while usually productive, do not appeal to all readers.

Hard Sell Versus Soft Sell

The variety of approaches within each category is a unique feature of *Lifetime Encyclopedia of Letters.* One fund-raising letter (which is a sales letter with a heart tug) consists of three short sentences:

> You make the difference between mediocrity and excellence.
>
> Think about it.
>
> Your considered gift to the Dorchester Alumni Fund supports the Campaign for Dorchester.

More common is a two- to four-page letter listing numerous reasons to make a donation, one of which the writer hopes will elicit a response from the reader.

Another contrast in presentations included in this book is the soft sell versus the hard sell, different approaches directed to different audiences. One real-estate sales letter begins:

> Once in a lifetime there is a special place.
>
> Reaching a gentle rise overlooking a flowering meadow . . .

A different realtor starts off:

> All fired up.

Contrasts in presentation offer you an opportunity to reach specific audiences. Analysis of appeals to human emotions can also help in directing your letter to a particular audience.

Model Letters Analyzed

For most situations, the explanations, suggested outlines, and analyses will make adapting the model letter easy. The fund-raising letters, for example, may not fit individual needs as precisely as many of the sympathy letters. Sympathy letters are short and general, while fund-raising letters are long and specific. In the latter, money is requested for a particular cause, and many separate reasons to donate can be included in one letter so that at least one will touch the wallet of the reader. Fund-raising letters are outlined, then analyzed to point out what techniques are used in each case. This enables the writer to list appeals, set them into the outline, and write the letter using one or more of the attention-getting techniques shown in the analysis.

One quick way to locate a model for the letter you want to write is to consult the Index.

Easy-to-Use Index

In this reference work, all the information in the Table of Contents can also be found in the Index. Many letters are indexed in several ways: by topic, category within the topic, alternate names for the topic and the category, geographic location, and company name. Having read a letter once, you can locate it in the Index by referring to one of several words. Double indexing is also used. For example, *reader's viewpoint* is indexed under both *reader's* and *viewpoint.*

Lifetime Reference Work

Through the use of suggestions and model letters, this book shows you how to write a letter that accomplishes your intended purpose.

Because the model letters in the encyclopedia are standards and can be adapted to your requirements for many years, this book will become a long-term investment and companion. The range of topics and the variety of treatments within each topic make *Lifetime Encyclopedia of Letters* a reference work that will last a lifetime.

Harold E. Meyer

Contents

Chapter 2   Declining Requests   21

Chapter 3   Sales   51

Chapter 4   Fund Raising 87

Chapter 5   Collection   137

Chapter 6   Information: Providing and Requesting   185

Chapter 7   Complaints: Making and Answering   217

Chapter 8   Employment 247

Chapter 9 Termination and Resignation 295

Chapter 13   Thank-You and Appreciation   375

Chapter 14   Other Business Letters   395

Chapter 15   Other Personal Letters   425

CHAPTER 1

Requesting Favors

Many people find it difficult to make a request that seems to impose upon others. Often, the person asked feels complimented that he or she is considered capable of helping to solve a problem. Therefore, assuming the request is reasonable, you should not be reluctant to ask. When making requests of a sensitive nature, as for a favor or cooperation, you must indicate clearly and persuasively why the request is being made. Let the reader know why you came to him or her for help and how you will use that help.

A letter requesting only information can be short and direct. For example:

We need quarterly SEC reports, our form C-140, for the year _ _ _ _. Submit these by the 20th of the month following each quarter.

A more willing response, however, would be received if the letter were expanded just enough to include an explanation of why the request is being made. A word or two, such as "please" or "would appreciate" is helpful in eliciting the desired response. This is illustrated in the following request that is also short and direct, but adds the reason for the request in a polite tone:

The year-end Tax Requirements report unintentionally omitted charitable contributions.

We would appreciate it if you would provide us with a schedule of donations made during the year showing the donee and the dollar amount.

The key to getting results from a sensitive letter of request is having a persuasive and convincing explanation of the reason for the request. Think before you write: What will appeal to the reader? How are the writer's wants tied to the reader's interests? A request is more willingly granted if the practical psychology of give and take is recognized. The reader may ask, "What's in it for me?" Whenever possible, offer something in return.

One of the model letters asks for financial statements and offers prompt deliveries of future orders upon receiving them. Other letters ask for information, implying that the reader knows more than the writer, and all readers like compliments. One letter requests a stepped-up delivery date for part of an order, "because we don't want to split the order with another supplier." This is not a threat of taking away promised business, but a suggested practical solution to a business problem, and of much interest to the reader. Another letter requesting a favor suggests an exchange of information about manufacturing plant operations. The reader of this letter is interested because he has an opportunity to receive information in exchange for giving information. In one letter a request is made by an alumnus doing research. Being an alumnus and doing research are both topics of interest to the college president to whom the letter is addressed. These offers of something in return or topics of personal interest to the reader can induce the reader to participate willingly.

When asking several questions in one letter, make the response easier by listing and preferably numbering the questions. In this way each specific question will result in a specific answer.

Another technique for getting a positive response is to write to an individual rather than to "Gentlemen." (The names of corporate officers can be found in reference libraries. Another method is to call the office of the person to whom you wish to write.)

When the request is mentioned early in a letter that includes an appeal of more than two sentences, repeat the request at the end. Make the reply easy for the reader by making the request specific and by providing an envelope or an address or a due date.

Never end a letter by saying, "Thanking you in advance" or the shorter "Thank you" or "Thanks." These phrases leave the reader with the feeling that the writer is terminating all interest in the request and that the reader is left to struggle on alone. Rather than ending with a curt "Thank you," make the reader happy to grant your request by clothing it with politeness and appreciation for the expected action. This can be done by using such phrases as, "It would be helpful," or "We would appreciate," or "Please."

Close the letter with confidence. Make no apologies. A letter ending with the statement, "I know you're awfully busy, and I hate to ask you this, but maybe you could find time to check this report for me," is likely to draw the response, "You're right, I don't have time." The ending should indicate confidence that the request will be granted, and it must be stated politely.

Closing a Request with Confidence—Examples

Your answer will be gratefully received.

We appreciate your cooperation.

Please mail the financial statements today.

Receiving a sample drawing would be greatly appreciated.

Please let us know when you can do this.

We will expect your answer soon.

Even a short visit with you will be truly appreciated.

Your answers to the above questions will be of great help to us.

Your filling in the blanks below and returning this letter in the enclosed envelope will be greatly appreciated.

How to Do It

1. Make the request specific, using a polite tone.
2. Explain persuasively the reason for the request.
3. Offer something in return.
4. Show appreciation for the granter's help.

Additional Information

Dear Mr. Hoskins:

Thank you for the operating schedule you made for conducting the market survey we discussed in April. All the bases seem to be covered.

I would like, however, to have you add calendar dates and costs for the various steps you have listed. As we discussed, timeliness is essential. The cost is also important because we have a definite and limited budget for this project.

With the added information on dates and costs, we can make a prompt decision on how to proceed with the survey. We hope to hear from you soon.

Sincerely,

Questionnaire

Dear Mr. Dawson:

Because you are one of our past trainees who has become successful, we recently sent you a questionnaire asking about your work and personal background, your work experience, and your opinions on several related matters.

We are eager to have your reply in order to better understand the characteristics of those entering our training program and to improve our program for future trainees.

If you have already returned your questionnaire, many thanks. If not, we hope you will do so soon.

Sincerely,

Dear Mrs. Testoni:

We are compiling a guide to the promotion of women in top firms in the nation and would appreciate your cooperation in filling out the enclosed questionnaire.

Given the timeliness and current controversy about the subject and the involvement of both Government and women's groups, the answers to our questions will be valuable to women seeking increasingly responsible executive positions.

Because we are already informally aware of your company's progressive policy, your response will be particularly encouraging.

Any additional information and comments you can provide will be appreciated.

Sincerely,

Consumer Survey

Dear Mr. Summers:

Thank you for taking the time to talk with us on the phone recently and for agreeing to participate in our survey.

We have sent one questionnaire to be filled out by each member of your household, twelve years of age and older. Please fill out the enclosed material and return it in the envelope provided as soon as possible. No postage is necessary.

We hope that you will enjoy participating in this survey. Your answers will become an important part of our scientific study.

Please accept the enclosed token of our sincere appreciation for your cooperation.

Sincerely yours,

Response to Inquiry

Dear Emil:

You should receive a phone call next week from our Washington headquarters. Please make every effort to supply them with the information they have requested from your plant.

The main office is drawing up a company profile. The exposure provided by our data should be beneficial for both the plant image and the individual personnel involved.

I look forward to seeing your response.

Regards,

Procedural Change

Dear Amos:

It seems there is a breakdown in procedures between our departments. We are not getting all the receiving records for scrap that your department receives after our department orders it. When inquiries are made directly to your receiving clerk, he complains that apparently he doesn't get all the copies of our orders to match with his receipts.

We have learned that our orders are sent through the company mail with the receiving clerk's name written in no particular place on them. Now we have instructed our order clerk to mail these in an intracompany envelope. This should eliminate misdirection of the mail.

Could you have your receiving clerk mail the receiving records to our department in an intracompany envelope? Please send them to the attention of Bob Smyth.

Sincerely,

Rescheduling Order

Dear Carl:

On July 24 we sent you our purchase order number AC 3341 for 100,000 tomato boxes. The requested delivery date, which you confirmed, is September 4.

Due to forecasted changes in the weather, tomatoes will ripen a month earlier than expected, and we will need 50,000 of these boxes before August 4 and the balance by September 4. Could you reschedule your production line to work in at least half our order to meet the earlier delivery date? I know your production schedules are full at this time of the year, but a profitable harvest depends upon boxing the tomatoes as soon as they are ready. We would certainly appreciate your help because we don't want to split the order with another supplier. Please let me know immediately if you can do this for us.

Best Regards,

Time Extension

Dear Mr. Mullen:

Enclosed is a copy of our option on rental space at the Furniture Mart. The option expires March 23.

The decision to renew must be made by our Board of Directors, and it is not possible for them to meet until March 28.

Would it be possible, therefore, to extend the option-renewal date to March 29? We will have the decision then.

Sincerely,

Dear Mrs. Janning:

I have received your notice to report for jury duty on August 16.

If at all possible I would like to have you put me on a later list of prospective jurors.

My sister who lived in Santa Barbara died recently, and I have to go there during the week that includes August 16 to work with her attorney to settle her estate.

I am willing to be considered for jury duty, but to do so on August 16 would seriously inconvenience many people besides me. I am asking permission not to report for duty on August 16. Please reply as soon as possible.

Sincerely,

Dear Ms. Chute:

Is it possible for us to obtain an extension of the initial trial-leasing contract for the 150 copier?

I am aware that the three-month trial period was provided at a reduced rate. Unfortunately, we could not take full advantage of testing the copier because the office was shut down for three weeks of the lease period.

The performance of the machine has, thus far, been satisfactory. There is, however, one special run to be made next week that will determine our decision either to buy the copier or to return it to you and end the agreement.

Please respond as soon as possible.

Sincerely,

Meeting Deadline

Dear Mr. Hartfeld:

Because of an audit by the Internal Revenue Service on September 27, I will need a transaction-by-transaction listing of all my stock purchases and sales made through Sanders and Sanders, Inc. for the calendar year _ _ _ _. Each transaction must include:

Name of stock	Date of purchase
Date of sale	Purchase price
Sales price	Brokerage purchase fee
Brokerage sales fee	

I know it will be a tight schedule for you, but I must have the report no later than September 26.

Your prompt attention will be greatly appreciated (by Uncle Sam as well as by me).

Sincerely,

Shorten Deadline

Dear Mr. Mollicone:

When we sent you the flat stock for 7,000 formed-steel channels, we told you that you could have 36 days in which to do the job. We now find, however, we cannot allow you that much time, due to the rescheduling of a U.S. Government bridge contract.

Can you get the job done by March 28? This cuts off 11 working days, unless you work Saturdays. Could you help us by shortening the deadline on this project? We really would appreciate it.

If this revised schedule is not possible, please ship back to us what you have completed and the remaining flat stock by March 18.

We hope you can do this favor for us. Please let me know immediately.

Sincerely,

Office Visit

Dear Ms. Jorgenson:

I understand you have a TM600 computer installed for use in your accounting procedures. We are considering several computer systems including the TM600.

I will be in Los Angeles September 25, 26, and 27. Would it be possible to visit your office then? I can arrange to come at any hour convenient for you. Even a short visit with you would be helpful and greatly appreciated.

Sincerely,

Manufacturing-Plant Visit

Dear Mr. Patterson:

We have had the Adenhaur starch-making system in operation at our plant for five months and understand you have used this system for about two years.

I will be in Memphis during the week of November 19 and would like very much to visit your operation. We have found interesting solutions to some of the problems posed by the installation of this system, and we could exchange information that would benefit us both.

I can arrange to visit any day during the week of November 19. Please let me hear from you.

Regards,

Share Experience

Dear Ms. Wallen:

Your firm has the reputation of having a workable and fair personnel policy. We are revising some of our personnel policies and are rewriting our personnel manual.

Could you share with us a few of your successful procedures? I would like to discuss this with you within the next two weeks. A short interview at your convenience, during which time we could exchange information, would be greatly appreciated. Please call me.

Sincerely,

Dear Ms. Goines:

Could you help us with a favor? Your Cincinnati office received computers almost two years before ours. Now an old problem has come back in a different form. In the past we had to continually admonish our clerks not to use the telephone and copy machine for personal business. Now we find our clerks sending and receiving e-mail and occasionally using the internet to participate in chat rooms.

We will be happy to look into any suggestions or solutions you can provide and to return the favor whenever you can use help.

Sincerely,

Financial Statement

Dear Mr. Bangor:

Thank you for your order dated August 20 for 5,000 pen-and-pencil sets. We especially appreciate orders from new customers. It will be shipped to arrive September 6 as you requested.

I would like to ask a favor of you before we fill your next order. We need a copy of your latest financial statements. It will take only a few minutes and will ensure prompt delivery of your future orders.

Next month we will have pen-and-pencil sets available for a promotional program. Our salesman, John Harvey, will show you these soon.

I would appreciate your mailing your financial statements today.

Sincerely,

Business Guidance

Dear Allen:

With the recent reduction in our staff that resulted from current economic conditions, we are finding it impossible to complete the monthly reports required by our headquarters office on time. Several steps have been taken to consolidate scattered information, to redistribute work loads, and to eliminate duplicated efforts. Our staff members realize the importance of making every minute count and of continuing to discover quicker ways to complete our reports.

In spite of all our efforts, we are continually falling behind. I would like to ask a favor. I believe you can help us. Would you come here for a day, or even half a day, to review our reports and to suggest some that might be eliminated? Some reports can probably be combined. Then, perhaps you could persuade the headquarters office that these reductions on our reporting workload would not eliminate any necessary management information. We would certainly appreciate your coming here, and we hope that the whole company will benefit. Please let me hear from you soon.

Sincerely,

Business Statistics

Dear Mr. Salvesen:

Our manager of marketing, Aaron Smith, asked me to write you for two statistics that he would like to incorporate in a marketing trend report for *Western Apparel* magazine. You will, of course, be given credit in the magazine for the information you provide.

To meet the magazine's deadline, we will need these figures by October 1.

What we would like is the following:

1. Number of leather jackets you shipped in the year _ _ _ _.

2. Number of plastic and simulated leather jackets you shipped in the year _ _ _ _.

Your help will be greatly appreciated. May we hear from you by October 1?

Sincerely,

Business Forecast

Dear Mr. Peterson:

Thank you for your help in making the year _ _ _ _ the most successful in our history. As you know, our sales exceeded all previous records, and because of the increased business we expanded our order-assembly and shipping departments. We also added four delivery trucks to our fleet. With this, we will be able to offer even faster service than before. Your business played a big part in our expansion.

To help us continue our fast service, could you provide us with an estimate of your needs for next year?

Please accept our best wishes for a prosperous New Year.

Sincerely,

Business Location

Dear Andy,

After listening to you at the Retail Hardware Association convention last fall, I have given serious consideration to our expansion plans. Your point about the price advantages of volume purchasing really struck home because our markup is low when we meet our competitors' prices.

I opened a branch store shortly after last fall's convention, and it shows promise of turning a profit in a few more months.

I am now considering a third store in a new shopping development, but I can't decide definitely to go ahead with the project. I am bothered by the store space available for expansion and the projected population growth in that area.

Could I ask an extraordinary favor of you? Could you possibly come here for a day or two to look over the situation and give me your opinion? Or make it three or four days and enjoy a mini-vacation. I want you to stay with us and of course bring Ethel with you. The lake and two golf courses are nearby.

Just talking over this decision with you would be a tremendous help to me.

Beth and I are eagerly awaiting your reply.

Best regards,

Business Opportunities

To Whom It May Concern:

Please send me information regarding business opportunities in the Jacksonville area for an unfinished-furniture store.

I am looking for a small but growing business community—and a place in which to live as well as work.

Any information you can provide to get my investigation started will be greatly appreciated.

Sincerely,

Sample Letter

Dear Dr. Abdi:

Could you do a small favor for an alumnus (1996)?

I am working on a research paper on the effectiveness of various basic appeals used in fund-raising letters, such appeals as pride, guilt, fear, and sympathy.

What I need is a sample letter asking for money for the University of Aberdeen. Any names and dates may be deleted from the copy or transcript mailed to me.

Receiving a letter written by you would be truly appreciated.

Sincerely,

Quote from Article

Dear Ms. Sanderson:

The immediate nature of your recent article on the subject of anxiety and performance makes it highly quotable. I would like permission to quote several paragraphs in my paper for the Psychology Association Workshop on psychological disorders most prevalent in affluent women.

As you are aware, too much misinformation has been common in the field. Thus, a well-written, logical evaluation of anxiety, such as you have produced, is extremely valuable.

Should you consent, full credit for your ideas will be given.

Your permission and any suggestions will be appreciated.

Sincerely,

Obtaining Interview

Dear Tim,

Can you help me obtain an interview with Dr. Jerson? I know you've worked closely with him for six months now, and you might at least be able to put in a good word or two for me.

The article I am writing is highly important to me because if it is successful, it will show that I really can handle investigative reporting. In addition, Dr. Jerson might feel relieved, at long last, to have the opportunity to tell his own story in his own words.

I'll be on edge until I receive your reply.

Sincerely,

Dear Mr. Kindes:

Because your industrial-design firm has a high reputation for innovative and practical work, I would like to ask a favor of you.

I have a daughter who is a high-school senior and is interested in becoming an industrial designer. Could you arrange for her to interview one of your employees? She is interested in learning the practical side of that profession, what school is recommended, and what subjects she should study. She has a good background (high-school level) in art and math.

She would appreciate your sending her a note or phoning her after 4 P.M. at 000-0000 to arrange for an appointment. She will be happy to hear from you.

Sincerely,

Request for a Speaker

Dear Ms. Alvarez:

Our club members have spoken highly of you as a speaker for our seminar on book publishing. You have written several books, been an author's agent, and had your books published by several publishers.

The seminar will be held in the Garden Room of the Settler Hotel on May 22 at 7:00 P.M.

We will leave the specific topic to you, but in general we would like a discussion—from the author's viewpoint—of the differences and similarities among publishers.

Please let us know if you can accept this offer and what financial arrangements you expect. You may call me at 000-0000.

Sincerely,

Dear Ms. Swinton:

You have worked a few years at the Abused Women's Shelter and have had many of your observations of abused women and their reactions to abuse printed in our local newspaper.

Would you be interested in sharing some of your thoughts with a group of older teenagers? About thirty of them participate regularly in evening basketball, volleyball, and Ping Pong at the Saxtom Gym.

Could you talk to them some Friday evening for fifteen or twenty minutes and then answer questions?

I could pick you up at about 6:30 P.M. and see you home afterward. Please think it over and call me at 000-0000 after 6:00 in the evening. The girls would be delighted to hear your comments.

Sincerely,

Dear Mrs. Nordstrom:

Your recent article in the local newspaper about your counseling sexually abused children was most interesting and informative.

Our Women's Counseling Service includes a number of volunteers who would be pleased and greatly helped by listening to some of the experiences and any advice you could offer.

We have meetings scheduled for March 15 and April 12. Would you be available to talk to the group on one of those dates? You could have a half hour for your presentation and another half hour for questions. The meetings are at 7:00 P.M. at the Bradley Hall on Twelfth Street.

Please call me at 000-0000. We all hope you will accept our invitation.

Cordially,

Dear Mr. Blackwell:

You are known in this area as a top salesman. Would you be willing to help some young people become better salespersons, to tell them some of the methods and techniques that have earned you your reputation?

The carriers for the *Marin County Times* are having a sales meeting Friday, February 22 at 7:30 P.M. at the *Times* office, 333 Silvera Way.

They would be thrilled (and I am sure educated) if you could speak to them for fifteen to twenty minutes and then answer questions.

I'm sure you will find the carriers an enthusiastic group. Please call me.

Sincerely,

Obtaining Speakers

Dear Jean,

Our seminar on the executive woman is scheduled for April and I'm in the process of putting together the list of speakers. Can you assist me here?

With your executive experience and your contacts with other women in the field, would you be willing to contact a few of them to speak at the seminar?

I would really appreciate it if you could use your influence to help me out. The more diverse our speakers, of course, the more productive the seminar.

My fingers are crossed in hope of your assistance.

Sincerely,

Entertaining a Friend

Dear Pete:

I would like to ask a tremendous favor of you.

Could you possibly spend part of a day with Jack Herald, who is one of our best customers as well as a personal friend of mine? He mentioned yesterday that he will be spending a week or more of vacation time in San Francisco, starting October 7. Jack is production manager for Aames Company here. He is still a bachelor, though I don't know how he manages to stay that way. Jack is an outgoing type, but modest and extremely pleasant. He would just about match you in golf. He is a camera bug like you and will surely bring along his new Nikon.

I'm sure he would like to take pictures from such spots as Colt Tower, Harding Park's 17th green the Cliff House, and Twin Peaks. Jack would also enjoy one or two of the tourist-type nightclubs, but that is not his strong suit.

Can I have him call you when he gets to San Francisco? I realize this is asking a lot, but you know I will return the favor whenever I can do something to help you.

Sincerely,

Alleviating Fear

Dear Mrs. Miles,

I am sending this letter to your office for the obvious reason that Mr. Miles should not see it.

In my opinion, and the opinion of Doctors Agnew and Danis, whose reputations as diagnosticians are excellent, Mr. Miles requires surgery as soon as possible.

It is understandable that you feel the way you do about surgery, Mrs. Miles. You expressed yourself clearly when we first met. We feel there isn't any other treatment, however, if you want your husband to recover his good health. Surgery isn't what it was forty years ago, or even ten, and you can be reassured by knowing the mortality rate for this particular operation, when performed in time, is less than 5 percent. The mortality rate for neglect of this condition is a certain 100 percent.

Please try to stop by my office with your husband Tuesday evening so that I may talk with both of you. If this is not convenient, please call my secretary this week for an appointment.

Sincerely,

Board a Relative

Dear Jo Ann:

Is there any chance that you and Tom could have Jane stay with you for a month this summer? You've offered in the past, but the need has never been so great. I have the chance to take on a really big account that requires a monthlong stay in Israel shooting fashion layouts and generally supervising the whole scene.

Jane has often talked of visiting with you, and I have felt that you would like to see more of her. If it can be arranged, count on me to take time off (I'll be due some if this goes through) to help you with the wedding in January. I already have some ideas.

Call me—even collect!

Sincerely,

Job for a Relative

Dear Tom,

Please review the enclosed résumé of my nephew, John Wentling.

John is an intelligent and ambitious young man whose college performance and initial work experience have been admirable. His work with Grande Company should prove beneficial to you.

Could you check around a bit to see if there is a place for John in the company in the areas of interest he has indicated. Anytime I can return the favor, or assist you in further contacts, you know you can just call.

I look forward to some good news.

With regards,

Please Send Money

Dear Dad,

Since starting my first job and being on my own here in Denver, I've managed to skimp by. But now my old Ford needs new brake linings, and I just don't have the cash. I have to work here six months—two more—before I can get a credit card.

I hope you can loan me $300, which should cover the brakes and another item or two mechanics always seem to find. I'll pay you back as soon as possible.

The job is going great, and there is promise of a small raise at the end of my six-month probationary period.

With love,

Tool Loan

Dear Morry,

I would like to ask a favor that I hope isn't imposing too much on you. Could I borrow your table saw for a week? The repair people say it will take that long to locate a new motor and some bearings and make other adjustments to my old (I think of it as ancient) table saw.

I'm in the middle of a project with a deadline, and I don't know where else to turn. I can bring your saw over here in my pickup truck if you can spare it for a week.

You know I'll return your saw in good condition and also return the favor whenever you wish.

Let me know tomorrow if possible.

Your pal,

Desert Rescue

Dear Steve,

Although you primarily report road traffic-conditions from a helicopter, television newscasts have shown you participating in the rescue of people lost in the desert.

I take small groups into the desert to show them the wild flowers and blooming plants. I also like to remind them of the dangers of the desert. When you have located and then approached a lost person, what is the first thing you do? Your reply will be appreciated.

Best regards,

(The answer was first to identify the person and then offer a drink of cold water.)

CHAPTER 2

Declining Requests

It is difficult to refuse or to say "no." The key to the successful no is tact. In a letter of refusal, the goodwill of the reader must be retained, and if the letter is tactfully written, the reader's disappointment will be lessened.

A customer receiving a flat no to a request for an adjustment will often not complain: He or she will quietly take his business elsewhere. The customer has bought a product or service and now asks for an adjustment. He or she receives a rejection. The disappointment that started with the unsatisfactory product or service deepens into distrust and then anger. This lost goodwill must be salvaged. The writer's task is to explain the rejection in a tactful way and to offer an alternative. He or she must combine the refusal with help for the customer. This will not please the customer all of the time, but the chances of alienating the customer all of the time are considerably lessened.

One good way to start a letter of refusal is to agree with the reader on some point. This establishes a feeling of working together as opposed to an "I'm-right-you're-wrong" confrontation. For example:

We agree that a watch running only part of the time is useless.

Another recommended opening statement is a thank you. This sets a tone of courtesy, pleasantness, and consideration for the reader. An example:

Thank you for your recent letter requesting a donation to the Redwood Girl's Club.

A combination of agreement and apology is a third introduction to model refusal letters. The message to be conveyed is that "we would like to help, but we can't." The use of this opening requires a reasonable and sincere explanation of why the request is refused. A strong alternative suggestion for obtaining help should follow the apologetic opening, as in this example:

We wish it were possible to provide door prizes for your second annual meeting . . . Perhaps we can help by advertising it in our store window.

After letting the reader know that you are aware of his or her request and have considered it from the reader's point of view, explain the reason for the refusal. Explain the refusal before making it. This takes the sharp edge off the refusal and prepares the reader for the disappointment that, to some extent, all refusals bring. The statements, "It is not company policy," or "For various reasons we cannot comply," are only slightly better than completely ignoring the request. If it is not company policy, the reader would like to know why it is not company policy. Perhaps it is that "Children under 12 years of age are not allowed to visit our plant because the safety hazards are too great to be covered by a reasonable insurance premium," or "We cannot continue in business if we extend our free-delivery policy to purchases under $100." A request for credit may be refused because of lack of information or not meeting certain qualifications. A request for a contribution may be denied because of lack of budgeted funds. Company procedures may not provide the data requested. A job applicant may be rejected because there is no opening, he or she is underqualified, or is overqualified. A pamphlet may be out of print. A request for a refund may be turned down because of an obvious condition excluded by the warranty. Whatever is being refused, the explanation to the reader must be straightforward, definite, and reasonable.

The next step is to state the refusal. The reader has been prepared by the explanation, and there is no reason to smother the refusal in a barrage of words. A few examples:

> I regret that we must decline this opportunity to help the Girls Club.
>
> I am sorry to inform you that we cannot supply the information requested.
>
> We hate to say no to your credit application, but we do not have enough information to say "yes."

Because the ending of a letter is the most emphatic position, a tactful letter of refusal should end on a positive or upbeat note. Consideration for the reader suggests that a sincere effort to offer at least some help or encouragement would be appropriate in offsetting the unavoidable disappointment. This helps the reader to save face, gives him or her an out, offers an alternative course of action, and reinflates the reader's ego. Closing statements such as the following are encouraged:

> We wish you great success.
>
> We are interested in your business venture.

Please keep us in mind for other ideas you may develop.

Many adjectives can be used to describe the proper tone of a letter refusing a request, but they are all brought together when the writer uses the persuasive power of a soft denial.

How to Do It

1. Agree on some point with the reader, offer thanks for the reader's interest, or combine agreement and apology.
2. Present reasons for the refusal.
3. State the refusal.
4. Offer a suggestion or an alternative that will help the reader.

Begin by Agreeing

Here are some agreeable beginnings for a letter of refusal:

As you requested, we are enclosing a tally of the monthly purchases you made during the past year.

Your Junior Chamber of Commerce *Sports Annual* is a commendable project.

A copy of the first-quarter issue of *Semiconductor Science* is being mailed to you today.

We like your approach to the consumer survey on garden tools.

Your questions are most interesting.

Begin with a Thank You

Using a thank you is another good way to start a letter of refusal:

Thank you for your recent request for a charge account at Liberty House.

Your enlightening comments on our Direct-Mail-selling series of letters are greatly appreciated.

Thank you very much for giving us the opportunity to consider you for employment.

Thank you for your interest in Inland Steel.

We are pleased that you thought of us as a source of information.

We appreciate your asking us to participate in your August meeting.

Begin with an Agreement and Apology

Agreeing with the reader while at the same time apologizing for not granting a request is a third beginning for a letter of refusal:

We would be happy to comply with your request for a sample of our new loan forms. May I suggest you write directly to our headquarters office.

We would like to grant your request for a copy of our booklet *Animal Husbandry*, but our supply has been exhausted. More will be available next year. To help you now, may we suggest you write to the Superintendent of Documents in Washington, D.C., asking for publications on this subject.

We are sorry to learn that the paint work on your car was not to your satisfaction. I have talked to Bob Anderson, and he suggests you bring your car in next Saturday for a complete inspection.

Statements of Refusal

Direct but polite statements of refusal include these:

At present, however, your financial condition does not quite meet Barrow's requirement.

He believes that meeting would not be helpful.

We do not have a position open that fits your qualifications.

I am sorry that we cannot accept the chairs for credit.

I am sorry we cannot provide the information you requested.

We hate to decline granting you credit, but we need additional information from you.

We regret declining this opportunity to help the Bay Area Youth Council.
I am sorry we cannot grant your request.

Close with Encouragement

A statement of encouragement for the reader is an effective goodwill gesture to offset the natural disappointment of a refusal. Some examples:

Thank you for thinking of Carl & Henderson.

I know you will find a suitable position soon.

I believe the Abbott Company could give you more detailed information.

Have you thought of asking Tom Anderson?

We will be glad to receive other ideas from you.

We are interested in your proposed new business.

We wish you great success.

We wish you continued success.

INVITATIONS

An acceptable declination of an invitation includes three important points. The first is brevity. Long explanations turn into excuses that become confused and hard to believe. The second is a polite thank-you for the invitation. Let the inviter know you are pleased to have been considered worthy of an invitation. The third is a plausible reason for not accepting—a reason that is believable by the person you are refusing.

Invitation to Dinner

Dear Andy,

Thank you for your personal invitation to attend the Old School dinner meeting on October 22. I regret that only yesterday I accepted an invitation to a meeting with a business group to which I have belonged for the past few years. Perhaps I can join you and our Old School gang next year. Thanks again for your invitation.

Sincerely,

Invitation to Speak

Dear Jon Larson,

Thank you for your invitation to speak before your fund-raising committee about our success last year. Unfortunately, I have been scheduled to lead our sales meeting in Atlanta that week. I would have enjoyed discussing our problems, solutions, and eventual success of last year's campaign. Perhaps Ron Lentler can help you. He was involved in all the details and could offer many suggestions. I sincerely appreciate your asking me.

With regards,

Dear Ms. Meacam:

Thank you for the invitation to speak at your investment club's annual dinner on May 3. I am sorry that because of previous obligations I will not be able to attend.

I am sure you can find another investment counselor to address your group, and I wish you good investing.

Sincerely,

Join a Group

Dear Mr. Adams:

I appreciate your asking me to join the Morgan Hill Toastmasters. I was a member of the Toastmasters a number of years ago but dropped out because of conflicts with my tax work.

I am new in town, am buying a new house, and have a new job. With all this piling up on me, I don't believe I could do my fair share as a participating member.

I will keep your kind invitation in mind and hope to join you at a later date. Thank you for asking me.

Sincerely,

Dear Mr. Rogers:

Thank you for inviting me to join the Delta Cost Accountants group. I am sure the monthly meeting to discuss mutual problems and solutions would be most helpful.

I have been on the job here for only four weeks and am up to my ears learning the job and clearing up the backlog of work. I would like, therefore, to decline your invitation at this time. After another year, please contact me again. I think the group is an excellent idea.

Sincerely,

Dear Beth,

It was nice of you to invite Frank and me to join your square-dance club. Some thirty years ago we were active participants in a group. We have considered starting again, but Thursday evenings are now reserved for tutoring under-achieving students at Logan High School. We find the pupils so appreciative of the extra help.

Thank you for inviting us to join you in this enjoyable activity, but we feel we can't right now.

Cordially,

TV-Program Research

Dear Josie,

I appreciate your inviting me to accompany you to a TV preview to obtain viewer responses to pilot programs. The presentation you describe sounds exciting, and it would be rewarding to present my ideas and preferences.

I have a reluctance, however, to spend a whole evening plus the hour's drive to the resort to provide an advertising promotional company with market research data when compensated only by an evening's entertainment. I have been involved in similar situations before and have concluded that I should be paid in dollars for my marketing knowledge and experience.

Thanks again for your thinking of me, but I wish to pass on this one.

Cordially,

Football Game

Dear Bob,

I am sorry Barbara and I cannot attend the Cal-Stanford big game with you this year. We have a previous commitment in Los Angeles that weekend, but I will have the radio tuned in. I am sure you can find another couple to share the excitement and the tickets you won.

Again, we appreciate your thoughtfulness.

Sincerely,

REQUEST FOR INFORMATION OR MATERIAL

Refusing a request for information, of whatever nature, should be done politely. The request may be inconvenient or seem useless or silly to the receiver of the request, but the fact that the requester has gone to the trouble to single out one company or person indicates that the request is of importance to the person making it. Respect for and a show of interest in the person asking for information can go a long way toward building goodwill for the organization or person answering the request—or refusing the request.

Information Not Available

Dear Mr. Newton:

At the present time, Tractor Mechanics, Inc., does not have an accounting-system program for its members, but we did in the past and would certainly recommend it for your review. If you are interested contact Mr. Robert Strong at Menson Accounting Systems. Their address is 000 Wescott Way, Portland, ME 00000.

We are in the process of compiling the type of data you requested. Initially, this information will be made available only to those who participated in the survey. It is hoped that the survey will be completed by the end of the year.

Sincerely,

Tree Disease

Dear Mr. Schaff:

Thank you for asking me for information about Valley Oak tree diseases or possible diseases. I do have hundreds of Valley Oaks on my acreage, but I'm not knowledgeable about what you say appears to be a disease.

My suggestion is that you write to the Agricultural Department of your state college or state university. They should be able to guide you in the right direction.

Regards,

Item Not Available

Dear Mr. Johnston:

We would be happy to comply with your request for a sample letter asking for contributions. However, Honourman Medical Center has just now received its full tax-exempt status, making us eligible for tax-deductible donations. Because we were not tax-exempt until now, we have not had an active fund-raising program and are only now reaching the final stage of our plans.

I would suggest that you contact Mr. George Appleton, Foundation Director, Boulder River Hospital, for sample letters. Boulder River has had an established and active fund-raising program for several years and could provide you with several examples. The address is: 111 Round Plaza, Boulder, California 00000.

If I may be of further assistance, please let me know.

Sincerely,

Dear Ms. Sibley:

Thank you for your order for our Model A701 bookcase. This model was discontinued three months ago, but advertisements for it are still in magazines and brochures. We are trying to locate a high-quality substitute at a reasonable price, and when we do, we will notify you by mail.

We are sorry we cannot accommodate you right now but hope to later. The check you sent is enclosed.

Sincerely,

Dear Professor Roland:

Your enlightening comments on our series of sales letters are greatly appreciated. We plan to use many of your suggestions as we continue the series.

This series was planned for a list of advertisers with only a few allocated to instructional institutions. The value of these letters as teaching material rather surprised us. We therefore do not have available the number of copies you requested, but two copies have been mailed to you today. Perhaps you can circulate these or make copies for your students.

After using these letters in class, we would appreciate your views on how to improve them for use as teaching material.

Very Sincerely,

Dear Richard,

Sorry we can't loan you our barbeque grill for your backyard outing in June. We don't have it anymore.

We hadn't used it for at least five years. Then, after three years trying to sell it, we gave up and took it to the landfill about two weeks ago. It wasn't much to look at, but it did work well.

We hope you can find one somewhere, and we wish you a fun-filled afternoon in June.

Cordially,

Application for Personal Credit

Always show an interest in the person applying for credit. Even if credit is refused now, potential future sales should never be overlooked. Let the customer know that thorough consideration was given to the application. Then state the reasons for refusal, clearly but politely. End with the fact that cash purchases or layaway plans are available or that credit will probably be available later.

Lack of Information

Dear Mr. Ames:

Thank you for your interest in Rankin's and your request for a line of credit.

Based on the information you supplied us and that from our normal sources, we are unable to grant you the open credit you requested. If you can supply us with additional references, however, and current financial statements, please do so, and we will be happy to reconsider our disappointing decision.

While waiting for this additional information we will welcome any orders accompanied by a cash payment.

Sincerely,

No Records

Dear Mr. Breaux:

Thank you for your order for two 5-foot by 2 ½-inch piano hinges.

Because we have no information about your work or payment records, we would like to suggest that you mail us a check for $89.20. This will include shipping charges. Alternatively, we could ship COD via United Parcel Service.

We can help you either way.

Sincerely,

Short Employment

Dear Ms. Lindstrom:

Thank you for your recent application for a charge account at Fordham's. Your application has received careful consideration but we find the information furnished by you does not meet our requirements for granting credit. Perhaps in the future, when circumstances have changed, we can again consider your request for a charge account. Our decision is based on the following reasons:

Length of employment

No credit file

I regret we could not be more helpful at this time. Meanwhile, our quality selections are available for cash, and you can take advantage of our layaway service.

Sincerely,

Slow Pay

Dear Ms. Tabor:

You have asked for an open line of credit. We appreciate your considering us for your household necessities.

The information we have been able to gather indicates that payments on your previous credit accounts kept getting further and further behind. We are afraid that by extending you credit, we would be adding to your debt problem.

Let me suggest that cash purchases require no interest payments, and you can still take advantage of our special sales.

Sincerely,

New in Area

Dear Mr. Wiria:

Thank you for your interest in Matson's Department Store and your request for a credit account.

We notice that you have been in this area only a few weeks and have just begun to work here. When you have lived and worked here a little longer and have established a bank account, we will be happy to review your application. We hope to open a credit account for you when you apply again in another two months.

In the meantime, please take advantage of our Annual Sale next month. We carry many lines of quality merchandise and are especially proud of our men's shop.

Please let us hear from you again.

Sincerely,

Current Information Lacking

Dear Ms. Esthers:

We appreciate your request for a Golden credit card.

It is a standard procedure with all companies issuing credit cards to check on the applicant's past payment record. We have found that you usually require more time to pay than our 25-day terms allow.

If we have not received current information, perhaps you could furnish us with the names of two or three firms from which you are now buying on credit. We will be happy then to reconsider your request for a credit card.

Meanwhile, we find that more and more of our customers prefer to pay cash and thereby avoid the high cost of interest on unpaid balances.

Sincerely,

APPLICATION FOR BUSINESS CREDIT

Future business must not be lost when refusing business credit. Be appreciative of the applicant's request. State any favorable elements in the application before explaining clearly the reasons for refusal. End with encouragement and suggestions that he or she may use to qualify in the future.

Financial Condition

Dear Mr. Colson:

Thank you for your application for credit at Barrow's. We appreciate your interest.

Your personal references are exceptionally good, and your record of hard work indicates that your business prospects are good for the near future. At present, however, your financial condition only partially meets Barrow's requirements. Therefore, we cannot extend the $5,000 open credit you requested.

Please come in and talk to me at your convenience. I am sure we can set up a program of gradually increasing credit that will benefit both of us. Meanwhile, remember that deliveries on cash purchases are made within two days.

Let me hear from you soon. We are interested in your business venture.

Sincerely,

Credit Limited

Dear Mr. Snelling,

We appreciate receiving your order of January 29 for 50,000 boxes.

This is our slack season, and we would like to receive several orders of this size. However, you have been in business only since October, and we feel that until we have had a little more experience with you, your open line of credit should be limited to $5,000. This limit can be raised as your business improves and expands.

We hope this is satisfactory as a starter, and we thank you for the opportunity to be of service to you.

Sincerely,

Company Procedure—Late Payment

Dear Ms. Arthur:

We received the copy of the past-due freight bill No. 278-089799 that you sent Wednesday, November 21. We have matched it with our purchase order and will mall it today to Central Freight Payment, Inc. in Atlanta, Georgia, for payment.

Although the bill is overdue because we did not receive the original bill, our corporate procedure requires that Central Freight pay the bill. This procedure speeds payment in practically all instances and includes an audit of all paid freight bills. We cannot write you a check from our local plant as you have requested.

We are sorry for the delay. You should have your money in less than a week.

Sincerely,

Guarantor Needed

Dear Mr. Almond:

We greatly appreciate the order you gave our Mr. Robbins. You will find that we have reason to be proud of our quality products.

We want to work with you and help you get established, but from the information we have been able to gather, you appear to be undercapitalized, which would make it difficult for you to meet payments on our terms.

One temporary solution we might suggest is for you to find a person or firm that would guarantee your open account with us. We have found this arrangement to work well with other customers until they become established. This could take care of your immediate needs. Later, we can work together on other arrangements.

Please let us hear from you soon.

Sincerely,

Previous Poor Pay

Dear Mr. Pappas:

We are pleased to learn that you are still interested in Allen's high-quality tools. We received your order on October 22.

You may recall that when you last purchased goods from us, we had a difficult time getting payment from you. In fact, some of your account was turned over to Dun & Bradstreet's collection department.

We realize, however, that times and conditions change, and we should probably not be concerned. To relieve the concern we do have, please send us a few current credit references and a recent statement of your financial condition.

If you are in a rush for the tools you ordered, please send us a check for $928.50. We still maintain the prompt delivery service you are familiar with.

Thank you for considering us again, and we hope to hear from you soon.

Cordially,

Bad Risk

Note that this letter follows an outline nearly the reverse of that suggested in the How to Do It section.

Dear Mr. Bankhead:

I am being completely honest when I say that many of our customers prefer to pay cash. This relieves them of any anxiety about having to make late-payment charges. I would like to suggest this method to you, because, as hard as I have tried, I just can't find a way to add you to our list of credit customers at this time.

The information we have gathered indicates that your payments have consistently been getting further and further behind during the past year. This may have been a bad year for you, but we cannot see adding to your outstanding debts. We hope that conditions soon improve for you.

We do, however, appreciate your considering us as a supplier. We will be most happy to do business with you on a cash-with-order-basis. You will find both our service and products outstanding.

Sincerely,

Bad Risk—No Hope

Dear Mr. Blair:

We appreciate your interest in Sampson's and your desire to establish credit with us.

However, based upon reports from our numerous sources of credit information, we can make shipments to you only when cash is received with the order.

We are sorry for this, but we are sure you understand. If we can be of any further service to you, please let us know.

Sincerely,

Franchise Refused

Dear Mr. Goodall:

We greatly appreciate your interest in obtaining an American Chicken franchise. Our present expansion rate exceeds our most optimistic expectations.

We, of course, make credit checks on all potential franchisers, and our information indicates that you might have difficulty meeting our payment terms for merchandise and supplies to be purchased from us. These payment terms must be met as well as those for the expected loan on the purchase price.

Past experience can be temporary, and we hope your financial condition improves soon. Perhaps we can review another application from you in the near future.

Sincerely,

Will Not Change Prior Understanding

Dear Mr. Donaldson:

We are very sorry to learn of your unsatisfactory experience with our Mr. Hanson's letters, but the bearings that we manufactured and delivered to you in Waterford became your property.

When Mr. Hanson and I visited you on February 17, there was no question that these bearings were left on consignment at your Waterford warehouse until December of this year and were used at that time by your customer, Central Trailer. The only unanswered question on your part was the problem of your pending bankruptcy and when you would be able to settle all the outstanding items. This was stated in your letter of February 24.

As far as we are concerned, Mr. Donaldson, these bearings were purchased by you and used by your customer. Our position has not changed, and this Invoice, No. 43332, in the amount of $3,459.90, is still outstanding.

Sincerely,

DONATION

Start this type of refusal with a thank-you, apology, or complimentary statement about the organization or event you are asked to help. Offer a plausible reason for the refusal, and end with alternative help or at least best wishes for success.

Discontinued Contributions

Dear Mr. Casals:

We are sorry that we can no longer contribute clothing and small household goods to your organization.

It was our understanding that all these goods were distributed to the needy immigrant farm workers. In an attempt to verify this, by checking written records and by interviews, three of our members learned that the goods that were salable were sold by your board members, and the proceeds were pocketed for their own use.

Therefore, you will no longer receive contributions of any kind from our association of churches.

Sincerely,

Dear Mrs. Alberts:

I am sorry I cannot contribute to the Children's Fund this year.

I am involved in several charities, including some for disadvantaged children. Your needs are real, I recognize, but my funds are limited and I have to make my own choice about the distribution of those funds.

I wish you well on your program to help these children.

Sincerely,

Use of Name in Fund Raising

Dear Mrs. Lansing:

Please accept my sincere regrets for having to decline the use of my name as a sponsor of Belmont Boys Home. I feel a little insincere about sponsoring something I am not actively involved in. I work with a number of charities now and just don't have the time to consider any more at present.

Your cause is worthy. I know, and I wish you well in your endeavor to obtain prominent names for your sponsor's list. Thank you for asking me.

Sincerely,

Company Policy

Dear Mrs. Melton:

Thank you for your letter requesting a donation to the Community Fund. Although we are a small business, we have a list of charities to which we give as generously as possible each year.

It is now established policy that this list will not be extended. We are sorry to decline your request, but our funds are limited. This is not in any way a criticism of your charity, and we wish you much success.

Sincerely,

Dear Mr. Sundston:

We wish it were possible to provide door prizes for your fund raising meeting. Your cause is commendable. We find, however, that as a national company we are asked quite often for donations of merchandise for worthy organizations. We feel that if we give to one good cause, we should give equally to all good causes. I am sure you recognize that this is not practical, and therefore we do not make door prizes available.

Perhaps we can help in another way: by advertising in our store window or preparing an advertisement for the newspaper. Let us know if we can help in this way.

Sincerely,

Budget Limitation

Dear Mr. Bates:

Your Junior Chamber of Commerce *Sports Annual* is a commendable project. We do budget for special advertising, but unfortunately, the money has been spent for this year. I am sure you can understand that we must operate by our budget to stay in business.

If you make this publication an annual event, please contact us early next year. We will consider you in next year's budget. The Junior Chamber of Commerce will receive our full help and cooperation.

Sincerely,

Political Donation

Dear Mrs. Sterling:

I understand your request for a donation to the Republican party: I am a registered Republican.

Recently, the Republicans added some "pork barrel" appropriations to a necessary disaster relief bill, thus causing the President to veto the relief bill. The Republicans, now in power in Congress, approved appropriations to bungling foreign dictators while cutting Medicare aid to our own senior citizens.

For these reasons, I wish to decline making a contribution at this time.

Sorry,

Disagree with Charity Project

Dear Ms. Eggmont:

I agree that St. Anthony University is badly in need of a new gym. I think, however, that this is an inappropriate time to request contributions for a building fund. The basketball team has not won a local conference championship in twelve years. I recognize that the gym is used for many activities besides basketball, but basketball is all the public hears about—and they haven't heard much about that in recent years.

When the team has won a local conference championship and a state championship and is headed for a national meet—then you can go to an enthusiastic public and meet little resistance. Big donors will also give more willingly at that time. Everyone loves a winner.

This may seem an unkind attitude toward a school in need of a new gym, but I feel a team must earn its right to a new facility. Best wishes for success in your campaign.

Sincerely,

CUSTOMER ADJUSTMENT

Customer adjustments must be made with tact. It is difficult to refuse the customer's request while retaining his or her goodwill. Open with something agreeable, a point you can agree upon or a thank-you for letting you explain your point of view. The explanation that follows must be clear and definite but not curt. Take enough time and space to make a complete and logical explanation. Completeness is important to the reader. Then let the reader know what he or she can do, or what you will do to make an adjustment satisfactory to the reader.

Damaged Product

Dear Miss Gerald:

We agree that a watch running only part of the time is useless. And we guarantee trouble-free operation of Serra watches for a year from the purchase date.

Your watch has been thoroughly examined by our service department. They report a dent near the winding stem, perhaps too small for you to have noticed. This indicates physical damage to the case, which is not covered by our guarantee. The dent is deep enough to touch the main spring regulator when it expands in warm weather. This can cause the occasional stopping of the watch.

Although not covered by our guarantee, we can repair your watch at factory cost and extend the warranty for a year from the repair date. The cost to you is only $15.

If you wish to have the repairs made, please return the enclosed card and attach your check for $15. We will repair your watch and return it promptly.

Sincerely,

Cash Discount

Dear Mr. Allsworth:

Thank you for your letter of February 28. You asked about our billing you for the 1 percent cash discount you took with your payment on February 17.

As you know, our terms for several years have been 1 percent 10 days, net 30 days. We offer these terms because we save interest on borrowed capital when we receive cash within 10 days. This is a savings we can pass on to our customers, but we have no savings to pass on when payment is received after the 10-day period.

The dollar amount involved in this case is small, only $32.10, but when multiplied by the number of our customers, the total is significant.

Our policy has always been to treat all customers equally, with discounts as well as service and reliable merchandise. I hope that you will see the consistent fairness in our bill for $32.10 and that we can both benefit from our 1 percent 10-day cash-discount policy.

Sincerely,

Credit Adjustment

Dear Mrs. Sajaro:

Thank you for letting us know of the plant-in-a-glass-bowl that you received damaged. We constantly review the procedures of our packers, but a rare shipment fails to meet our standards.

We sincerely apologize for our negligence and enclose a check to cover your cost.

We appreciate your being a regular buyer and will try even harder to please all our customers—that is our goal. We are glad to help you any time we can.

Sincerely,

Special Product

Dear Mr. Mills:

Your memo requesting credit for the gear housing we made for you in October has been given to me by our sales engineer.

Although we realize that machinery-rebuilding plans are sometimes changed at levels above that of the purchasing agent, we are sorry we cannot accept the gear housing for credit. It was cast to your specifications, and there is no market for it among our other customers.

If we do get an inquiry for this type of casting we will get in touch with you immediately. I'm sorry we can't do more for you.

Cordially,

Poor Workmanship

Dear Mr. Wilson:

We are sorry to learn that your application of Thickwall to your house was not completely to your satisfaction.

Applying Thickwall is a specialized job, and that is why we request all our dealers to make this part of our warranty clear to each customer. Mr. Bob Johnson, salesman at your dealer, Appley Building Supplies, recommended application by John Sanders, a specialist who works with Appley Building Supplies. Our warranty states clearly that Thickwall must be applied by a specialist.

I have talked to Bob Johnson, and he suggests that John Sanders inspect your house and make recommendations for correcting the work. Mr. Sanders can then make the necessary repairs at a reasonable cost or perhaps suggest how you can make the repairs yourself.

Please talk to Bob Johnson at Appley Building Supplies. I am sure you can work out a satisfactory arrangement for getting the application of Thickwall corrected.

Sincerely,

Slow-Selling Product

Dear Mr. Lunsford:

Thank you for writing us about the Country Gentleman chairs you purchased on September 3 and wish to return for credit. These are the chairs you ordered. In fact, you paid for them early and took our 2 percent cash discount.

As I understand the situation, you wish to return them because of slow sales. I am sorry that we cannot accept the chairs for credit. We discontinued this line six months ago, but most of our dealers found them to be good sellers during the winter promotion we sponsored. We are sending you additional promotional material and ideas that proved successful with others. If there is anything else we can do to help you sell these chairs, please let our salesman, John Ballard, know. He will be calling on you next month and will have some helpful suggestions.

With regards,

OTHER LETTERS OF DECLINATION

The following letters cover a variety of refusals, from sample letters to a church volunteer. They follow the general outline: agreeing with the writer or showing appreciation for the writer's interest, offering a plausible reason for refusing, and ending with an alternative or expression of goodwill.

Can't Fill Order

Dear Mr. Porticellini:

Thank you for your order for 50 Baldwin 27"×1¼" bicycle tires. That brand has been so popular the manufacturer is not able to keep up with demand. We are told it will be from 30 to 45 days before we will receive our next shipment.

In the meantime, we have the Kinston brand available. The quality, we know, is slightly lower, but so is the price. If you can use these, we can ship immediately. Please let us know.

Sincerely,

Special Assignment

Dear Ms. Wilshire:

I deeply regret the amount of time that has passed before responding to your letter of November 26.

After careful consideration and the exploration of some possibilities, I find that we cannot handle this particular assignment.

Please accept my best wishes for your success in this endeavor.

Sincerely yours,

Business Meeting Unnecessary

Dear Mr. Verdon:

Mr. Talbert has carefully considered your request for a group meeting to discuss a change in your property settlement. If a meeting would be of benefit to you, he would be happy to arrange it. He has asked me to write and tell you that he believes another group meeting at this time would not be of any help to you.

With regards,

Magazine Subscribers Limited

Dear Mr. Ludwig:

A copy of the first-quarter issue of *Computer Chip Science* is being mailed to you. Please accept it with our compliments.

Your interest in our publication is appreciated, but we discourage subscription by those who are not directly engaged in the production of computer chips. This quarterly manual is highly technical and expensive to produce. We find that those outside the industry do not continue their subscriptions, and this makes the printing difficult to schedule and unduly costly.

I am sure you understand our position, and we sincerely thank you for your interest in *Computer Chip Science*.

Sincerely yours,

Manuscript

Dear Ms. Veal:

Thank you for sending us your book proposal for *Everyday Grammar*. Unfortunately, it is not right for our current list of books.

Thank you for considering Wilson Publishers.

Sincerely,

Publication—Editorial Program

Dear Mr. Smythe:

Thank you very much for inquiring about Wilson Publishers' possible interest in your proposal for a textbook: *Essentials of Psychology*.

I very much regret that we must decline the opportunity to publish this interesting work. Our editorial program is, unfortunately, unable to accept an addition of this kind.

Please understand that this response to your idea is the reaction of only one company. Opinions vary widely among publishers. and I hope you will continue to develop your material toward a successful publication. I also ask you to keep Wilson Publishers in mind for any other textbook ideas you may have.

Sincerely,

Publication—Needs Reworking

Dear Professor Nelson:

Enclosed are three reviews of your proposed *Cost Accounting* text. I share them with you for the benefit of the text's development.

Based on the reviews, you have the basis for a fine text. While the concept of a brief book is sound, it is my opinion that it does not go far enough, which limits the value and marketability of the text.

Should you be willing to expand the text's coverage and appeal, I would be pleased to reconsider the text for publication. I would also appreciate receiving more information on how your text would compare to existing competing books.

Cordially,

Refusing a Volunteer

Dear Ms. Lester,

We appreciate very much your volunteering to head the Junior Youth Fellowship for the coming year. Looking at the overall program, however, we believe you could serve the church better working with Mrs. Holbrook and the Senior Youth Fellowship. She is in need of someone with your background and willingness.

We hope you will consider working with Mrs. Holbrook. The Seniors need your helping hands.

Yours in Christ,

Declining a Friendly Loan

Dear Bart,

I sympathize with your need for a small loan, but there is a principle involved. Too often—and I have had this experience—when loaning money to a friend both the money and the friendship disappear. I could survive without the money, but losing our friendship would be unbearable.

I don't like to disappoint you, but in the long run we will both be happier if we don't have to fret about your returning the money.

Sorry this time, my friend,

No More Babysitting

Dear Ellen,

It's true that at my age I am home most of the time. That's why I agreed to baby-sit little Lisa once in a while.

She is a sweet girl, but I must decline to continue because "once in a while" has become "too often." Last week you brought her here three times, twice without calling me first. That is taking undue advantage of a person willing to be helpful.

Sorry, but I am no longer available to baby-sit Lisa.

Sincerely,

Lying

Dear Frank,

I'm disappointed, Frank, that you would think me capable of stating an outright lie for you.

I can't do it. That would put both of us in jeopardy. You got yourself into a bad situation, and it's your job to get yourself out.

Good luck,

Loan of Personal Item

Dear Eva,

Saying "no" to a simple request disturbs me, but I've been disappointed when loaning shoes and bracelets to friends. My shoes came back with a missing heel plate, and my bracelet catch was jammed. So I said to myself, "No more, not even to my best friend."

I would like to loan you my favorite blue dress for your Saturday-night party, but just feel I can't. I hope you can make some other arrangement.

Jeannie,

Freight Claim

Ladies/Gentlemen:

Please refer to your Claim No. 00000:

Our records show your bill of lading 0000 bears a January 3 signature. Your claim is dated November 29.

Section 2(b) of the Bill of Lading Contract Terms and Conditions requires that claims be filed in writing within nine months from the date of delivery or, in case of failure to make delivery, within nine months after a reasonable time for delivery has passed.

We are sorry we cannot honor your claim. We have checked all possible sources for a prior filing and can find no record of an earlier claim related to this shipment.

If, however, you can provide proof of an earlier filing, we will be happy to reconsider your claim.

Sincerely,

Miscellaneous Request

Dear Mr. Walkup:

In reply to your recent letter, while we wish you success with your project, we must decline the opportunity to participate.

We appreciate your interest in Smith Company, Inc.

Sincerely,

Dear Mr. Stofer:

Your letter of March 3 has been referred to me.

In the past, we would have been pleased to accommodate your request. However, due to the increasing volume of inquiries from governments, universities, and other parties, plus requests for data not readily available through our current reporting network, we regret we have found it necessary to discontinue discretionary reporting services. Your understanding of our situation is appreciated.

Thank you for thinking of National Plumbing Contractors.

Sincerely,

Financial Aid

Dear Mr. Ohlsen:

Thank you for your letter describing the need of Sandia Youth Homes. I am sorry that we will be unable to assist you at this time with your farm project. I would, however, be interested in hearing more about the vocational training program you mentioned.

I am enclosing a copy of our Grace Foundation annual report, which includes our guidelines for financial-assistance proposals. I think it will be helpful to you in sending us more information on your program.

Our next cutoff date for new proposals is June 30. The board meeting is scheduled for the early part of September.

If you have any questions after looking at our guidelines, please do give me a call. I hope everything is going well with you and the boys and girls, and I wish you success with your farm project.

Sincerely,

CHAPTER 3

Sales

A sales letter is one of only many factors in the sale of a product or service. A need must exist—or be imagined; the customer's interest must be aroused and a choice must be made among competing salespersons and products. A sales letter probably won't accomplish all these things, but it can persuade the reader that he or she will be helped by buying the product or service.

One technique for persuasion is to use POWER words. Using words to make people DO things is the key to business success. Listed here is a sampling of power words, effective in pepping up a sales letter:

able	free	powerful
absolute	great	professional
advantage	guarantee	proved
brilliant	hard-sell	quality
confidence	help	quickly
controlled	immediate	results
delighted	impelling	satisfaction
detail	insight	scientific
different	instant	solved
economical	know	stunning
effective	largest	successful
electronic	latest	super
emphasis	lowest cost	today
expert	money-making	tremendous
extensive	new	value
fact	now	volume
fair	oldest	you
flare	persuasive	yours

As will be observed in the models, sales letters also take advantage of visual aids. These include such devices as CAPITAL LETTERS, *italics*, **bold-face**, "quotation marks," <u>underlined words</u>, dashes—, dots . . ., short paragraphs, phrases punctuated as sentences, indented paragraphs, exclamation points, bulleted lists and postscripts.

The purpose is to hold the attention of the reader, who thus becomes eager to read on to find out what is interesting enough to deserve this special presentation.

Insurance sales letters and advertisements often emphasize fear—fear of what *could* happen—"so you had better be prepared with *our* insurance coverage." Fear is one basic appeal. Other basic appeals, which are general themes or topics running through the letter, include love, pride, greed, ambition, sex, hate, and loyalty. An emotional appeal is usually more effective than an intellectual presentation.

A word of caution when appealing to these various emotional feelings; don't belittle the reader, exaggerate, trick the reader, be flippant, or abuse competitors. A little puffing of your item or service is good, but respect the intelligence of your reader.

However intelligent the reader, he or she has a limited attention span. Cover only a few selling points in each letter (or preferably only one). Trying to tell everything only confuses the reader.

What you say should be directed toward the audience you have chosen. Sell an elitist magazine to college-educated people, sell farming equipment to ranchers, sell wrenches to mechanics. Your audience can be targeted geographically down to specific postal Zip Code numbers.

The reader will want to know *why* he or she should buy; not what the product or service can do, but what it will do *for the reader*. This statement can be strengthened by a guarantee. Present a testimonial from a well-known person, offer a free trial period or a moneyback guarantee. Let the reader know you are interested in his or her welfare.

The proper length of a sales letter is debatable. One theory is that no one reads past the first page, so don't make it any longer. Another theory is that if the first page gets the reader's attention, the fourth page will clinch the sale. One standard suggestion is to tell the story and then stop, regardless of length. Another standard is to tell only enough to make the reader ask for more information. The proper length, in the final analysis, will be determined by the writer's best judgment of the presentation to which the majority of the selected readers will respond.

Selling the reader must begin with a strong statement of interest to your particular audience, be he or she a druggist, accountant, housewife, business executive, dog lover, or doctor. Also, the first sentence must relate to the statements that follow.

There are many types of attention-getting opening sentences:

- Reference to a previous personal contact
- A sentence encompassing who, what, when, where, why
- A question
- An unusual remark
- A story
- Invoking a well-known personality
- A well-known quotation
- Using the reader's name (if not obviously inserted into a blank space that doesn't fit the name)
- Use of gimmicks, such as enclosing a stamp, pencil, or address labels; or a question on the envelope that is answered inside

Endings are also important. Having presented your sales story and gotten the reader interested, he or she must be moved to action. Tell the reader exactly what to do and when: "Mail the enclosed card today"; "This offer ends June 30"; or "Phone us right now at 000-000-0000." Of most importance, make the action easy: "Phone us toll-free at 800-000-0000"; "Use the enclosed postage-paid envelope"; or "We are open 7 days a week."

When reviewing your written letter, a few checkpoints may be helpful:

- Are sales points presented clearly and simply?
- Are enough *facts* presented to make the letter convincing?
- Are the strong points emphasized in short, two- or three-line paragraphs?
- Is the appeal enthusiastic? A great salesperson is one who sets into motion the contagious emotion of enthusiasm.

How to Do It

1. Use an effective attention-getting opening.
2. Develop a central selling point.

3. Be vivid and specific in talking up the product.
4. Present proofs of your statements.
5. Close by moving the reader to specific action.

Model Opening Sentences

The following are ideas and suggestions for sales-letter openers:

It's your money that's involved and the stakes are HIGH!

Here's an indispensable invention for anyone who . . .

Strength in numbers may be good for the military, but not for the fashion-conscious woman. Barbara's Exclusive Fashions promises what the name implies.

This letter is unlike any we have written before.

Select any three books from the list below. I'll send you two of them *free*.

If you're not sure you want ___, I can understand.

If we have selected our prospects as carefully as we think, you qualify on two accounts.

Have you looked at mountain property and failed to buy because . . . ?

We would like you to select any three important professional books—value to $93—for only 99¢ each.

We nurses can never know enough about IV therapy, can we?

I wonder if you have ever had an experience like this one—

Here are nine hard-sell secrets to triple your advertising results.

This may be your last chance to . . .

You're hard to find, Mr. Anderson.

Lyons has opened a great new store in . . .

Just a little note to say HELLO and to let you know what's happening at Todd Valley.

A mortgage is a wonderful thing.

You don't know me from Eve.

Today I feel like a salty sailor.

I feel like the flinty old mule skinner.

Has your eye ever been caught by a picture so beautiful you couldn't look away?

Mark Twain once remarked. "Always do right. This will gratify some people and astonish the rest."

The two most abused words in manufacturing sales are *quality* and *service*.

This letter will keep you from being fined . . . severely penalized . . . or deprived of your livelihood under the current Tax Law.

You can well imagine the kind of quandary we are in.

Would you like an estimate of the present value of your home?

The average home is now for sale every three or four years.

You couldn't have chosen a better time to request the enclosed booklet.

I am most grateful to loyal customers like you who have made the past year the greatest year in our history.

We live in an age where there seems to be a club for just about every purpose you might imagine.

The San Francisco area has long been known for its cosmopolitan tastes.

You probably get a lot of mail like this—and it goes in the round file—but don't be too hasty!

Do you know Socrates' chief attribute? Pertinacious curiosity—and with it he came to represent the highest achievement of Greek civilization. This quest for answers has drawn Zellwell Chemicals into the search for relief from the common cold.

You can buy a Stone's lifetime battery today, next month, or probably ten years from now. But not at our special price of $85.20. That price ends February 28.

Have you ever looked in the mirror in the early morning and said, "There has to be a better way"? We have said that too. And we can help you. Jones Correspondence Courses can prepare you . . .

Did you know that the average person uses a mere 10% of his or her brain power? Why not double that, or even triple it? You can. Our new book tells you how.

So many of us are tired of the day-to-day dull routine of a salaried job. Now you can do something about it! Chicken Little Franchises offers . . .

Too many expenses have doubled in recent months. Why not double your income? Our training course has doubled the salaries of a great many men and women. It can do the same for you.

As chairman of the Board of Trustees, I'd like to personally invite you to . . .

When General Electric calls on us for information, that is something to be proud of.

Wilcox and Associates has changed its name. We thought you might be interested in the story.

Model Closing Sentences

Here is a list of suggestions to spark the reader into action:

So do the right thing for yourself—mail the card today.

Your credit is good. Just tell us what you want.

Won't you take advantage of it *now*—to put a quick stop to costly losses?

Save yourself some time. Just initial this letter and return it in the business reply envelope enclosed.

Allen Albright, a fellow you are going to like, will be around Tuesday morning to show you samples and to write your order.

Your copy of this interesting publication is ready for you. Just initial and mail the enclosed card.

Send no money. Simply mail the card.

We take all the risk. You enjoy the food.

This letter is your guarantee. Keep it but send us the card—today.

The enclosed order blank should be mailed immediately.

Do not delay—send the order blank now.

Simply check the card and put it in the mail today.

Remove the coupon below and mail it with your order at once.

Mail your check today in the convenient envelope enclosed.

We've cut all the red tape—simply mail the card.

Break out of the summer slump. Return the order blank right away.

Don't write a letter. The enclosed check-off card is for your convenience.

Before you put it aside, sign and return the card.

Just sign the card and have your secretary mail it promptly.

Our supply is limited. Act now!

Send no money. If not satisfied, don't pay.

There are no strings attached to this offer. It is simple. Just mail the enclosed postpaid card.

Put the card in the mail to start the ball rolling.

It's your move. Telegraph orders are filled overnight.

If for any reason you're dissatisfied, simply return . . . and owe absolutely nothing.

When it comes to service. ABC Corporation produces results.

We will be happy to assist you. Please give us a call.

Investment—Real Estate

Dear Friend:

Although their incomes have climbed during the passing years, many people today are living beyond their means. Some try to help themselves by taking on extra work, but there is a limit to what a person can earn in an eight- or even a twelve-hour day.

An excellent solution is to make a sound investment that will provide enough READY CASH for increasing future needs. Listed below are a few of the more popular types of investments:

STOCK MARKET   In spite of a current booming economy, in the long run stocks are somewhat speculative

SAVINGS BANKS   Yields up to __% annually: the bank then often takes YOUR money and invests it in Real Estate

REAL ESTATE   Although the market fluctuates, long-term profits are made by following these rules:

1. LOCATION As close to a MAJOR CITY as possible
2. POPULATION City requires a past and present history of growth

3. HIGH GRADE PROPERTY Not desert or swamp, but good, usable land
4. UTILITIES Water, roads, electricity, gas, phones
5. PRICED RIGHT Buy UNDER comparable land prices, if possible

We would like the opportunity to prove to you that even as little as $000 monthly may bring substantial returns over the years. Billions have been made with land located in the path of progress. In these days of high taxes, the opportunity *to keep big profits* is due to the many favorable tax concessions allowable in Real Estate.

Mailing the enclosed card may open your eyes to a new path leading to attractive long-range profit opportunities for you and your family in years to come.

Sincerely,

Business Magazine

Dear Executive:

How does your business compare with similar ones? What are you doing right? What are you doing wrong?

Read the monthly *Business Journal* and know where you stand—and why.

This magazine contains a wealth of information to help you operate more efficiently.

We feature interviews and profiles of business people, your peers—and also your competitors. Are they doing better than you? Why?

Articles about individual businesses reveal successful as well as not so successful policies and strategies. Are you placing too much emphasis on one aspect of your operation and neglecting others to the detriment of the company?

Business Journal keeps you abreast of governmental activities that affect your business, international business opportunities, financial markets, and business statistics, with special emphasis on trends, political changes and investment strategies.

Business Journal is a monthly magazine with complete economic and business coverage. The competitive advantages of reading this publication are yours for only $46 a year. We have enclosed a copy for you to examine. Do you want to continue in business without being this well informed? Please mail the enclosed card now.

Sincerely,

Magazine—Elitist

Dear Mr. Deskins:

World Journal reveals the influence of the world's best minds on our politics, science, environment, cities, and the couple next door.

Become a part of this intriguing world by learning what the great thinkers are accomplishing.

True, ideas from the world's greatest minds will conflict, but that stimulates other minds—including yours—when you read this exceptional magazine. Even with its sophistication, it is well written and easy to read.

What subjects does *World Journal* embrace? They vary from written portraits of great people and their ideas to what you as an individual can do to improve our environment. The articles and departments cover Books, Art, Poetry, Short Stories, Essays, Commentary, Medicine, Environment, Politics, Humor, and the great dissenters who write letters to the editor.

This entertaining and stimulating magazine is yours for only $34 a year. Please mail the enclosed card today. We will bill you later.

Sincerely,

Mortgage Insurance

Dear Mr. Hodges:

A mortgage is a remarkable obligation.

Do you have a mortgage? Most families do. Few families could afford to live in their comfortable homes without a mortgage and its monthly payments spread out for twenty to thirty years.

You are making regular payments from your salary, and your family is secure. But what would happen if suddenly you were no longer there? Who would continue the payments? Would the family continue to feel secure?

We have the answers. We can provide you with a simple insurance plan that in the event of your death will pay off the mortgage. Your family can continue living in their home. They can retain their feeling of security.

All this is available for only about 1 percent of your mortgage annually.

Surprising? Yes.

Simple? Yes.

Your neighborhood representative. Mr. Al Hoerner, will phone you soon to arrange a time to allow you to see how this plan works—how simple it is—and how inexpensive—especially when you consider the potential benefits.

Sincerely,

Homeowner's Insurance

Dear Neighbor:

Your homeowner's insurance is due to be renewed next month. Before you renew, please ask yourself these questions:

Is my agent a neighbor and friend?

Am I underinsured—or overinsured?

Does my coverage meet my particular needs?

Am I paying more than necessary?

If you are unsure of any of your answers. please call me at 000-0000. You can become better informed with absolutely no obligation.

Sincerely,

Flood Insurance

Dear Mr. and Mrs. Carlson:

In recent years floods have damaged untold numbers of homes, many in areas dismissed by owners who thought they were beyond danger because of the 100-year-flood myth. In 100-year-flood zones, catastrophic floods don't always wait 100 years. Can you—for flood insurance?

Nearly 30 percent of flood-insurance claims come from so-called low-risk areas. Peace of mind is the knowledge that if a flood strikes your home, recovery is possible. This requires foresight in buying flood insurance.

Call your insurance agent today and ask about the National Flood Insurance Program, administered by the Federal Emergency Management Agency. Be prepared.

Sincerely,

Health Care

Dear Mrs. Womak:

Health care is serious business, especially for seniors. And health care is being taken over more and more by HMOs (Health Maintenance Organizations).

The popularity of HMOs is due largely to the fact that they provide more services than Medicare does without charging higher monthly plan premiums. There is only a small fee at ABD Health Care for some of the extra services: $5 for annual eye exams, $7 for prescription medicines, $5 for office visits, $6 for hearing exams.

The most important part of health care is the diagnosis of a doctor. Availability of competent, medical-board-approved doctors is the main strength of ABD Health Care. We have a large staff of doctors from which to choose. And these are supplemented by a vast network of specialists to whom you can be referred.

Recent articles in news and health magazines have confirmed that ABD Health Care is one of the country's best HMOs.

To learn more about the ABD Health Care program, please call 1-800-000-0000. We can answer your questions, mail you details, or make an appointment for you to attend one of our free seminars near your home.

Sincerely,

Dentistry

Dear Mr. French:

Professional dental care is the first step to a lifetime of healthy teeth, overall health, and an appearance you can be proud of.

Robert Samoto. D.D.S., and I, Martin Hardwich, D.M.D., are established dental practitioners in this area, having worked as a team in one location for fourteen years.

We can do cosmetic dentistry to repair chipped or broken or darkened teeth or to repair unsightly gaps. We will be happy to discuss in detail how these techniques can be used in your particular case.

Of course, we are professionally trained to help you with general dental care, including cleaning, cavities, gum care, crowns, and the old fashioned toothache.

As part of our service for you, we will obtain your dental records and request from your previous dentist any medical problems or special care you require. This eliminates unnecessary examinations and X-rays.

We have a pleasant office with soft music in the background, a relaxing decor, and tropical-fish aquariums for your viewing interest. You will find our staff helpful and friendly.

Sincerely,

Book Club

Dear Reader:

Can you get current best-seller books from a book club?

You can from the Personal Book Club. This is a personal invitation to readers who like to make their own selections.

Every three months you will receive a list and description of 500 to 800 books from which you can select books for the following four months. We do not decide what books you will receive.

Topics covered include: reference, health, spirituality, memoirs, history, biography, self-help, literary fiction, mystery, classics, humor, psychology, science, art, language, economics, politics, fiction, cooking, creativity, computers.

Our new-member offer is four books for five dollars with shipping and handling included. This offer expires December 31.

Regular prices are 30 percent off publisher's prices for hardcover books and 60 percent off for softcover books. Shipping and handling costs are added. You will be billed later. However, if you pay with your order, we will pay the shipping and handling.

Purchase requirements are four books each calendar year. Free bonus books are available after you exceed certain dollar amounts of purchases.

What better way to keep informed and entertained at a reasonable cost?

Please fill in the enclosed enrollment card and mail it today.

Sincerely,

Real Estate—Homes

Dear Mr. and Mrs. Sutherland:

Once in a lifetime there is a special place.

Just beyond the gentle rise overlooking a flowering meadow you come upon a secluded setting of prestigious homes. The tree-covered slopes are fenced and guarded, ensuring protection and peace of mind.

The custom-built homes are designed by A.I.A. architects and are priced from $795,000. Homesites of from two to five acres are also available from $280,000.

These are the Wallingford Estates of Saratoga—telephone 000-000-0000.

Sincerely,

Dear Mr. Sommers:

All fired up.
Desk piled high.   Morning gone.   Energy too.
Day pushes on.   One last call and out the door.
Goodbye traffic.   Goodbye smog.   Honking horns turn to silence.
Quiet mountains.   Skittering quail.   Quiet time.
Scampering rabbits.   Time to think.   Time to breathe.
Relax.   Unwind.
       Regroup.
         Recharge.
          At Tatum Ranch. Phoenix
          A master-planned community.

               (signature).

(Reprinted from a magazine advertisement, with permission from SunCor Development Company.)

Dear Mr. and Mrs. Woodwise:

Greene Meadows Ranch is now building upscale log cabins at the western edge of the Ranch. The cabins are designed as a second home, a summer home, or a vacation home. The floor size ranges from 1,000 to 2,500 square feet. The interiors can remain rugged or be finished in contemporary styling.

Ranch activities include horseback riding, 4 × 4 back-country tours, horse-drawn wagon rides, hay rides, an all-day working ranch experience, a two-day cattle drive, and less rugged activities such as hiking, nature walks, lawn games, horseshoes, and evening campfires with marshmallows, singing, and story-telling.

For a change of scenery and activities, within one or two hours' drive you will find four national parks, a large lake with unlimited water activities, and two large cities with all the usual city amenities, tours, and recreational facilities.

If all this activity should tire you, sit back, relax and enjoy the mild sunshine, and let the world go by.

Phone 000-000-0000 for information introducing you to a new way of living.

Sincerely,

P.S. The Ranch area includes an 18-hole golf course.

Real Estate—Mountain Property

Hi Folks,

Just a friendly note to let you know that we aren't really in the high mountains. More like nestled in the foothills. But you can see the mountains and the wild-flowers from your back porch and hear the birds chirping and the afternoon breeze whispering through the trees.

Property values are rising monthly, so don't wait too long. The number of homes Rancho Verde has built now exceeds 600, and our qualified local sales staff has increased to meet the growing demand. We know you want to talk to salespeople who own cabins and houses here and who know this area. John was born only ten miles to the north. Tim has owned a cabin here for seven years. Sarah has lived for twenty years adjacent to our estates and just can't bear to move next door. I tramped through these woods as a child and live in the third house to the left down there. You are not dealing with strangers when you drop in to visit us.

If you are interested in buying a lot for future development, a comfortable cabin, or a completed home, any of our salespeople will be glad to help.

Write your name and address on the enclosed card, and we will mail you a few pictures of these foothill estates. Or just call us at 000-000-0000.

Your friends at Rancho Verde,

Camera

Dear Ms. Won:

Accept no limitations.

A horse and jockey breaking from the pack, stopped at full speed by the auto-focusing Minolta Maxxum 8000i. Because both rider and camera rose to the challenge.

Here, Maxxum's Predictive Autofocus anticipates the horse's charge for exact focus in a split second. While our Sports Action Card, one of 14 unique, computer-like Creative Expansion Cards, automatically pre-programs Maxxum to take advantage of its unsurpassed shutter speed. Freezing every detail, even at the pace of a wire-to-wire winner.

Maxxum, the world's most comprehensive autofocus system, offers more than 30 lenses to help you unleash your creativity as never before.

The possibilities are as limitless as your imagination.

For details or product information, see your Minolta dealer or write: Minolta Corporation, 101 Williams Dr., Ramsey, NJ 07446. in Canada: Minolta Canada, Inc., Ontario.

Sincerely,

Computer Modem

Dear Mr. Alvarado:

USRobotics—incredibly fast. Incredibly available. Incredibly connected. (Did we mention it was fast?)

Speed. It's the only reason to get a 56K modem. But what good is extra speed if there's nobody to connect to? That's where the new ×2 Technology 56K modems from U.S. Robotics are different.

×2 has already earned the backing of most of the top Internet service providers, including America Online, CompuServe, Prodigy, MCI and NETCOM. (Not to mention more than 400 others who have pledged their support—many of which are live now, with local access.)

So you can connect immediately at high speeds with ×2. And since ×2 is software upgradable, you'll stay connected for a long time to come.

Visit our Web site at www.usr.com/x2now or call l-800-525-USRI to find a provider near you that supports ×2 today.

Now download up to twice as fast with the company that connects more people to the Internet than any other. What are you waiting for?

Sincerely,

(With permission of Neilk Clemmons, U.S. Robotics)

Specific Customer—Roofing Tile

Dear John:

This confirms our conversation concerning real-estate developer Allen Company's plan to close down their roofing tile operation in Oakland, California, and go to the open market for their tile requirements.

The Johnson Corporation is in a very good position in the Bay Area to be a dependable long-range source of supply for roofing tile. Johnson has two tile plants in the immediate area of the Allen Company's housing developments. One plant is in Dublin, which is 30 miles east of your development, and the other is in San Jose, which is 35 miles south of your current operation. These two tile plants are under one resident manager who correlates the two operations to give the best possible service to our customers.

At your convenience I would like to arrange a tour of our Bay Area operations for you and for anyone else from your company who would be interested in seeing what Johnson has to offer as a source of supply.

You stated that your national director of purchases will visit Oakland the week of December 6 to discuss with you the procedures and guidelines for acquiring quotations on your tile requirements. You also asked me to contact you the following Monday, December 13, to further discuss what our next steps should be.

If, during the visit of your director of purchases, he or she would like to see some of Johnson's operations, we would be more than happy to make any arrangements that would be convenient. If not, John, look forward to talking to you on December 13.

Best regards,

Sales-Promotion Book

Dear Mr. Elender:

Would you like to make big money using the incredible power of the hard-sell approach that gets ACTION from your prospects? . . . actually doubling or tripling the effectiveness of your ads, sales talks, or merchandising techniques?

You will quickly learn from *The Ten Keys to Money* the clues to advertising—and selling—and be ahead of your competitors whether in retailing, wholesaling, manufacturing, or servicing. You will learn the hard-sell approach that it takes to get ahead these days. Immediately, you will write powerful and absolutely persuasive ads and promotional materials.

You will be able to look at the ad you or your associate—or your competitor—wrote and know that "this is a selling ad" or that "this needs reworking, and I know exactly how to change it."

You want to be skeptical? The *10 Keys* are time-tested, scientifically sound and success-proven techniques used for more than twenty years by the country's few most highly successful—and rich—sales people.

The *10 Keys* are explained in simple language by Tom Morlick, a successful salesman himself, in his book *The Ten Keys to Money*.

The book is yours for only $19.95. Money back if not absolutely delighted beyond your wildest expectations.

Rush the enclosed postpaid card today!

Sincerely,

Gift of Food

Every year 'bout this time . . .

we start feeling downright sentimental . . . start taking time to think of the special ladies in our lives. Lots of other folks do, too—and that's why we put together this special booklet of gifts for Moms of all kinds, on their day.

Harry and I picked these gifts especially for Mother's Day. We think there's something special here to please every Mom you want to remember at this special time of year. You'll find truly original gifts of the finest quality—such as our tangy Royal Gala Apples, imported fresh from New Zealand . . . flowers and exotic foliage plants she can grow in her home . . . our new Sweets and Sentiments, a delicate hand-crocheted pouch filled with a box of our luscious

Mint Truffles . . . and our famous homemade food gifts from the kitchens here at Bear Creek!

Best of all, our prices include everything . . . all the extras you usually pay for at stores. Harry and I will gift pack and deliver in the nicest way . . . and every gift will be sent with your own personal greeting.

Mother's Day is May 11 this year . . . and that's just around the corner. Harry and I need your instructions just as soon as you can get them to us. So please fill out your order right away . . . and return it in the special postage-paid envelope enclosed. We guarantee *you'll* be pleased . . . and so will *she*!

David

(Reprinted by permission of Harry and David, Medford, Oregon.)

Bakery

Greetings:

San Francisco has long been known for its fine foods. Barocchio's Bakery will become a part of this tradition. We recently moved into a most modern bakery with a team of exceptional baking specialists whose two concerns are quality and taste.

Our bread line is complete with varieties from bleached to black, from white enriched to 12-grain, from extra sour to honey bran.

Each day we bake a selection of cookies, pies, and sweet rolls. Choose cakes from white angel food to German chocolate fudge.

The enclosed sheet of coupons will enable you to sample a wide range of our products at a 50% discount.

We value our customers and are certain that once you have tasted our bakery goods you will know they are a part of San Francisco's tradition of fine foods.

Sincerely,

Income-Tax Consulting

Dear Mr. Tiffany:

You're probably going to pay too much in personal income taxes this year.

You are, if you're the kind of totally involved executive we think you are.

With everything else on your mind, there's a good chance you may fail to take some perfectly appropriate steps to minimize your taxes.

This makes it all the more important that you get the advice and counsel of the professionals at Deloitte, Haskins & Sells.

To start with, we'll systematically review your current financial picture and your returns for previous years. (Who knows? We may very well find refunds you've overlooked.)

Then we'll go further and help you devise financial strategies to meet your long-term business and family needs—your needs for trust arrangements, perhaps, or the sale of a family business, or exercising some stock options.

At Deloitte, Haskins & Sells, we think income tax and estate planning is a very personal matter.

When we say we don't stop at the bottom line in serving clients, we include thousands of business people and professionals among them.

They're individuals who look to us for planning for the years to come—just as much as for our help in filing this year's return.

Of course, not everybody requires our kind of help. But if you do, perhaps we should talk.

The sooner the better.

Please call the above phone number or write to the above address.

Sincerely,

(Adapted, with permission from a magazine advertisement.)

Service Contract

Dear Mr. and Mrs. Cody:

Just a reminder that your Service Contract will expire soon.

Don't let it!

Actually, your service contract is more valuable to you as your appliances get older. That is when repairs get more complicated and are therefore more costly. One service call may cost as much as the annual contract.

Renew your contract now. You will save time and money and be assured of fast, efficient service from Terry's Appliances.

We are enclosing a renewal contract for one year. You can sign and return it in the enclosed, postpaid envelope. You pay only $00 for our low-cost renewal policy.

Don't worry any longer about uncertain appliance repairs—which are always needed at an inconvenient time. You may use your credit card for easy payment.

Why not sign and return the contract today?

Sincerely,

Inactive Customer

Dear Andy,

The loss of a business friend may not seem as tragic as the loss of a personal friend, but still a part of one's self fades away when a friend is gone.

We seem to have lost you as a business friend, and we feel the loss. Is there something we have done, or something we have *not* done? As a personal favor, could you give us, briefly, the reason for apparently leaving us. Just a short sentence or two on the back of this letter is all we ask. You can mail it in the post-paid envelope enclosed.

We have recently expanded our warehouse capacity and increased the variety of paper and stationery items to serve you better. A request for a quote or an order for a carton of Scotch tape would be most welcome. We will do everything possible to become a business friend of yours again. Please let us hear from you.

Sincerely,

Collection Service

Dear Mr. Caplan:

Tylenol may be replacing aspirin as a headache remedy—but headaches remain. Especially collection headaches. Perhaps your collection remedy should be changed.

If you are plagued with "headache" accounts, let us help you. We have many years of experience and an outstanding track record of clearing up old accounts.

Our method is as simple as it is effective. First, we send out a letter that is both imaginative and skillful. It commands respect. And it gets results. Most collection problems are solved at this point.

For more reluctant debtors, we send a trained expert who is tactful and persuasive and can hold your goodwill.

Give us a try. Send us a list of your past-due accounts. If the first letter succeeds, you pay us nothing. We must, however, charge a modest fee for sending our personal service representative. If we collect nothing, you pay nothing.

With nothing to lose but your "headache" accounts, and the probable recovery of your inactive assets, give us a call today at 000-000-0000.

Cordially yours,

Public Official

Dear Mr. and Mrs. Baker:

I would appreciate your serious consideration of my candidacy for City Council when you vote on April 8 this year. You have been among the few who take the time and interest to vote in Municipal elections, which indicates your concern about local government.

Forecasts show that I have an excellent chance of winning a seat in this forthcoming election, as my years of volunteer involvement in community affairs and present position of Planning Commissioner have provided the name recognition and background that is necessary to be a viable candidate in our town.

As it is physically impossible to contact every voter personally, and as the press gives only equal and therefore minimum coverage to any candidate, I have to communicate by using signs and mailed campaign literature. To reach every voter with just one message requires over $10,000.

I hope to be able to provide each voter with sufficient facts upon which to base his or her selections on April 8. If I miss your house, it's because I did not have the funds to supply all the literature and postage necessary to mail it to you. If this happens, please understand. I cannot spend any campaign funds unless they are donated by supporters who want to see me on the City Council.

If you really want to help me and yourself for the next four years, $1 or more now and your vote on April 8 will do it.

I have always said that the way to keep an elected public official honest is to have his campaign financed by $1 each from 10,000 people rather than $10,000 from 1 person. I am sure you share that opinion.

Sincerely,

Executive Recruiter

Dear Mr. Butler:

Is your valuable time wasted in interviews and background checks of potential executives who later prove unqualified for the job? Has questionable information by a candidate slipped through the hiring procedure only to surface when the performance record of an executive is called into question weeks or even months later? Do you find too few qualified individuals from which to choose?

James and Jordan can assist you in recruiting qualified candidates for your available positions—and often with less cost to you in both time and money.

Here is why:

- James and Jordan's executive-search service covers the nation.
- We have referral agreements with other recruiting agencies.
- We are on top of the current salary market: what is being asked and what is being offered.
- We know the latest labor and fair-employment laws, rulings, and court decisions.
- We refer to you only qualified and motivated candidates.
- We practice complete confidentiality.
- We approach our work from our client's viewpoint.
- We have a large number of satisfied clients to whom you may refer.

In taking over the search for executives, James and Jordan completely eliminates one of your business problems.

Further information is available by returning the enclosed postpaid card. We look forward to working with you.

Sincerely,

Personal Credit

Dear Mr. Nordstrom:

Very likely you have heard about Individual Financing. This is our bank's special finance service created for people with an above-average income and credit standing. It occurred to me that you might be interested in hearing a bit more about it.

With Individual Financing you enjoy the remakable independence of administering your own long-term credit needs. If your annual net income is $40,000 or better and you also qualify in other respects, you'll have a credit line of somewhere between $8,000 and $40,000. Use it whenever you want to for personal, family, or household purposes simply by writing a special check of $500 or more.

Individual Financing can give you the flexibility you want through these valuable benefits:

1. There is no charge until you use it.

2. You can pay more than the minimum monthly payment, if you wish, thereby reducing the amount of future financial charges.

3. No collateral is required.

4. There are no prepayment penalties.

5. No bank visits are necessary each time you need a loan.

6. Credit life insurance of up to $40,000 is available.

Please take this opportunity to complete and sign the enclosed application and financial statement. You can be sure this information will be handled in confidence. By signing this application, you are under no obligation. Mail it in the prepaid return envelope provided. Soon after we receive your application, either a loan officer or I will call you.

Cordially,

Furniture, Retail

Dear Mr. Mosland:

Parsons has opened a great new store in Phoenix at 00000 Camelback Road. Although we're new to this area, Parsons has been satisfying home-furnishing needs since 1919. These years of experience have shown us that when you shop, you want selection, availability, and value. Parsons can offer you all that, and more!

We have expanded our selection of 200 room groupings to include our new Formal Gallery. This collection features American of Martinsville, Hibriten, the Burlinghouse Globe Collection, Thomasville, and the many other famous name brands that complete our three-million-dollar inventory.

As an introduction to our new Phoenix store, we're offering you a 20% discount on ALL regularly priced merchandise. In addition, we have a get-acquainted gift for you. It's a beautiful piece of native Indian pottery, absolutely FREE with any purchase of $200 or more.

To make shopping at Parsons even more convenient, we're inviting you to open a charge account today. With this card you can charge your purchases and never have to worry about a down payment, or tying up your credit lines on other charge cards. And your card will be welcome at any of our ninety-eight locations nationwide.

All you have to do is complete the coupon below and return it in the enclosed postpaid envelope. It's so easy, why not do it today?

Sincerely,

Art Object

Dear Alumnae:

We are pleased to announce that the University of Washington Alumni Association has commissioned world-renowned Reed & Barton Silversmiths to create in rich and precious metals a Limited Edition Damascene Insculpture (metal etching) of our famous landmark—the Rainier Vista.

This uniquely beautiful metal etching, handcrafted in pure silver, 24kt. gold electroplate, burnished copper, and bronze is being produced exclusively for Washington alumni—and for no one else. It is being offered at this time only, through this single announcement, and will never be issued again.

Each richly detailed Damascene etching of the Rainier Vista will be faithfully re-created by skilled artisans in Reed & Barton's famous patented process. The rare art medium of Damascene involves more than twenty separate hand operations in the creation of each metal etching through the painstaking blending of silver, gold, copper, and bronze.

Mounted to produce a handsome three-dimensional effect, each Insculpture will be in an antiqued gold-and-silver leaf frame, dramatically displayed against a rich velveteen background, as depicted in the attractive brochure enclosed.

A Certificate of Registration will be affixed to the reverse side of the Rainier Vista frame and will bear your name, your class year, and your limited-edition number.

Since this is the only time that the Rainier Vista Damascene Insculpture will ever be offered—and since only Washington alumni will receive this information—these exquisite works of art are almost certain to become collector's pieces.

Reed & Barton will honor all orders postmarked on or before March 31. They cannot guarantee to honor orders postmarked after that date.

The original issue price of this framed etching is just $200, including delivery. We have made arrangements to have all orders entered directly with Reed & Barton Silversmiths. You may pay for your University of Washington Insculpture with a $50 deposit, if you prefer. After you have received your insculpture, the unpaid balance of $150 will be billed at the rate of $25 a month for six months. All of these details are described on the enclosed postage-paid Reservation Form.

Please mail it before March 31.

Sincerely,

Life Insurance

Dear Wells Fargo Master Card Customer:

As you know, Wells Fargo Bank, known for its service to Californians since 1852, makes available to you many financial services including your convenient Master Card account. We are pleased that Wells Fargo has selected us to add to these services by making available to you a product design for the protection of your estate and the future security of those dependent on you.

You are undoubtedly aware that what you can buy with one dollar today is hardly more than half of what you could buy with that same dollar ten years ago. The other half has been lost to inflation.

With this in mind, we offer you a unique Term Life Insurance Plan that is competitively priced, has a special anti-inflation Benefit Protection Option, and features convenient premium payment through your Wells Fargo Master Card account.

Let me tell you about the highlights of this special plan:

Adults under 60 can select up to $50,000 of Term Life Insurance benefits.

You and your spouse, if under age 60, can protect your insurance benefits against inflation by including the Benefit Increase Option in your coverages. This option will automatically increase your insurance benefit until the total benefit doubles.

You can cover the balance in your Master Card account with your insurance benefit.

You have the convenience of having the monthly premiums billed to your Wells Fargo Master Card account.

Medical examinations are not required to apply for this insurance.

You will own your policy—it is your personal property.

You can have lifetime protection, regardless of any change in your health, because at any time prior to age 60, while your coverage is in force, you can convert this policy to a whole-life or endowment policy without evidence of insurability and without a medical examination.

We are proud to offer this Term Life Insurance Plan to you and to support it with the strength of our company, a member of AMEX Life Assurance Company group that, for 137 years, has provided Californians with quality insurance plans at competitive rates.

I urge you to read the enclosed material, which further explains the Plan, then evaluate your insurance needs, complete the enclosed application, and mail it to us today.

Sincerely,

Cost Savings

Dear Customer:

Valley Truck Supply is now in a position to reduce the cost of your truck replacement parts. This is due to our growing number of satisfied customers over the past few years.

Volume discounts are available to customers buying as few as six of an item with, however, a dollar minimum per order.

Please refer to the enclosed sheet for a list of commonly purchased parts and the discount rates.

We hope this program will help you provide faster service to your customers. We look forward to continuing to serve you in the future.

Sincerely,

Retail Sales

Dear Mr. and Mrs. Letterman:

Just a note to let you know that we at Smythe's Family Store are already having our After Christmas Sale—before Christmas so you may enjoy your savings before the holidays.

These will include shoes, shirts, blouses, slacks, and everything in the Children's Department.

This is Smythes' way of wishing you the best Christmas ever.

We look forward to meeting you during this season of good cheer.

Sincerely,

Kitchenware

Dear Mrs. Kowalski:

WHAT'S NEW IN THE KITCHEN?

    besides recipes, which change many times daily?

The answer is kitchenware. Inventors and designers are never happy. They must constantly think of something new, not only new but helpful to family cooks, to make their time in the kitchen more interesting—and shorter.

The enclosed copy of our newsletter/catalog, *Kitchenware Monthly*, shows you the latest and most practical kitchen utensils available anywhere.

The great appeal these items have will increase your retail sales and give you repeat customers.

For only $10 per year you will never be at a loss for new items to interest your customers.

Please return the business-reply card and we will bill you later, or mail your check for $10 in the enclosed envelope, no postage required. Your customers will be glad you did.

Sincerely,

Envelopes

Dear Mr. Diaz:

When I visited you six months ago, you showed an interest in our large envelopes for mailing posters flat rather than rolled. These have now been produced and are available padded or with cardboard inserts. We also have a wide variety of heavily padded envelopes for shipping small items and a collection of pleated envelopes for bulky items. All of these are made from serviceable and tested heavy paper.

I would like to call on you late this month, perhaps on the 26th, to show you samples of these envelopes. I'll phone you a week ahead so we can agree on a date and time.

It will be nice to visit with you again.

Sincerely,

Letterhead Design

Dear Mr. Bennion:

A well-designed letterhead is an effective sales tool. It is a first impression that no reader forgets.

We have real artists and designers who can add life and sparkle to your letters. Our many happy customers will attest to this.

Company logos can also be improved and modernized, either by designing a new logo or, more often, by bringing your presently recognized logo into the current era with contemporary treatment.

Just send us a copy of your current letterhead and logo and we will, with no obligation, suggest a few changes to modernize your customer's first impression of your company.

Please contact us at the above address or phone number for further information.

Sincerely,

Pest Control

Dear Mrs. Atwood:

You hate to admit it but most homes are bothered with unwanted insects. Peter's Pest Control can get rid of these pests for you.

The primary problem in many areas varies from crickets to red ants to termites to field mice—yes, even those in new-home areas adjoining open fields. Peter's knows your area and gives your problem special attention.

We spray your yard and can treat the inside of your house if you wish. We guarantee results and offer references, and our prices are competitive.

Call Peter's Pest Control now at 000-0000 and we will send an expert to discuss our guaranteed solution to your problem.

Sincerely,

Weight Loss

Dear Mrs. Cargill:

If you have a weight problem, do not despair. The Federal Drug Administration has approved the weight-loss medication Ionamin, which is effective and doesn't have the harmful effects of other medications.

But this is only a part of our complete procedure that promises proper weight loss. We perform a medical physical examination, including heart-rhythm tests, blood tests, and basic medical history.

From this we can prescribe the proper medication—if needed—diet, and exercise. Each person is different, and you will be treated as an individual.

Weight loss can be promised, but keeping your weight at its proper level can be achieved only with your cooperation and persistence.

Call us at 000-0000 for a free consultation. We can help you maintain your desired weight.

Sincerely,

Beauty Salon

Dear Mrs. Brett:

For new customers only, Helen's Hair Salon offers several exciting discounts on our much-admired hair styling.

A soft personal styling, including haircut, set, and blow dry is discounted $20.

A full set is reduced $15.

A pedicure or manicure is $10 off our regular low price.

For all our customers, we also offer wigs, complete nail care including fiberglass wraps, and razor cuts and hair coloring.

Phone 000-0000 for an appointment for our guaranteed services at a friendly place to have your hair done. Kathy, Jean, and Linette will make sure you are pleased with the results.

Cordially,

Produce Containers

Dear Mr. and Mrs. Ballam:

Crave a fresh peach when the snow is four feet high at your kitchen window? It's possible. The secret is packaging.

Storage and shipping containers for fresh produce must be ventilated—not too little, not too much. That's the secret. Riverside Forest Products designs thousands of different containers for each storage and shipping situation.

Apples from eastern Washington, figs from Palestine, grapes from Chile, oranges from California, dates from Iraq, olives from Italy; temperature changes, humidity changes, and occasional rough handling are all considered when we at Riverside design storage and shipping containers.

Yes, and we didn't forget fresh peaches from Greece to pamper your snow-bound appetite.

Sincerely,

Toyota Camry

Dear Mr. and Mrs. Wendell:

Life in the fast lane just got a little smoother and quieter.

Why start with a clean sheet of paper when you can have what *Automobile Magazine* called "The best car built in America" as your inspiration. That's why the design of the all-new Toyota Camry was dedicated to a very simple proposition. In a car, performance is the greatest luxury of all, no amount of leather and wood trim can compensate for too little power or poor handling. Which is why the new Camry offers a choice of more powerful engines. And why a refined suspension package, strengthened chassis, available traction control and standard Anti-lock Brake System are all designed as part of a single unit intended to optimize driver input and control. Camry's chassis and suspension refinements also make it one of the most comfortable cars in the fast—or any other—lane.

The NEW Camry better than ever, by Toyota. I love what you do for me.

Sincerely,

(With permission of Beth B. Henning, Toyota Motor Sales, U.S.A., Inc.)

Mississippi Welcome

Dear Mr. Coughlan:

The South's Warmest Welcome is in Mississippi, heading down the Natchez Trace with a full tank of cheese grits.

It was getting late. The sky had changed from blue to orange, and the Mississippi moon was signaling us to pull over and rest.

The sign said another 15 miles to Tupelo. We kept our car at a leisurely pace, taking in the beauty of the country houses with their rolling pastures and fishing ponds.

After all, our century-old bed and breakfast wasn't going anywhere.

Stepping through the tall doors of the majestic antebellum home was like wandering into a Norman Rockwell painting. A small chandelier hung in the foyer, and a wide circular stairway lined with paintings of distant relatives swept from the balcony.

Our room had a huge mahogany bed with big goose down pillows and an old set of family china laid out on an antique table. The window was above the garden, which by now was sprinkled with fireflies. I have to admit, somehow, this house did feel like home.

This morning, my hunch was confirmed: Southerners like big breakfasts. Really big. Our hosts made cheese grits, eggs, toast, country sausage and cinnamon apples. I suppose we'll need it. There are a lot of stops along the Natchez Trace between here and the casinos. And we're not going to miss any of them.

For your Mississippi Travel Planner, call l-800-WARMEST. To visit The South's Warmest Welcome on the World Wide Web, go to http://www.mississippi.org. See your travel agent for Mississippi vacation plans.

Cordially,

(With permission of Vaughn Stinson, Mississippi Director of Tourism Development)

Phone Service

Dear Ms. Bairley:

"Save on long-distance calls." "Sign up now and save 25%." "Save 20% on all calls." "No restrictions." "Save on weekends." "Save after 7:00 P.M." "Only $5 per month access fee." "No access fee." "United States calls only." "Twenty cents per minute." "Fifteen cents per minute." "Ten cents per minute." Etc., etc., etc. You have heard them all. Let's be sensible. Stop and think for a couple minutes.

The "fine-print" restrictions seldom appear in printed, TV, or phone-call ads. All phone companies are in business to make a profit. The competition is fierce, causing the net cost to you, the subscriber, to soon level out: Give a little here, take a little there.

Your total long-distance phone bill is determined by how many calls you make, their distance and their duration.

If you can provide us with a close estimate of:

1. How many phone calls you make per month,
2. The average length of your calls,
3. The most common destinations,

we can calculate what your monthly bill would be from several of the new long distance phone companies.

Our promise: We can undercut all competitor's prices by giving you a special rate. You will not have to dial extra numbers, pay access fees, limit your calls to certain days or hours, or pay for minutes not used.

Please contact our Customer Service department at 000-000-0000. We are here to help you and save you money.

Sincerely,

FOLLOW-UP SALES LETTERS

A successful salesperson is likely to be one who uses follow-up letters. They are effective because they generate orders from current customers and new prospects, build goodwill, iron out misunderstandings, and provide written records that may forestall future disagreements.

Additional purposes of follow-up letters are to thank buyers, to remind customers that it is time to reorder, and to introduce new products.

Because the ending of a letter is the most emphatic position, close your letter in a pleasant manner.

How to Do It

1. State the reason for the letter.
2. Explain the subject of the letter.
3. Indicate the steps you are taking to assist the reader.

Follow-Up

Dear Policy Holder:

As you know, it's almost time to renew your Comair Service Policy. It has been a pleasure serving you this past year. Enclosed you'll find a new contract form with simple instructions. Please read it carefully, then sign and return it with your check to ensure uninterrupted service coverage.

We are enclosing one of our current brochures with all of the options and prices listed. If you have any questions please feel free to call, and one of our representatives will be glad to stop by your home and assist you.

Again. it has been a pleasure serving you this past year, and we look forward to doing so for many years to come.

Sincerely,

(Reprinted with permission from Bob Unruh of Comair Service Systems, Peoria, Arizona)

Dear Mr. Tucker:

It is with genuine pleasure that I thank you for your purchase of our Model VII tractor. Choosing Normans as your dealer represents your faith and trust in us, and I, personally, would like you to know that that is a matter of great importance to us.

Please be assured that we shall endeavor to deserve your confidence and friendship. It is our company policy to conduct our business in a manner that gives full attention to providing the best service to our customers. Our personnel are chosen for their enthusiastic and pleasant attitudes and are trained to give courteous and efficient service on which you can depend.

I hope it never happens, but should Normans ever fall short of your expectations, I would consider it a personal favor if you would let me know about it.

Sincerely,

Dear Mrs. Spencer:

It has been some time since we have been in touch with you. I hope this note finds you well and ready to enjoy the holiday season.

We have been busy at Sun Ridge. You may have noticed our dramatic landscaping and seen ads locally for our many special events. Rio Salado College is now located on our campus, and Sun Ridge is bustling with activities.

We would be delighted to have you stop by for a new look at our community. I look forward to hearing from you. In the meantime, I wish you the happiest of holidays!

Cordially,

CHAPTER 4

Fund Raising

A written request for a contribution to a charity is a sales letter with a heart tug. Like a sales letter, the fund-raising letter first arouses the interest of the reader, then convinces the reader of the need for buying the product or service (or making the contribution), next tells how the product or service will help the buyer (or giver), and finally makes positive action by the buyer (or contributor) easy. The heart-tugging part is the second step—convincing the reader of the need to give.

Let us follow the steps in order, using the first letter in this chapter to explain them. The opening sentence excites the reader's interest with the intriguing statement:

Right now, the people best equipped to help runaway kids are pimps.

The first three phrases are straightforward and suggest a problem of interest to many people, but the surprising last word of the statement snaps the reader awake and arouses his or her curiosity. The reader is eager to read on.

Another letter begins:

This is the story of Ella.

Because the stories hold the promise of being interesting, the reader looks for that promise and finds:

Ella is lonely.

Now the reader wants to know *why* she is lonely. A startling first sentence is not mandatory in a good fund-raising letter, but the reader's interest must be aroused if the writer expects the letter to be read. Here are more interesting first sentences:

How much is your life worth?

Mentally retarded children may have no braces, no scars, no physically observable defects.

We don't like asking for money anymore than you do.

Having captured the reader's interest, the heart-tugging second step begins. The reader must be convinced that the cause is good and just and worthy of opening his or her checkbook. Referring again to the first letter in this chapter, how a pimp can help is mentioned, as well as why the children seek anyone's help. What happens to the child is described, arousing the sympathy of the reader, who also becomes emotionally involved with the helplessness of the runaways. Here are children as young as nine, searching for love, but hooked on drugs, selling their bodies, cast off by society, beyond the reach of family or government, helpless in the hands of brutal pimps. Any one of these treatments is reason enough to open the pocketbook of the reader.

The third step in a fund-raising letter is a statement of the benefit for the giver. The community problems of juvenile prostitution and pornography will be alleviated through the organization REFUGE. Most fund-raising letters, including this one, indicate that one of the reader's benefits will be the personal satisfaction of helping someone in need. Many letters mention the deductibility of the gift for tax purposes—definitely a direct benefit.

Making positive action by the giver easy is the fourth step. In our model letter, the chore of deciding how much to give is done by the writer when he suggests five or ten dollars. The assumption is that less will be gladly accepted and that more is hoped for. The *postscript* requests that the contribution be mailed in the enclosed envelope and states that the postage is prepaid. Envelopes and stamps are small items, but they can be exasperating inconveniences when not provided. The giving must be made easy.

Positive statements should be used in any request. Imagine the potential giver's lack of enthusiasm when reading, "We can't build a new Intensive Care Unit if you don't contribute something." It would be better to say, "Your contribution, added to those of our other donors, will assure starting our Intensive Care Unit early next year." A positive attitude in the letter promotes a positive attitude in the giver.

The first model fund-raising letter may seem emotional—and it is intended to be that—but in it, several unemotional techniques are used to induce the reader to give. A friendly, conversational tone is carried throughout the letter. Three devices are used to accomplish this: informal language, short sentences and questions, and contractions. Some contractions used are *it's, isn't, we're, can't,* and *won't.* The short sentences and questions include *It's ironic, isn't it? It really doesn't have to be that way*; and *We need your financial support.* Informal language also adds to the conversational tone: the use of the word kids, phrases such as maybe get hooked on drugs, it's an ugly scene, and beat the pimps on their own turf.

Additional sales techniques are used in other letters, and some recommended techniques even contradict others. How effective any particular one is depends on the audience to which it is directed. Here are some examples:

- Be brief.
- Fully state the need.
- Avoid gimmicks.
- Attract attention with an unusual letter layout.
- Prod the reader into fulfilling his or her pledge.
- Remind without undue pressure.
- Have the letter signed by the highest official of the organization.
- Make examples specific.
- Make the request specific.
- Have a specific use for the donation.

As these persuasions are used in the model letters, they will be mentioned in the introductions to the various sections.

Many of the model letters have a *postscript*. This is not an afterthought, but a planned part of the letter. The reason for using a postscript is to attract attention. This is accomplished by placing the added remarks outside the body of the letter and at the end, where emphasis is strongest. Just how much emphasis is added is a matter of choice. Some writers of sales letters use it constantly and some not at all, but it does add a little punch to the end of a letter.

One fact of "direct-mail solicitation" should be noted: It is one of the least effective solicitation methods. If 5 percent of the letters elicit a response, the mailing is highly successful. This fact does not diminish the dollar importance of this method, however, because a large number of small donations can add up to as much as a few large donations. The return percentage can be improved by directing specific letters to specific groups. For example, a series of three letters in this chapter were sent to doctors who work in the hospital making the solicitation, and the appeals were directed toward the doctors' involvement in that hospital. Many solicitations by colleges are addressed to alumni with the appeal made to their interest in the college. In spite of limitations, fund-raising letters do bring in large sums of money.

The following are thoughts from successful fund raisers. Keep them in mind when preparing a campaign or a letter:

- In general, 90 percent of giving is done by 10 percent of the donors; therefore spend 90 percent of your time on that 10 percent.

- Always assume that your prospect has more money than you estimate. Flattery may get you somewhere.
- It is reported that when one millionaire was asked by an alumnus why he gave a large donation to one college but only a small one to his own alma mater, he replied, "Because no one from your school asked for a large donation."

How to Do It

1. Start with an interest-arousing first sentence.
2. Explain convincingly the need for the donation.
3. Indicate how the giver will benefit.
4. Make positive action by the giver easy.

CHARITABLE HELP FOR THE DISADVANTAGED

Runaway Children

The letter to Mr. Longworth from REFUGE appeals to the reader's sympathy. The sales (or pleading) techniques, describing the dangers to runaways, tax deductibility, and informal language have been described. The letter is directed toward a wide, general audience, as indicated by the conversational style and the mention of many reasons for the reader's being sympathetic, at least one of which should appeal to any reader.

My Dear Mr. Longworth:

Right now, the people best equipped to help runaway kids are pimps.

A pimp can come off like a father figure to a kid who never had much love at home, particularly when he or she is scared, lonely, and right off the bus.

All he needs is a week to break the kid in, maybe get him or her hooked on drugs, and put the youngster out to work on the street. It's an ugly scene, and it's getting worse all the time.

Keep in mind that these are kids we're talking about, both boys and girls as young as nine who sell their bodies in the squalid marketplace of commercial sex.

It's wrong for these kids to leave home, of course, at least for most of them. Some can't really be blamed: They leave separated parents, alcoholic parents, or drug-abusing parents. Sometimes the child just can't cope with the inconsistent confusion of present-day pressures. Is it any wonder they run off, searching for the love many don't even know they're seeking?

They're society's castoffs, beyond the reach of family, church, school, or government. It's ironic, isn't it? In the richest nation on earth, the people best equipped to help runaway kids are pimps.

It really doesn't have to be that way. We think it's time to take the responsibility for their futures out of the hands of the pimps and put it where it belongs: in the hands of the people who care enough to give them a second chance—people like you.

With your help, REFUGE can make the difference. REFUGE is a nonprofit program to help communities cope with the growing problem of juvenile prostitution and pornography.

REFUGE is based on a simple idea. Every community has at hand right now the resources to help runaway children. Through REFUGE, these resources can be integrated into a network of critically needed services that will start these kids back toward useful lives.

Given enough support, we can beat the pimps on their own turf, with streetwork counselors, crisis housing, professional guidance, medical care, and psychiatric care. The point is to reach these kids before they fall prey to the pimps, advocate for their rights, and get existing institutions to take an interest.

We need your financial support.

Five or ten dollars won't make much difference in your life, but it will make a big difference in the life of some runaway child.

Do it now, please! You'll be giving us a weapon no pimp will ever have on his side: simple human decency.

Sincerely,

P.S. Please mail your tax-deductible check in the enclosed envelope. It is for your convenience, and we pay the postage.

(With thanks to the National Office for Social Responsibility, Alexandria, Virginia)

The following letter about Ella is an intriguing story of a teenage tragedy. The story technique leads the reader easily to the last two paragraphs, where the request for help is made. Requests for contributions using teenagers as the basis of the appeal are most effective when directed to people who have or work with teenagers.

Disadvantaged Girl

Dear Mr. and Mrs. Wallan:

This is the story of Ella and a teenager's loneliness. Ella does not feel isolated from her friends, but she feels trapped—as though confined inside a crowded bus: The doors are locked, the driver is missing, and no one speaks. Each turn of her head reveals only blank faces. Confusion swells inside her mind, struggling desperately to release itself when she hears voices at the other end of the bus. For a moment hope dawns—but each word is contradicted by the next. The voices seem to say one thing but obviously mean quite another.

Ella's life is like that. She is no longer a child, but not yet an adult. She is experiencing the struggle of an adolescent for identity. Actually, she is searching for a solid base upon which to make her own decisions. But in this era the search is so often in vain. Her father tells her to attend college and find a career she can happily follow, but he implies that a woman's place is in the home. Her parents say, "We'll teach you to drink in our home," but the obvious message is, "Stay away from bars and drinkers." Her mother says, "I'll help you get birth-control pills," but the thought is clear: "Sex is sinful."

Because a solid base for decisions cannot be found at home, Ella turns to her peers and friends. They have a simple solution: If it feels good, do it. She tries alcohol, she tries sex, she tries marijuana. These become intriguing, then comfortable, then compulsive.

Ella is still locked inside a crowded bus with strangers talking only in contradictions, but she is coping—she thinks.

You are the one who can help unlock the doors. Youth Service Groups has psychologists and counselors, some volunteer and some paid, working with adolescents like Ella. Your dollars are needed to help these youths who are trying so desperately to find a solid base upon which to build their lives—lives that will become self-rewarding and self-supporting. Well-chosen guidance for Ella now will forestall a future of institutionalized care.

Please use the enclosed, postage-paid envelope to make your contribution to Youth Services Groups. Even a small donation helps.

Ella is waiting.

Sincerely,

Dear Friends:

Teen Girls Rehab is a halfway center for teenage girls who are without a home due to parents leaving, past abuses, or plain neglect. We have a program that gives them a sense of security and self-respect while we help them adjust to a normal, self-supporting way of living.

The girls are offered basketball, volleyball, and quilt-making activities plus counseling and vocational guidance. Most of our counselors and coaches are retired professionals, but two are paid staff supervisors. The girls enjoy the physical activities and are happily intrigued with designing quilt patterns.

To support this project we need quilting materials, sewing machines, volleyballs, basketballs, basketball shoes, and girls' clothing. Many girls come to us with no change of clothes.

Money is also needed to pay for salaries and items not donated. Money and donations are the basis for the rehabilitation of many homeless girls. Please help them. We can pick up your donations. Give us a call at 000-0000.

God bless you,

Troubled Boys

Dear Friend:

While our youngsters prepare to observe our fiftieth birthday in December, those of us privileged to actually live and work with them have been looking back with fond memories at Hanna Boys Center's past and ahead with great hopes for its future.

I assure you that we have thought with affection and pride of the more than 2,700 troubled boys who found a measure of love and care here, and we have thought with gratitude and admiration of the literally thousands of warm-hearted people who have made our home possible through their support.

The boys who come to us are troubled and face problems too difficult for them to resolve without help. They are going through hard times. They are struggling with feelings of worthlessness, confusion, frustration, sadness, and anger. Successes are few and far between. The danger of their developing a delinquent behavior pattern is real. Unaided, they will have difficulty moving from childhood through adolescence and into manhood.

Our job here is to provide assistance—to extend the helping hand our boys and their families need at a crucial moment. The help we offer is available around the clock, provided by a skilled and understanding staff working to develop an effective program for each boy and his family. It is help that they have been unable to find in their home communities. The staff has worked closely together to improve the quality of child care, counseling, academic and vocational education, and recreation.

We have the capability of providing a large measure of love and badly needed special care for some lads whom few other individuals and organizations can help. This is true only because of the support given to us over these many years by so many people having compassion for these children. This support is principally in the form of modest gifts and bequests. Any contribution you can make to our work would be most welcome and most appreciated.

Sincerely,

Homeless Children

Dear Ms. Rizzo:

Being a homeless child does not mean the loss of parental love. It means a house is replaced by a tent, the bed of a truck, or the back seat of a car.

In this city, Child Crisis Care has started a school for homeless children. Former schoolteachers have volunteered to teach these children, who have a vastly varied educational backgrounds and mental abilities. Some children stay for most of the year and some only a week, depending on how soon the parents find a job or decide to move on.

While they are with us, the children are delighted to have something specific to look forward to each day. They are eager to learn.

As you can imagine, they have little in the way of clothing—or food. We desperately need children's clothing of all kinds and sizes. We are working with local warehouses, stores, and restaurants to get a daily supply of food for their breakfasts and lunches.

We also need school supplies: children's books, paper, pencils, crayons, round-pointed scissors, library paste, colored paper.

Because volunteer gifts come in irregularly, money is needed to fill in the gaps and to purchase items not contributed.

Please send what you can in the way of clothing, food and supplies, and add to that with a generous check to help educate those who will control our future.

The enclosed card is a reminder of what to give and where to send it.

Sincerely,

Mentally Retarded

Dear Mr. and Mrs. Cantrell:

Mentally retarded children may have no braces, no scars, no physically observable defects. But these handicapped children desperately need our help.

With proper training, many can be helped to perform small tasks and thus become more useful citizens of our community. Our training center has done much in the past and will continue to do as much as our funds permit.

Another need is research. That is the only hope for future generations. Much more needs to be learned about the causes of birth defects, and progress is being made.

I know you must consider many requests for donations, but the needs of the mentally retarded are greater than ever.

Please give this request serious thought. Your contribution, added to that of our many other contributors, can add up to real help for those otherwise so helpless.

The enclosed envelope is for your convenience. Please use it today.

Sincerely,

Disabled Children

Dear Mr. and Mrs. Jackson:

Sameness can be monotonous: it can also be wonderful—when it is the same people each year giving to the Disabled Children's Home.

You gave last year, and we feel sure you will want to give again this year. Perhaps you can give more than last year. We have more children to care for, and operating costs just won't stay down.

In addition, we are expanding our physical therapy program. We have some new equipment and need more. We need another professional therapist as well as more volunteer assistants.

All this takes more of that same commodity: money.

The children respond well to our help, and their parents are appreciative of the benefits from your contribution.

Please be as generous as possible, and use the enclosed envelope for your tax-deductible gift. Do it today.

Cordially,

Home Support for Disabled

Dear Mr. Poole:

Home Support Services provides numerous services for those who can't leave the house or haven't the physical capabilities for complete self-care.

Here are some of the services provided by our volunteers:

Grocery shopping for shut-ins:
Grocery lists are picked up on Mondays and deliveries made on Tuesdays, A.M. or P.M., as requested

Friendly visits:
One-on-one friends to visit, read mail, relieve a caregiver, accompany or take shopping

Handyman:
All minor household repairs. Faucet washers, sticking doors and drawers, shelf building, furnace filters, door locks

Transportation:
One-time shopping trips, alone or with client

Business education:
Teaching bank reconciliation, insurance-claim forms, business policies and situations

Although the helpers of these services are volunteers, we need funds to pay full-time social-service supervisors, office rent, office supplies, phone bills, and insurance.

We are a self-supporting social-service corporation, meaning that your contributions are tax deductible. Please mail your gift today in the enclosed envelope. The less fortunate will thank you.

Sincerely,

Hungry Children

Dear Mr. and Mrs. Addison:

Two ragged children sharing a can of creamed corn for dinner. A photo of that scene was printed alongside a recent, local newspaper article.

Joseph, Manuel, and Jose were left with a kindly aunt due to a family tragedy. The aunt was a widow surviving on meager social-security payments, and although she appreciated the children's needs, she could not buy enough food for them. Riverside Food Bank provided their food.

Joan was seven months old. Her abusive father disappeared, leaving her and her mother with no income. Until the mother could find work and a place for her child, Riverside Food Bank provided their food.

The sole mission of Riverside Food Bank is to feed the hungry. We distribute up to 1,000 nutritionally balanced food boxes each week to those who have nowhere else to turn.

To continue this aid to the needy, we require donated food, and money to buy additional food. Children who go to bed hungry cannot study. Parents who go to bed hungry cannot work well. They need YOUR help. For your concern and generosity, they and the community thank you.

Please use the enclosed return envelope for your thoughtful sharing.

Sincerely,

Arthritis

Dear Mrs. Fiorello:

Two years ago you volunteered to visit your neighbors to remind them of the work being done by the Arthritis Helpers and of the need for funds to continue our research.

Any of the many who suffer from arthritis can tell you of the desperate need for continuing research to find a cure for this crippling disease.

Our regional volunteers raised over $200,000 last year, and we expect to raise $250,000 this year.

You will be called when the annual campaign starts. We look forward to your favorable response.

Cordially,

Heart Disease

Dear Ms. Trail:

How much is your life worth? Consider the odds:

Heart and blood vessel disease claims an American life every 32 seconds, almost a million lives a year—including about 180,000 under retirement age.

In fact, cardiovascular disease claims more than twice as many lives as cancer. And almost as many lives as all other diseases and causes of death combined.

When it comes to giving, you're one in a million.

Your distinctive financial standing makes you one of those rare individuals who can help shape history by influencing the course of medical research. Research that has already reduced the age-adjusted death rates from coronary heart disease by 28.7% and the stroke mortality rate by 36.6%—both since 1977.

Yet as encouraging as this progress is, worlds of work still need to be done. Simply stated, we need to intensify ongoing, primary research if we are to understand, control, and ultimately prevent the underlying causes of this insidious and complex disease.

That is why we so urgently need your help now. Because far more than the average person, your generous financial support can help us unravel the mysteries that still confound us. Moreover, your gift can help give you and your family a lasting legacy of life and health—today and for years to come.

Heart disease is a monumental problem.

For instance, in the United States alone, nearly 66 million people have one or more forms of heart or blood disease. *That's more than 1 out of every 4 Americans—people just like you and your family.*

The cost is staggering: More than 88 billion dollars this year in lost wages, productivity and medical expenses.

Sincerely,

(Reprinted with permission. How Much Is Your Life Worth, 1989 Copyright American Heart Association.)

American Veterans

Dear Friends of AMVETS:

Today you and I—all Americans—have reasons to be thankful. The guns of war are silent. Our nation is at peace.

But walk the wards of any VA Hospital. Visit the men who served those agonizing years in Desert Storm—in Vietnam—in Korea—in World War II. Then you'll know why their battle is not over.

Time does not cure what a mortar shell does to a man's legs—or what two years of P.O.W. interrogation does to his mind.

- AMVETS offers a nationwide counseling service to any veteran, widow, or dependent *entirely without charge.*

- In 48 of the 50 states, there are AMVETS Service Officers, and their job is to help veterans. Whatever the problem involves, hospitalization, compensation, vocational rehabilitation, or any of a hundred other things, AMVETS is ready to give them the hand they need.

- AMVETS volunteers reach the 75,000 veterans who are hospitalized today. More than tax dollars are needed to fill the lonely hours that sometimes stretch into years.

As Americans, we must remember and be willing to help, even beyond tax-supported hospitals or a pension check. The support you give to AMVETS is one way to show how much you care.

Whatever you can give—$10, $20, $30, or more—means so much to those who gave so much, and please remember, YOUR CONTRIBUTION IS USED DIRECTLY BY VETERANS TO SERVE VETERANS—and our nation.

Please don't forget. These are the ones who paid a high price for the peace we enjoy today.

Sincerely,

Cerebral Palsy

Dear Friend:

You probably don't think of a trip to the market as anything special, but for my friend Sue, it is a learning experience.

Sue and I are attending the Cerebral Palsy Center for the Bay Area where we are learning skills to help us lead more independent lives. Through these classes, my friends and I are learning how to travel, cook, manage money, and shop—things common to you, perhaps, but that are new horizons for us.

The funds raised during Capella Auxiliary's annual Carousel Capers helped make it possible for us to attend these classes. Now in its fourteenth year, Carousel Capers is three days of fun, carnival rides, family entertainment, and, of course, good food. Capella Auxiliary is again sponsoring its country fair benefit September 21, 22, and 23, and I hope you will attend.

If you can't attend, you can still help. This year's grand prize is a new Mercury. This car, donated by a generous friend, could be yours simply by filling out the enclosed ticket stubs and mailing them with your donation of $5, $10, $20, or whatever you can. Your ticket might win you a new car.

Your donation will help make it possible for us to receive important vocational, recreational, and daily-living training. Although no contribution is required to win the car, please remember your dollars do make a difference.

We are looking forward to your coming to Carousel Capers, but if you can't, won't you still help by sending your check today?

Sincerely,

P.S. This unique Center is one of the oldest health agencies in the United States serving the cerebral palsied and others with developmental disabilities. It is independent of any other organization. Please make your checks payable to Cerebral Palsy Center for the Bay Area. Your contribution is tax-deductible.

The following letter to Dear Fellow Employee takes advantage of a specific situation to make an appeal for the United Way Campaign. The specific situation is a labor dispute during which office employees are doing manual work normally done by "blue-collar" employees. The third paragraph is a transition from the labor dispute to the request for a contribution.

United Way

Dear Fellow Employee,

I recently read a publication that stated "Colfax people are pretty special." Never has this been any more evident than during our current labor dispute when almost everyone has had the opportunity of learning more about how our plants operate and of becoming more physically involved in the actual operation.

We've all discovered new uses for our eyes, arms, and muscles in our dedication to keep the plant going. It is hoped that most of the original aches and pains have disappeared and our muscles and senses are toned up, putting many in the best physical condition they have experienced in recent years. This is one of the fortunate aspects of the labor dispute in addition to our need to help one another.

Some of the local residents do not have the eyesight to learn as we do. Some do not have the muscle control to wrap a carton, push a broom, or even push a button. Most of these good people, and I've personally seen many of them recently as they attempted to contribute to a working society, would give a fortune to walk, run, talk, write, or see as you and I do each living day. We can help them and others feel that they have a place in the sun, a place to meet and work and earn, and offer them some means of upholding their dignity.

One of the unfortunate aspects of the labor dispute is that it prevented us from early participation in the United Way Campaign, which enables us to help our neighbors and local communities. I now plead with you to help our plant contribute 100 percent to this cause by whatever monetary means you feel is fair. By single-payment or regular-payroll deduction beginning January 1, you can support the local agencies through United Way. If you wish, you can designate the agency to which your tax-deductible donation is given. This is a new option, so feel free to make your choice on the enclosed card.

Thank you for taking the time to consider this.

With appreciation,

Disaster Relief

Dear Mr. Marcum:

Wherever disaster struck last year in the United States, we were there.

Emergency Relief, Inc., helped over half a million individual victims, providing them with clothing, food, shelter, and moral support. We helped them locate family members and gave them temporary financial help. In many cases we coordinated our efforts with the larger national relief agencies.

However, our specialty is getting to disaster areas before other agencies. Immediate help is often of great importance to the victims.

Our ability to arrive early, often before destruction has hardly started, requires your help as well as ours. Please give generously. Use the enclosed card and envelope for your tax-deductible contribution.

Sincerely,

Sponsor a Child

Dear Friend:

At last! Children International offers a $20 sponsorship program for Americans who are unable to spend $40 or more a month to help a needy child.

And yet, this is a full sponsorship program because for $20 a month you will receive:

- a 3½" × 5" photograph of the child you are helping.
- two personal letters from your child each year.

- a complete Sponsorship Kit with your child's case history and a special report about the country where your child lives.
- issues of our newsletter, "Sponsorship News."

All this for only $20 a month? Yes—because Children International believes that many Americans would like to help a needy child. And so we searched for ways to reduce the cost—without reducing the help that goes to the child you sponsor.

For example, unlike some of the other organizations, your child does not write each month, but two letters a year from your child keep you in contact and, of course, you can write to the child as often as you wish.

Also, to keep down the administrative costs, we do not offer the so-called "trial child" that the other organizations mail to prospective sponsors before the sponsors send any money.

We do not feel it is fair to the child for a sponsor to decide whether or not to help a child based on a child's photograph or the case history.

Every child that comes to Children International for help is equally needy!

And to minimize overseas costs, our field workers are citizens of the countries where they serve. Many volunteer their time, working directly with families, orphanages and schools.

Will you sponsor a child? Your $20 a month will help provide so much:

- emergency food, clothing and medical care.
- a chance to attend school.
- help for the child's family and community with counseling on housing, agriculture, nutrition, and other vital areas to help him or her become self-sufficient.

A child needs your love! Fill out the enclosed coupon today.

Then, in just a few days you will receive your child's name, photograph, and case history.

May we hear from you? We believe that our sponsorship program protects the dignity of the child and the family and at the same time provides Americans with a positive and beautiful way to help a needy youngster.

Sincerely,

(From a magazine advertisement; used with permission)

Lung Disease

FIGHT LUNG DISEASE WITH CHRISTMAS SEALS®

For more than seventy years, people have used Christmas Seals® as festive additions to their holiday mail. But their real purpose goes far beyond decoration.

Your contribution means vital support of Christmas Seals programs against Emphysema, Bronchitis, Air Pollution, Smoking, TB, and Asthma.

Your gift will bring victories that will enable children to breathe better on long nights and develop into healthy grown-ups—victories that will help you, and millions of others, enjoy healthier lungs in later years.

Strengthen this work. Use Christmas Seals®.

It's a Matter of Life and Breath®.

Mail your contribution in the enclosed envelope.

Thank you for your gift in any amount. It is tax deductible.

Sincerely,

(Reprinted with permission from a 1979 brochure. Christmas Seals® is a registered trademark of the American Lung Association.)

Working Mothers

Dear Mr. Alexis,

Your firm has given generously to the Seattle Children's Society each year.

The Society provides needed daytime facilities for the small children of working mothers. It furnishes play space seven days a week and offers counseling services to families and individual children in need of help.

We are sure Alexis, Inc., will want to continue to support this work. For your convenience we are enclosing a pledge card. You have previously subscribed $500 a year. Any increase this year would be greatly appreciated by the children.

Sincerely,

Inner-City Children

Dear Mr. and Mrs. Chevalier:

Love! That is something missing from the lives of too many inner-city children. How can you share your love with these children?

Since 1880, Rural Life has sent children from the crowded, unfriendly inner-city streets to a country ranch or estate for two weeks of fresh air, sunshine, and loving guardians. We have provided over a million disadvantaged children with a true "summer vacation." They return healthier and more contented.

Your love and only $350 will do all this for a deprived child.

Rural Life's activities and finances are recorded at the State Registration Department. To help, please call the above phone number or write to the above address. An exposure to rural life will make an inner-city child happier.

Sincerely,

LIBRARY

Often a series of letters will succeed better than one in raising funds. One letter might be discarded or put aside without further thought, but the second letter reminds the reader of the first, and the third of the first two.

A series like this one for libraries should be planned for mailings covering a full year. Send one each two months until a contribution is received. Watch two things: (1) send letter three, Thank You, only if contributions were received during the previous year, and (2) when money is received, cancel further mailings for the current year.

If the first letter doesn't open the reader's checkbook, a subsequent one may. Constancy in fund raising as well as in advertising produces results.

Letter One—What We Offer You

Dear Mrs. Roth:

The Meadowvale Library has much to offer you, even though it has been here only three years.

We have 40,000 books in a range wide enough to satisfy nearly every reader's interest: general fiction, detective, western, biography, history, hobbies, travel, health, arts, nutrition, and a complete reference section on (your state). Large-print and talking books are available for the vision impaired. A small selection of braille books is also available.

Several hundred records, cassettes, and compact discs have started fast-growing collections of music and topics of current interest.

New books and those in high demand may be rented for a small fee. An inter-library loan can get you practically any book in print.

Paperback books are available on an exchange basis operated on the honor system: You return the number of books you check out.

We have growing newspaper and periodical selections, and an extensive financial-reference section.

To provide all this, and more to come, we need your help. We are NOT tax supported. We depend entirely upon your membership, your gifts, your memorials, your bequests by will, and your volunteer help. All financial donations are tax deductible.

We can serve you in proportion to the support we receive from you. The enclosed envelope is for your convenience.

Sincerely,

Letter Two—Seeking Memberships

Dear Mrs. Roth:

I am sure you join us here at the Meadowvale Library and your friends in the community in wanting a first-class library.

We have made a good start. We have an excellent selection of fiction and non-fiction books, many current magazines and metropolitan newspapers, financial periodicals and advisory services, ample table space and comfortable chairs, an extensive cassette and compact-disc collection, and a willing and helpful group of volunteers. Other services are planned: weekly movies, book-review discussion groups, lectures on current and historical subjects, and a genealogy section.

Because we are not supported by taxes or other public funds, we need your contributions to continue and to improve our services to you.

You can become an important part of the Meadowvale Library by joining our membership, helping us to expand and become more responsive to your needs. The Library is yours. It can use your help.

A membership card is enclosed with suggested levels of membership. Select the one you feel comfortable with and return it with your tax-deductible contribution in the enclosed envelope.

Sincerely,

Letter Three—Thank-You

Dear Mrs. Roth:

Thank you for the contribution you made to the Meadowvale Library last year. The response from the whole community was heartwarming.

We are pleased that we nearly reached our goal for last year—but now it is this year—and a new goal of $55,000 has been set. It would be most thoughtful of you if you would continue to include the Meadowvale Library in your tax-deductible "giving" plans.

The value of your giving is returned to you in our many library services that benefit the total community: a wide selection of books, home-town newspapers, cassettes, compact discs, financial-planning aids, plus plans for lectures, movies, a genealogy department, and more in the future.

Thank you again for your helpful support in the past and for the support you will provide for this year. Every dollar counts.

Cordially,

Letter Four—Magazine Campaign

Dear Mrs. Roth:

The friends of the Meadowvale Library urge you, your business, or your organization to join with us in donating money to the library's magazine campaign. Contributions make it possible for Meadowvale Library to maintain a broad range of magazines for the use of everyone in the community. During the campaign, the librarians also welcome suggestions from you or your group about any periodicals you would like to see included in the library's magazine collection.

We hope that you will contribute to the Meadowvale Library's magazine campaign of this year and that your donation will be generous since subscription rates for most magazines have risen steadily over the last few years. Our campaign for donations will continue through September of this year.

If you wish, your name or that of your organization will be displayed prominently in the library along with the name of other magazine campaign donors. Remember, your donation is tax deductible.

Please make your check payable to the MEADOWVALE LIBRARY MAGAZINE CAMPAIGN.

If you have any questions or suggestions, please call Jean or Barbara at 000-0000.

We know that caring people will give to the Meadowvale Library Magazine Campaign for 0000 because they want to promote quality library service in our community.

Sincerely,

Letter Five—Need Volunteers

Dear Mrs. Roth:

This is an invitation to you and other area residents to participate in the continuing growth of Meadowvale Library. Our library is the information, research, and recreational reading center of Meadowvale. It is here for your use, and it needs your volunteer help.

Most of our staff are volunteers. Only the head librarian and two assistants are paid. Checking books in and out, reshelving returned books, handling the information desk, and even housekeeping is done by our dedicated volunteer staff. Most work one or two days a week, but even a half day a week is a big help to our growing number of book borrowers.

Volunteers alone, however, will not keep our library operating. We need money for the three salaries, for new books, for magazine and newspaper subscriptions, and even for such mundane necessities as water, lights, and heat.

We urge everyone in the community and especially our library users to consider seriously our current funds appeal and to become annual participants in an orderly expansion of library facilities. Any amount you can contribute will be most welcome.

Please use the enclosed envelope and the slip with its suggested giving levels to mail your tax-deductible donation. And, if you can donate some time, please call Roger Smith, our head librarian, at 000-0000.

Yours for a better library,

Letter Six—Exceed Last Year

Dear Mrs. Roth:

Our Meadowvale Library circulates approximately 12,000 books monthly from its 40,000 book collection. The library is expanding, the community is growing, and our needs increase.

Last year's solicitation resulted in contributions of over $46,000. This year we hope to exceed that amount. We need $55,000 if we are to continue to serve our expanding population.

We are finding more and more people using the reference section, and we hope to increase it to meet the needs of our library users. We pride ourselves on being able to answer so many questions, but continually find we lack this or that reference work.

An increase in your annual donation would go far toward improving our reference department. Please use the enclosed slip and envelope to mail your tax-deductible donation. You will benefit from your own gift.

Cordially,

CHURCHES

In addition to God's blessings, churches, to survive in our era, need cold cash. The most successful solicitation letters include a secular appeal. An appeal made strictly from a religious or Godly or loving or intangible basis will, however, bring forth gifts from certain donors. As with other solicitation letters, the use to which the money will be put should be spelled out. One church letter makes a request for two specific, tangible items: seats and an altar rail—both to improve the worship area.

Secular Appeal

Dear Mr. and Mrs. Helverson:

We don't like asking for money any more than you do. But when the cause is just and the Christian spirit is there, the asking is easier.

As we have mentioned in recent Sunday worship services, the Sommersville Community Church needs your help in making it a better place to serve you. In particular, we need new pews at the back of the sanctuary and a new altar rail. (It's the rail, not our faith, that has been wobbly.)

The members with whom I have talked agree that these worship-area improvements are necessary. The amount needed is $6,500. This money can be raised quickly if each member family contributes $55.

Please join your fellow members in accepting this invitation to make our worship facilities more pleasant. Please use the enclosed envelope, which you may mail or place in the collection plate on Sunday.

The entire congregation will appreciate your efforts to continue His work in Sommersville.

Sincerely,

P.S. We hope all contributions will be made within sixty days. Then the improvements will be completed for our Christmas services.

Dear Dr. and Mrs. Mehdi:

A mosque's roof does not shut out Allah. Allah is omnipresent. But a leaking roof does let in water. And that's the problem.

Our forward-looking budget committee anticipated three years ago the need for a replacement roof. A new roof fund is in operation, but the recent, unusual wind storm loosened so many shingles that more than patching is now required.

We urgently need more funds to replace the roof before the winter rains begin. Please consider additional donations now or an advance on your regular giving. It's the rain we're trying to shut out.

Cordially,

Fund-Raising Start

Dear Mr. and Mrs. Evans,

You will agree, I am sure, that the enclosed proposal for our church sets forth a program of which we can be proud. We believe we can do this job with the help of the other members and you. Note especially the new local Missions program and the expanded youth-activities program.

The Finance Committee of our church, reflecting the mood of our church members and friends, is interested in making this one of our most significant years. Your giving will supply the tools for building the programs that will positively help our community.

A few homes will be visited during the week starting September 7, in advance of our general solicitation. I know you will be giving serious thought to your share in our enlarged program.

Your gift not only brings hope to many others at home and abroad, but it also enriches your own life.

Sincerely,

Every-Member Canvass

Dear Mr. and Mrs. Elender,

On Sunday, September 16, our church will take an important step forward. In a spirit of consecration and worship we will dedicate ourselves to greater service for Christ during the coming year.

We hope that you will be present to join with us in the simple service. Although no financial commitments will be taken then, the occasion will start our Every-Member Canvass. This year we have two obtainable goals:

1. Every member pledging to support current expenses and missionary goals.
2. Every pledge increased.

We are enclosing a copy of the proposed budget. It shows you both needs and opportunities.

During the week starting September 16, church visitors will call on all members and friends to discuss our plans for the coming year. We invite you to consider with concerned prayers your part in our enlarged program. Let us face together the challenge that economic need has thrust upon our church.

Plan to be with us on Dedication Sunday, September 16.

Cordially,

Budget Can Be Met

YOU HAVE RESPONSE-ABILITY

To: Members and Friends of Temple Sinai

From: Bob Baskin, chairman of the Finance Committee

With the knowledge that the work of the temple *will* be done and with the knowledge that an informed congregation *will* respond, the financial condition of your temple is presented below:

Our budgeted income through 10-31-__	$99,590
Our actual income through 10-31-__	*90,746*
We are short of our goal by	$ 8,844

At least $7,500 of this shortfall must be collected. Each member MUST consider his or her individual responsibility in this crisis situation and respond accordingly.

If 250 members and friends give an extra $30 during the month of December, the $7,500 will be raised.

With the knowledge that a response to this request IS possible, we can move ahead with far greater hope and assurance.

We appreciate the concern and RESPONSE-ABILITY we know you will share with YOUR temple at this time!

Sincerely,

The following letter is a lighthearted reminder to fulfill a pledge to the church. The layout is intended to attract attention and to lead the reader pleasantly to the realization that a pledge is a promise that must be kept.

Delinquent Pledge

Once upon a pledge card . . . Mrs. Aronson.
You promised your support to the Riverside Youth Building.
And then, the architects were called in
    and a contractor found (we signed);
    the cement arrived one sunny day,
    the foundation was laid, solid and square.
The passersby observed·
    the floor that was poured
    and troweled so smooth,
    a two-by-four here,
    a rafter truss there.
    the roof was on.
Let's move in!
    an office desk in that corner,
    a class held here,
    a meeting there;
    a pot-luck supper is planned.
And then it happened—
    we found that you were behind
    in meeting your pledge—made
    once upon a pledge card.
Now, what do you think we should do about that?

(Signed)

Dear Mr. and Mrs. Hickerson:

On October 2 we received your pledge card for the year _ _ _ _. It is now mid-April and we have received none of your monthly pledged amounts—and they have already been committed to our local Parson School for homeless children.

For your convenience, we have enclosed a postpaid envelope. Please reply with whatever amount you can contribute at this time.

Sincerely,

Stewardship Committee

Love Is a Reason for Giving

Dear Church Friend:

> Loving, Sharing
> Giving, Caring,
> This is what the Lord
> Meant Christians to be.

Have you ever given love and not had it returned? Then you know how God must feel much of the time. Love is sharing. Think of the happiest moments of love—moments with your children, with your spouse, with God, at Christmas time—and you realize that giving stands out. God's love was demonstrated by the ultimate gift, "For God so loved the World that he gave his only begotten Son."

> Love is sharing.

You have an opportunity now to share your love with your Church. As we enter the period of stewardship emphasis, I appeal to you to show your love by making a financial commitment to God's work for the coming year.

> Care deeply for
> Christ our Saviour.
> Care for the Church as
> The Lord cares for you.

Sincerely,

Mission Potluck

Dear Church Friends:

Our fourth annual Missionary Potluck Supper will be on April 30 at 5:30 P.M.

Our feature for this meeting will be an informal talk by Dr. Joseph Bair, founder of Boundless Hope, a Christian mission in Peru. Dr. Bair has spent over thirty years as a missionary in South America. He and Boundless Hope's chairman, José Arrendondo, will describe the mission's efforts and successes in aiding the homeless street children of the cities in Peru. The two men are fascinating speakers and will present a short movie of the streets of Lima, Peru.

To sign up, please fill in the enclosed card and bring it to the church office or place it in the basket in the Meeting Hall.

A box for donations to Boundless Hope will be at the door.

Cordially,

HOSPITALS

Both public and private hospitals feel the need to solicit the public for funds—funds that it is hoped will approach the need. The basic appeal is to the satisfaction that the giver receives from helping someone in need. A secondary appeal is the selfish one of helping oneself by giving to a hospital in which one has been or may become a patient.

The first letter from Mount Zion Health Systems, Inc., San Francisco, is to a prospective donor. The uses to which the donor's money will be put are listed and explained. The last paragraph suggests how much to give and mentions the convenient mailing envelope. A suggested amount and a return envelope are standard techniques—and they are effective; they should be included in all solicitation letters.

Updating Facilities

Dear Friend:

If you made an inspection tour of Mount Zion today, you would see the activity that has already taken place or is getting underway in the hospital's second-year program of updating facilities and equipment. For example:

- Renovation of patient rooms

- Moving of fifty patient beds from "C" Building (which can no longer house patient-care facilities because of new earthquake requirements) to the new seventh floor of "A" Building
- New Courtyard Building under construction to house new lobby, Admitting Office, Dispensing Pharmacy, and kitchen
- Construction of new quarters for Geriatric Day Care
- Completion of four floors of the Mount Zion Pavilion for the Prenatal Center, including Obstetrics, Intensive Care Nursery, Regular Nursery, and Alternative Birth Center

All this work and much more has to be done to modernize and renovate our hospital. Space that is today handling a greatly increased volume of patient-care programs with new lifesaving technology has not been changed in fifteen years and must be expanded.

We are not adding any new beds, but are seeking to preserve the quality of medical care for which Mount Zion Pioneer, a core group of supporters, has contributed in the historic first two years of our Annual Campaign.

A reply envelope is enclosed for your convenience. I hope to hear from you at an early date and to welcome you as a member of the Pioneers. A gift of $100 would be most appropriate—$1 for each of the hundred years Mount Zion has been serving the community.

Sincerely,

The second letter is to former patients who may appreciate their hospital care enough to contribute to the care of others. The persuasive technique is the use of success stories.

Success Story

Dear Friend:

Do you like success stories? We hope that your stay at Mount Zion was one, and we would like to share with you just two of the many at Mount Zion's Senior Day Health Center:

Mrs. W.S.

65-year-old widow. Residing with employed daughter since husband's death. Adjustment to this living arrangement complicated by a physical condition that worsened, severely limiting mobility and increasing dependency. Since becoming Center patient, occupational therapy with use of adaptive equipment has decreased dependency greatly. Able to assist daughter in meal preparation. Has developed many new interests. Contributes regularly to Center Newsletter. Involved in writing life history and recently has been learning to weave. Only complaint is that days are not long enough.

Mr. C.H.

75-year-old married man. Confined to wheelchair following stroke three years ago. Referred to Center by his disabled wife to whom he has been married 55 years. She attempted to care for him at home but even with maximum allowable homemaker assistance was unable to do so and he had to be admitted to nursing home. Lost interest in life; both he and wife finding separation extremely stressful. Based on availability of Day Health Center services, discharged from nursing home. Motivation increased immediately. Now ambulates short distances with supervision. Enjoys copper enameling and has delighted wife with gifts made for her at Center. Couple now able to give each other emotional support that was integral part of their lives for 55 years.

The Center changes the lives of its patients from hopelessness and despair to happy, fulfilling days of newfound physical activity, new interests and new friends and sociability. This is why we are so anxious to make its new home, about which we told you in my preceding letter, comfortable, cheerful, and suited to the needs of its patients. Won't you please help us furnish and equip it by making your gift to the 0000 Annual Campaign today? An envelope is enclosed for your convenience. We suggest $101—$1 for each year Mount Zion has been serving the community—but any amount is most welcome.

Sincerely,

The tone of the next letter is direct and positive. This candid approach will appeal to many, but the recipients of this frank letter must be carefully chosen.

Expansion Costs

Dear Mr. and Mrs. Halstrom,

The hospital staff wants to help you!

To provide medical help they must have adequate facilities. Clayton Hospital is expanding to provide you and those you love with better medical care.

Our recent expansion includes a new Intensive-Care Unit for the critically ill and a modernized Pediatric floor. During the next two years, a Cardiac-Care Unit for patients with heart trouble will be built.

The value of lives saved cannot be measured, but the cost will exceed $6 million. Much of this money must come from the community and donors like you.

How much should you give? That, of course, is up to you, but we suggest a tax-deductible minimum of $50.

This is an opportunity I hope you will take to invest in medical help for your community and for you.

Please send your contribution soon in the enclosed postage-paid envelope.

Sincerely,

P.S. The staff and patients, present and future, are looking forward to the help your donation will provide.

Maintain Quality Service

Dear Mrs. Finnegan:

Renovations to our Medical Center have just been completed. We invite you to visit the "new look." The lobby has been repainted and a new rug installed. The wall pictures were donated by Mrs. Dolores Arquette and the Northwest Museum of Art.

All patient rooms have been painted in pastel colors and include new carpeting. Interest is added to the hallways with pictures loaned by the city's many art groups.

A new feature is a series of ramps for quick exiting. They are designed so patients' beds can be rolled down them instead of relying on elevators, always danger spots in emergency situations.

Community hospitals belong to all of us, and we never know when we may need them ourselves. It therefore behooves us to make sure they are properly staffed and maintained at all times. This requires money. Your donation is needed and will be appreciated by all the patients.

The enclosed postpaid envelope is for your convenience in mailing your tax-deductible gift.

Sincerely,

The three following letters are a series mailed to doctors who work at the hospital that is making the request for contributions. The mailings were approximately one month apart. The first letter appeals to our human need to be part of a group: "because you belong to the hospital family." The second letter appeals to the doctor's business experience (rare is the doctor who is not well versed in the business aspects of medicine). The third letter is a short review of the first two. The statement in the first sentence that this is the "last invitation" is both an appeal to give *now* and a relief to the doctor that no more solicitations will be received.

Doctors Join in Giving

Dear Doctor:

As a member of the Mount Zion family, you benefit from the contributions that the hospital receives in terms of improved facilities for the care of your patients. Therefore, I am sorry that up until now I have not had the opportunity to share with you what happened last year in one area of support.

For the first time in its history, friends of Mount Zion were asked to participate in an Annual Giving Campaign. Annual campaigns have long been a tradition in many hospitals throughout the country, and they provide a dependable source of support for current pressing needs.

By contributing $1 for each of the 99 years we had been serving the community, a donor could become a Mount Zion Pioneer. The response was so gratifying that we decided to reopen the ranks for the second year. After this, they will be closed.

You were not asked to participate last year, but because you belong to the hospital family I thought that you, too, might welcome the opportunity to Join the Pioneers.

This is my invitation to you to become one by contributing $100 to the 0000 Annual Giving Campaign—$1 for each of the years we have served the community. I hope you will accept. Your support will help your hospital serve you better.

Sincerely,

Doctors as Business Persons

Dear Doctor:

I am writing again to invite you to join the Mount Zion Pioneers by contributing $100 to the Second Annual Giving Campaign—$1 for each of the 100 years the hospital has served the community.

In some ways a hospital is like a business—its facilities and equipment must be improved constantly. As you know, many of Mount Zion's facilities have not been changed in fifteen years but are today handling a greatly increased volume of patient-care programs with new lifesaving technology. They must be modernized.

The recent Capital Funds Campaign raised a substantial amount to assist with renovation and new equipment, but campaign goals are seldom realized, and this one was no exception. Rising costs are another problem.

Notwithstanding, the work in progress must be completed as soon as possible and other phases of modernization must be gotten under way (see the enclosed Fact Sheet).

The real business of Mount Zion is LIFE—helping it to be born; strengthening it; saving it. Please help us provide you with the most effective medical facility possible in which to do it. Send your gift today and become a Mount Zion Pioneer.

Sincerely,

Last Appeal to Doctors

Dear Doctor:

This is your last invitation to become a Mount Zion Pioneer. This year's Annual Giving Campaign is ending soon, and I hope that when it is over your name will be on this year's list of contributors.

Mount Zion is your hospital and it needs your support in keeping abreast of advances in medical research and technology.

As you know, your gift will help provide optimum facilities for the care of your patients, and it is urgently needed to carry on the modernization and renovation program now underway.

As a member of the Mount Zion family, please do become a Mount Zion Pioneer: Give $1 for each of the 100 years this hospital has served the community and mail your check in the enclosed envelope today.

Sincerely,

Using a Specific Example

Dear Friend:

A broken arm . . . severed above the elbow in an automobile accident . . . a small incident in our troubled world—but of more than small importance to Janet Collins.

Two years later she has nearly full use of her arm and hand, thanks to the expertise of the microsurgery team at Cantebury Hospital.

Janet's severed left arm was picked up by a police officer at the scene of an accident and packed in ice from a nearby restaurant. The police sped her to the nearest emergency medical station from which she was rushed by helicopter to the downtown heliport, then by ambulance to Cantebury Hospital. The microsurgery team spent fourteen feverish hours reattaching Janet's arm.

The microsurgery team inserted a steel rod at the elbow, then brought the rod out of the cut and into the upper part of the arm. Then an artery and three veins were connected. Major nerves were tied, and finally the skin was sewn.

Nearly two years were required to get full feeling into the fingers. Therapy and slow progress are Janet's future, but she is happy to have the use of her arm again.

Cantebury Hospital is doing its small part to serve this troubled world. Will you share in the Hospital's efforts? The enclosed envelope is for your convenience in making a gift to Cantebury Hospital. You will receive the gratitude of our many patients.

Sincerely,

Need New Equipment

Dear Friend:

Our medical equipment does not belong in an antique shop—it merely seems that old. The rapid advance of medical technology is the reason for the early obsolescence of much of our medical equipment.

On the other hand, many of our beds have wobbly wheels, and some will crank only halfway up. The floor covering in three rooms is worn through.

Ordinary equipment does wear out, and lives depend on having the latest diagnostic equipment available when needed—when *you* may be the one in need.

Obsolete medical equipment must constantly be replaced, and that is why we appeal to you each year to do what you can to aid the community and yourself through a donation to West Center Hospital.

Contributions last year were generous, and we anticipate that they will be even more generous this year. The enclosed envelope is for your convenience. Whatever you give will be deeply appreciated and will ensure continued medical care for all of us.

Sincerely,

Dear Ms. Toelken:

One of the recent diagnostic medical tools is the MRI (Magnetic Resonance Imaging). West Center Hospital does not have one.

Hadassa Degani and colleagues at the Weizmann Institute of Science in Israel have developed a procedure using MRI that promises to detect breast cancer. This is a noninvasive procedure that could reduce the need for biopsies.

Although not proven yet, this procedure points the way to other diagnostic advantages of an MRI machine.

A fund has been established to collect contributions for the purchase of this medical tool. We hope your generous gift to West Center Hospital will be an important send-off to our fund-raising campaign. A postpaid reply envelope is enclosed.

Sincerely,

Appeal to Ego

Dear Mr. and Mrs. Yang:

We recently received a donation of $75,000 toward the purchase of an MRI (Magnetic Resonance Imaging) machine for Riverside Medical Center.

Donations of this size are rare but also encouraging: It indicates the willingness of people to help others. Diagnostic tools have advanced greatly in recent years, but they are also expensive. An MRI scanner costs about $2 million. The scanners are noninvasive diagnostic machines used to obtain clear pictures of the interior of a person's body.

If you don't have $75,000 to contribute to the continuing support of our medical center, whatever you can give will be appreciated. The purchase of this machine is within sight, and its benefit to our patients is immeasurable. Please give enough to make yourself feel good.

Cordially,

Join Hospital Foundation

Dear Friend:

Everything in the health-care profession is changing—except the need for funds to meet today's demands and be ready for tomorrow's needs.

Today's health-care institutions face unprecedented changes. These changes involve new concepts in medical care and treatment, increasing specialization in services and equipment, development of service-training programs, government partnership in medical insurances programs, population growth, and changing sociological patterns. A program to develop critically needed supplemental income for our health-care institutions is imperative.

The Foundation, an agency through which such a program is to be projected, has been created. The Wheeler Hospital Foundation is a completely autonomous, nonprofit, nongovernmental organization established to support Wheeler Hospital. The Foundation would afford a means for accepting in a legal, orderly manner the philanthropy of donors who have the spirit and will to give.

Through a permanent Foundation, the independent financial security of the Wheeler Hospital may be achieved.

Through this Foundation, a fund will be built up year by year that will be available continuously for essential capital and supplemental operational needs. This Foundation, as the responsible agency for a continuing financial program, will embark upon programs that may extend far beyond the life span of any one individual.

The Foundation will involve many influential persons from all walks of life.

The Board of Trustees, consisting of 48 representative citizens of the area who volunteer their time and talents, invites you to regard the Foundation as one of highest priority. It will be both life-giving and lifesaving.

When you join with other leading citizens of this area as a member of this new nonprofit corporation, you will be part of a team dedicated to the development of the finest health-care facilities possible. What could be more worthy of your wholehearted support?

Sincerely,

P.S. The enclosed card and envelope are for your convenience in requesting more information about ways you can help.

SCHOOLS

The "old college spirit" often leaves the campus right along with the sheep-skin. In an attempt to recapture that spirit, colleges write to alumni with requests for donations to the "dear old alma mater." To be successful, a request for a contribution must be for a specific project or purpose. The first letter requests increased giving to combat inflation and attract a more competent faculty. The main appeal is to pride.

Give More than Last Year

Dear Mr. Warner,

Difficult choices must be made during difficult times. Increasing inflation rates coupled with reduced tax revenues make the choices of where and how much to give truly difficult. It is especially difficult for those of us who care deeply about Harcourt College and its 140-year tradition of excellence.

This year you are being asked to increase your annual gift by 20 percent. Last year's gift of $100 was encouraging—and we did manage to balance the budget. But, with 3 percent inflation, we need more than that even to think about strengthening our traditional standards of academic excellence, community service, and social responsibility.

Our tradition of excellence and responsibility is ours to improve upon or to let fade away. As president of Harcourt College, I feel a special and personal responsibility to future generations of students. It is through past and continuing efforts of people like you that we can meet the expectations of future students. They, too, will want to experience the basic qualities of Harcourt College: a sense of honor and decency, a pride in academic proficiency, a feeling of joy and pleasure in both work and play, a love of growing and learning together, and the acceptance by our community. These qualities, although partially intangible, can be realized only in a climate of financial security.

Our strength has been the ability to attract students and faculty of the highest competence. This we must continue if we are to keep Harcourt College what it is today; but the cost will be greater tomorrow.

Viewed this way, perhaps our choices for giving are not too difficult. An increase of 20 percent in annual giving will maintain our tradition of excellence and assure its continuation for the benefit of our students, faculty, and community.

Sincerely,

Library Needs

Dear Graduate:

Quality in a university depends to a great extent upon the information available to its students in its libraries. We, as well as you, Ms. Garcia, are aware of how rapidly new information is discovered and published. Budget restrictions and inflation are putting a squeeze on available library funds, but we strive hard to buy current publications and computer services required by our serious students. The quality of Riverside University is dependent upon our having access to the latest knowledge. Help from you and other graduates is essential.

Enclosed is a brochure describing our library, the study facilities, the friendly assistants, the quick service, the special-department libraries, the areas in immediate need of funding, the plan for future growth, and items of particular interest to library users.

Your gift, Ms. Garcia, whatever its size, will improve the educational quality of the Riverside University Library. Please mail your tax-deductible donation in the enclosed envelope today.

Sincerely,

P.S. Don't forget, for a donation of $40 or more we will send you a copy, upon request, of the book plate showing your name that will be placed in a book purchased with your gift.

Alumni Solicitation

Dear Alumnus, dear Alumna:

YOU make the difference between mediocrity and excellence.

Think about it.

Your considered gift to the Dorchester Alumni Fund supports the Campaign for Dorchester.

Sincerely,

Haven't Given Yet

Dear Fellow Alum:

The Texon University annual-giving campaign ends April 30. Just noticed that your name is missing from the list of this year's donors.

To date, 30,000 alumni and friends have donated nearly $6 million. A gift of only $25 from those who haven't given would add at least $500,000 to this year's total, further enhancing Texon University's position as one of America's leading centers of higher education.

Please mail your check in the postpaid envelope, now! The students will appreciate your help.

Sincerely,

Dear Ms. Hasland:

I am happy to have been asked to get in touch with classmates who have not yet responded to this year's campaign. Too few of us have given. The Fund this year will provide capital improvements to the Johnson and Guthrie Halls.

In recent years, the prestige of Cleveland Dental School has risen substantially. One indication is the number of articles published in medical and dental journals that are written by our faculty and former students. Another is the increasing number of highly qualified applicants for admission. Also, the number of graduate students choosing Cleveland Dental for research has shown a steady increase in recent years. Your prestige improves right along with that of the School.

Considering your interest in your profession and in your school, I am hopeful that you will use the enclosed card to pledge your support. Several convenient giving programs are suggested on the card. The enclosed envelope is for your convenience.

Working together, we can meet the capital-improvement goal and enable Cleveland Dental School to continue its growth in education, service, and prestige.

Sincerely,

Minorities Program

Dear Friend:

Olin College has a strong program to help Mexican-Americans . . . to give them hope and to break the pattern of impoverishment and hopelessness.

The College is using everything from private consultants to county farm agents.

The Minorities Department is giving assistance to 300 Mexican-American students in Practical English, Everyday Mathematics, and Farming. Other campus programs are helping these minorities in agriculture, drug education, and small-business practice. The College is currently looking at other beneficial programs.

As you are well aware, the need is great, and it is real. Better education makes better citizens, and better citizens make a better country in which to live.

Your financial help will benefit all of us in the near future.

Sincerely,

P.S. For making your tax-deductible contribution right now, we have enclosed a postpaid envelope.

Operational Funds

Dear Mr. Mann:

You have kept us going! While many colleges in recent years have been closing, Whittington College has remained open with generous contributions from alumni.

But the crisis of inflationary costs coupled with a declining enrollment has not bypassed Whittington. We have fought the financial crisis by delaying faculty-salary increases, reducing service personnel, and putting off needed maintenance

These can be only temporary solutions. We need your contributions now to keep Whittington from joining the growing number of closed colleges.

Please use the enclosed postpaid envelope to mail your gift, perhaps larger than the one you gave last year. But gifts of all sizes are needed and appreciated.

Sincerely,

Building Fund

Dear Ms. Cross:

Your gifts to the Computer Science Building Fund of Norfork University are now showing on campus in the form of a new building. We have reached 80 percent of our goal, with contributions coming in daily.

A visit to the building site will let you experience the excitement of dollars being turned into a facility for the advancement of computer knowledge.

We thank you for the gifts that are making the long-time dream of a computer science building an accomplished fact.

Sincerely,

Dear Mr. Ko:

We recognize your helpfulness to the fund-raising committee for the restoration of the Wayne Science Building two years ago. The campaign manager, Welton Jules, praised your efforts highly.

Also, we were impressed the year before when you managed the city's Senior Citizens Center fund-raising campaign.

As you know, the Computer Science Building Fund has reached 80 percent of its goal. The bad news there is that the fund manager, Walter Ralston, had to resign for health reasons.

The special favor we would like to ask of you is to continue the good work of Mr. Ralston and lead the fund drive to its completion. We know you are capable and pray you will say "yes."

Best regards,

Student Union Building

Dear Humboldt Parent:

As the parent of a student living away at college, how often do you get a phone call from your son or daughter that is for the sole purpose of exchanging pleasantries? Occasionally, we hope. Usually the call is for a little extra cash or transportation home.

This week, however, you will get a phone call from one of our students who is not your son or daughter. Humboldt students will phone each parent, asking for a donation for furnishings for the Student Union Building. The goal is $40,000 to complete the building for use next year.

A Student Union Building can contribute so much to the education of a student. A college education is not limited to classroom academics. Making new friends, sharing new experiences with old friends, trying a new hobby or activity, enjoying a lively discussion with one's peers—these are all a vital part of the college experience. A center for social activities encourages participation in this part of college life. A Student Union, run by and for students, is an ideal center for college social activities.

When you receive your call from a Humboldt student this week, please respond favorably. It is your son or daughter who will benefit.

Sincerely,

Financially Disadvantaged Students

Dear Mr. Stone:

This appeal is on behalf of the students of Webster Technical Institute who might not be able to complete their technical training without additional financial aid. Many of our 21,000 students support themselves and members of their families with part-time and temporary jobs. When any emergency occurs, a family illness, a job layoff, or a medical bill there is no way for them to cope without temporary financial aid.

Many students enter Webster Tech directly from high school and lack the necessary skill for jobs that are available. But they, too, must buy books and school supplies. We find that many of these students run out of money before the school term ends. Often, $200 or $300 is all it takes to keep a student in school through the end of the year.

We do have a Student Fund Program, supported by donations from concerned groups and individuals. Your help is needed: our Fund is running low, and we don't expect all the money to be returned. All requests for money are thoroughly investigated, and no money is lent or given unless the need is real.

Your contribution is, of course, tax deductible. Please use the enclosed envelope. We appreciate your consideration of our many needy students as they struggle to learn a trade so that they can make their own way in this world.

Sincerely,

Each of the following three letters opens with an interest-arousing sentence. These are good, but the writer must take care not to overdo a good thing and let the sentences get cute.

Every Little Bit Helps

Dear Mr. Allen:

Some alumni have never given to the University of Oregon! Their explanations go something like this:

> Well, I never contributed because, well, because I didn't think my few dollars would be noticed.

I want you to know that the University of Oregon needs *your* financial support, however small. Small gifts have a way of adding up to large sums.

Our immediate needs are two endowed professorial chairs in the social-science field and scholarships for Oregon residents.

Please take this opportunity to continue the improvement of your university and your state. Many others are giving. I hope you will too.

Sincerely,

Pledge Not Received

Yes—we are concerned, Mr. Hampton.

We have not recorded your pledged contribution to Ellsworth College. Time is short. The Anniversary Fund closes October 31. The Fund this year will provide new seats for Landon Hall. The need has long been obvious to us and to those attending public performances.

I hope you know that we need *your* help. All donations are needed—and appreciated—however small or large. We depend primarily on gifts from individuals: from you.

Please take a moment now—right now—to send your pledged contribution.

Your consideration and thoughtfulness are appreciated by the Fund committee, the students, the faculty, and the community.

Sincerely,

Worthy Projects

Dear Mr. Bronson:

We really don't mind asking for money—when the project is worthy.

At Cornwall College, all projects are worthy—or they don't get started. And we feel this one merits your special attention. A fine-arts performing center will bring together our scattered fine-arts department. The stage and auditorium will be available to the public so that they as well as our students will benefit. Our goal is $800,000 to be raised through donations from foundations and the public. This center has long been needed by both our college and our community.

Please take a moment to consider this. Then use the enclosed reply card to make your pledge or contribution.

I know you'll feel glad about helping.

Sincerely,

COMMUNITY

The following letters are designed to elicit funds for causes that give pleasure and raise the morale of the whole community rather than applying to one organization. The fund-raising techniques are the same as for other charities because the appeals are still to individuals.

Art Museum

SUN CITIES MUSEUM OF ART

Dear Members and Friends,

DID YOU KNOW . . .

. . . that the proposed new road to the Museum (to be started this September) will be a tree-lined, four-lane boulevard?

. . . that the Heard Museum has discovered us and is now displaying at our Museum?

. . . that an anonymous Sun Cities couple has generously agreed to put in an expanded new parking lot for the Museum, to be completed by this summer?

. . . that the Museum is providing the only art education to the entire Dysart elementary-school system, with generous and gracious help from Del Webb and our "picture ladies"?

. . . that professionally catered Sunday brunch is now being served twice a month in the Charles and Ruth Stone Tea Room . . . as well as lunches every Thursday?

. . . that the Dean of the ASU College of Arts and Sciences, the Mayor of Surprise, our State Senator, the Superintendent of Dysart Schools, a County Supervisor, and the CEO of WESTMARC are all now advisers or Trustees of our Board?

. . . that the developer of the property in front of us has proposed the construction of a magnificent archway spanning the avenue leading to the Museum, with a sixty-foot high obelisk in the traffic circle abutting the Museum property?

. . . that the Afternoon Museum Tea is coming back this summer by popular demand?

. . . that yellow busloads of students from Peoria, Glendale, and Dysart schools now make scheduled, docent-guided visits to the Museum, sometimes at the rate of 500 students a day?

. . . that the Museum now does over fifty shows, receptions, and exhibits a year, plus constantly changing displays of our own art work in the Great Hoover Gallery?

. . . that these wonderful programs, displays, school-outreach projects, receptions, etc., must be, and are, largely underwritten by our many generous donors and members?

As is the case with virtually all institutions of our type, we find that admissions, membership fees, Museum League projects, etc., provide only about 80% of the total, carefully monitored cost to operate the Museum. The rest comes from contributors and donors.

We are grateful that we have so many generous supporters like you who share the vision of making our Museum such an important part of this exciting time for our Museum. Twenty percent ($60,000) of our total operating cost needs to come from our own financial support . . . people like you and like me who understand the great need to keep this "Jewel of the Desert" shining brightly!

Will you please help? Please return the attached coupon in the enclosed envelope. Payments by both check and credit card are gratefully appreciated and are, of course, tax deductible. If you should wish to give a major gift, it will also count toward a $1,000 Annual Hoover Membership and/or a Life Membership.

On behalf of our hundreds of volunteers as well as the staff, we thank you! Please let us hear from you now in order to help us reach our goal of $60,000. . . to help ensure that these many programs, receptions and projects continue.

Best wishes,

L. Birt Kellam, Trustee
Chairman, Resources Development
Committee

P.S. We have just received wonderful news! To kick off our campaign, a longtime museum member has agreed to *match dollar for dollar* all donations received during our Annual Operating Fund Campaign. So please, while this offer is in effect, send in your donation now so that it can be magnified 2 for 1!!

(With permission of L. Birt Kellam, Trustee, Sun Cities Museum of Art, 17425 North 115th Avenue, Sun City, Arizona 85373-2501)

Community Theater

Dear Miss Keltner:

Here is your opportunity for you to play a leading role as a contributor to the Merrill Community Theater. The theater group is forming under the direction of the longtime star and director on Broadway, Emil Vittorio.

Rehearsals for the first play, *Little Mary Sunshine*, are underway. Upcoming plays will include *Richard III*, *Beehive*, and *Music Man*.

The theater group is a local amateur organization. Setting ticket prices to cover the production costs would prohibit many interested people from attending these exciting plays. That's why we must rely on personal and business donations to bridge the gap between ticket income and production costs.

Your contribution will help expand an interest in the arts in your community. With your gift you will play a leading role.

Sincerely,

Local Symphony

Dear Mr. and Mrs. Ropelato:

A symphony orchestra in *our* small city? Yes. We start small, and as our reputation builds we attract more and better musicians. Really? Yes. I have witnessed this growth in such diverse communities as Fort Smith, Arkansas, Concord, California, and Sun City West, Arizona.

We are fortunate to have as our conductor Dr. Arturo Salzetti, who has a Ph.D. in music education and has led two university orchestras as well as three of the smaller city orchestras. He has decided to come out of retirement to help this community develop an appreciation of the arts, specifically symphonic music. His efforts will enhance the way of life in our community. Will we back him? With enthusiasm, publicity, and a few dollars?

For starters, a new community symphony needs such mundane items as music, music stands, chairs, newspaper ads, rehearsal- and performance-hall rent (we have been provided, rent free, a practice space at a local church for the rest of this year), and volunteers to help with myriad organizational details.

We have enclosed a card with suggested amounts to contribute and a postage-paid envelope for your easy response. Let's do it today.

Sincerely,

Security Patrol

Dear Spring Meadows Resident:

During the past three years you, your neighbors, and local businesses have provided financial support for our security patrol. Two former police officers and a few dedicated volunteers have provided night patrols to this growing community.

It is now time to expand this service to include daytime patrols for your increased safety and protection. Our crime rate is one of the lowest in the nation, and we want to keep it that way.

We receive no public funds and therefore must rely on your financial support to meet our goal of 24-hour worry-free security for Spring Meadows.

Your generous past contributions have enabled us to have only one fund drive per year, and we hope that will continue.

Please return the enclosed card indicating the amount of your contribution and, we hope, your willingness to volunteer to help with patrol driving, dispatching, phone answering, or other details of keeping your patrol on the streets looking out for your safety and security.

Sincerely,

Middle East Peace

Dear Friends,

Israel has a historical claim to the "West Bank" area of what was once a part of "Palestine." This statement is disputed, especially by Arabs. But is the settling of Jews there the main reason for delay of peace in the Middle East? Yes? No? Maybe?

The history is long and confused among Great Britain, France, Syria, Lebanon, Egypt, the League of Nations after World War I, and the United Nations after World War II.

For a tax-deductible contribution to the above address you will receive a printed, detailed article on this problem. Your generous gift will also permit continued publication of related discussions in popular magazines. Please use the enclosed card. An informed public is our goal.

Sincerely,

Immigration

Dear Concerned Citizen:

Why do we allow our government to receive over a million immigrants each year? Because we have not found political leaders who will follow the wishes of the majority of our citizens.

A Roper poll released early this year reports that 70 percent of Americans want immigration reduced to not over 300,000 persons a year. Congress must be urged to pass legislation to reduce annual immigration.

Illegal immigration rums rampant. One estimate is that over 350,000 people enter this country each year illegally. Most of our citizens, 74 percent according to the poll, want the illegals deported. Why does Congress ignore the people's mandate?

You can help. Mail the coupon below indicating your contribution to a fund for lobbying Congress to pass restrictive immigration laws. We will use the money wisely and also mail you the addresses of your Congressional Representatives and Senators along with suggestions of how and what to write to them.

We must work together to persuade the Congress to support the will of America's citizens.

Sincerely,

Public Television

Dear Mrs. Clegg:

Just a personal note to thank you for watching public-service television on WKWK. We know you enjoy it—the science programs, the children's programs, the classical music, the pop music, the nature studies, the old and new heroes of our country, the high-quality current news programs, and on and on.

Your annual membership brings you all this plus a program magazine and valuable gifts. Annual memberships start at $50 and can go on up until it feels good. (This is more than "until it hurts.")

A full 60 percent of our operating costs come from our viewers. We could not continue our superb programming without your tax-deductible gifts. Please use the enclosed card and envelope to join your generous friends of WKWK.

Sincerely,

Visitors' Center

Dear Resident:

Our retirement community opened its Visitors' Center last year. A dedicated group of volunteers work to promote this community and our lifestyle. They do this because of the large turnover of homes due to deaths and residents returning to "where the children live."

We average several hundred visitors each week. In addition to the many volunteers this takes, we have operating expenses including water, electricity, phones, office supplies, insurance, building maintenance, printing, and advertising.

We need your financial support to attract new people who will maintain property values and spread the word about our most pleasant lifestyle.

If you cannot make a large contribution, we realize that many small gifts add up quickly. Please mail the enclosed card with your contribution. Sorry, it is not deductible for income tax purposes.

Sincerely,

CHAPTER 5

Collection

The primary function of a collection letter is to collect money. To accomplish this, the writer must retain the goodwill of the debtor. This is especially true of personal-collection efforts, directed toward individuals or businesses managed by one or two persons. A collection letter to a large business firm, however, need not put as much emphasis on empathy with the reader.

For purposes of comparison, let us for a moment explore the essentials of a business-collection letter. The most important thing is to identify exactly what is delinquent. The letter should include:

the delinquent customer's order number and date,

the items purchased,

the seller's invoice number and date,

the dollar amount that is past due,

the original due date.

These items are essential to the reader in identifying the delinquent invoice. The following letter was written by a collection agency to a company that receives over a dozen freight bills daily. The bill referred to could be one of several hundred, either paid or unpaid. Imagine the difficulty of tracing this particular bill:

Your past-due account in the amount of $22.06 has been brought to our attention by Freight Agencies.

Please mail your check for this amount to Freight Agencies by May 5 so that no future action will be necessary.

The tone of a business-collection letter takes second place to the identity of the delinquent item. This is true because in a large-business organization a collection letter is delegated to the lowest ranking clerk capable of searching for the bill and determining if and when it was paid. The following letter displays an overly aggressive tone for a first reminder, but the research clerk ignored the letter's harshness and checked the facts stated in the letter.

Gentlemen:

In reviewing our records again, I find that your account is more than forty-five (45) days past due in the amount of $162.94 for statement dated 7/7/_ _.

OUR TERMS! ALL ACCOUNTS ARE DUE AND PAYABLE UPON RECEIPT OF OUR STATEMENT.

Please forward payment immediately.

Thank you.

(signed)

Credit Manager

ALL ACCOUNTS ARE DUE AND PAYABLE UPON RECEIPT OF STATEMENT

For the first three notices to a large-business organization, a copy of the delinquent bill or a short reminder is as effective as a letter of persuasion. For the fourth notice, a letter explaining the delinquency, with a copy of the overdue invoice enclosed, will be helpful.

Do not, however, construe this functional approach to business-to-business collection letters to mean that politeness, fairness, and consideration for the reader can be ignored. The primary difference is that a business-collection letter must contain more technical identification of the delinquent items than is usually necessary in a personal-collection letter.

The last example would never do as a personal-collection letter, in which the reader's goodwill is of paramount importance. The personal-collection letter should excuse the debtor while requesting payment. The delinquent person may have merely overlooked the due date, may be in temporary financial difficulties, or may even be a "professional procrastinator" (one who operates his or her business on money that should have been used to pay the bills). Whatever the reason, let the debtor save face and assume that the delay has not been spiteful.

Continue thinking well of the customer and omit any harsh and abusive language. In addition, omit words and phrases of this nature:

cannot understand	delinquent
remit promptly	ignore
failure on your part	require

we insist	compelled
our demand	wrong
unsatisfactory	cancel

Positive words sound better and bring you more favorable results:

respond	your payment
fairness	your check
you	mail today
your credit	please

A personal-collection letter must be considerate of the reader. Therefore, give him or her a reason for paying promptly. Rather than saying, "We would appreciate prompt payment so we can clear our books," apply the "you" attitude and write, "Your prompt payment will keep your good credit rating intact," or "Your paying early enough to take the discount will allow us to continue our low prices for you."

Collection letters are a standard part of the collection process. The first notice to the delinquent is usually a copy of the bill with or without a sticker or rubber-stamp impression stating "past due" or "have you forgotten" or "second notice." Following this are short and gentle letters, each one successively insistent upon a payment. Phone calls may be interspersed with the letters. The third or fourth letter is often long, making a sincere appeal to sympathy, pride, justice, fairness, or self-interest. The final step is turning the account over to a collection agency or to an attorney for legal action.

How to Receive a Prompt Reply

The surest way to receive a prompt reply is to enclose a postpaid, self-addressed envelope. Mention in the letter that one is enclosed.

An additional device for making the reply easy for the reader is to include a card or note showing the amount and date of the next payment. Leave a space for comments. This will be returned to the writer and will save the reader the trouble of writing a letter.

A third technique is to enclose a phone number with the name of a person who can be called.

Attention-Getting Openings—Humorous

The opening of a collection letter must attract the attention and arouse the interest of the reader. The techniques for doing this are limited only by the imagination and research efforts of the writer. Opening statements can vary from "Just a reminder that we have not received your last payment" to slapstick comedy in personal letters:

Dear Mr. Wilson:

"Hey, look at this, Bud!"

"Bad news, Joe?"

"Yeah, this guy wants my autograph."

"But, gosh, that's a compliment. Aren't you proud?"

"But this guy wants it on a check."

We, too, would like your autograph on a check—$45.60 for the toaster you bought on February 7th. Please use the enclosed postage-paid envelope.

Other stories and fables like the following can be used as attention getters for readers who will respond favorably to the lighthearted and humorous.

An official whose garage delivered his car every day received a card on his windshield one day. "Merry Christmas from the boys at the garage." Two days later he received another card, "Merry Christmas, second notice."

This is a second notice to you about your overdue payment of $99.80 . . .

One mathematician to another, "Now that you have invented zero, what do you have: nothing."

Nothing is what we have received from you for your purchase in June . . .

In a similar vein, here are three snappy collection letters:

Are you holding on to that check for $29.70?

Might makes right. Right for us is a payment of $52.50. Might for you is a good credit record.

We think a collection letter should be short and successful. We hope you do too. $32.95.

Other Opening Sentences

When they ask about you, what can we say?

I am as embarrassed to write this letter as you are to receive it.

Is our Fiery Kilowatt heater working well for you this cold winter?

I am sure we both agree that a good reputation is essential to a prospering business.

Again, may we call attention to your loan payment due March 30.

Why haven't you paid? Why haven't you written? Why haven't you phoned?

Could you tell us why you haven't paid your account?

We cannot in good conscience carry your account any longer.

Strong Closing Sentences

The end of the letter is its most emphatic part; make the last statement or request strong and definite. Be specific about *what* you want, *when* you want it, and *how* you want it done. At the same time, keep in mind consideration for the reader: An offended reader pays slowly. Examples for specific purposes follow.

Prompt-Action Sentences

In order to open your account for further purchases, please let us hear from you today.

To avoid additional expenses and unpleasantness, we expect to hear from you within ten days—before August 12.

Because we are anxious to provide fast service, please let us hear from you promptly.

We can help you just as soon as we hear from you.

Goodwill Sentences

We are glad to cooperate with you, and look forward to serving you for many more years.

Thank you for bringing the problem to our attention. We are always happy to help.

We appreciate your cooperation.

Thank you for letting us help.

Soothing Sentences

The mistake was obviously ours. We misunderstood your complaint. We have taken steps to correct the situation and hope you will bear with us for a few days.

We cannot disagree with your feelings; we would have felt the same in your situation.

We are sorry we had to take the action we did, but under the circumstances we had no alternative. We hope you understand.

This action may seem unnecessary at this time, but later I am sure you will appreciate what we had to do under the circumstances.

We would sincerely like to grant your request, but we are unable to do so now. We are, however, looking forward to serving you in the near future.

Apologetic Sentences

We are sorry for the inconveniences we caused you, and you can be sure we will make every effort to prevent it from happening again.

We feel bad about the trouble we caused you and hope you will accept our sincere apologies.

Thank you for calling the error to our attention so we may correct it. We are sorry for causing you an inconvenience.

Your patience is appreciated, and we thank you for your consideration.

Please accept our apologies. We have corrected the cause of our mistake, and you can be assured it will not occur again.

Reassuring Sentences

We appreciate the business you have given us, and we trust you will understand that we cannot be of service to you at this particular time.

Of course we are sorry to have to turn down your request, but we do look forward to serving you in future months.

We dislike, as all business people do, turning away a sale, but I am sure you understand why we must at this time.

A lost sale leaves us with an empty feeling, but, as you know from the circumstances, it is not possible for us to help you at this time. The near future may look more promising.

Repeated Thoughts—Sentences

Again, prompt payment will retain your good credit rating.

To repeat, the sooner we receive payment, the sooner we can help you again.

Which of these two suggestions appeals to you? Please let us hear from you right away.

To prevent these added expenses and the inconvenience to you, please let us hear from you within ten days.

This order cannot be released until we receive your financial statement, Please mail it today!

To forestall bothering you again about this overdue balance, please mail a payment today in the enclosed envelope.

Repeated reminders are a lot of trouble for us and a bother to you. Please help us both by mailing your payment today.

Briefly, a partial payment now will keep your account open.

Promoting the Future—Sentences

Now that we have your financial data, it will be a pleasure to approve your future orders promptly.

We are available to serve you at any time, so please call at your convenience. We will work hard to make you a happy customer.

We appreciate your prompt payment for your recent order. We look forward to more years of serving your needs.

Now that your account is on a current basis, we look forward to approving your future orders promptly. A continuing business relationship will benefit both of us.

Suggestions for Effective Credit Letters

A nearly unlimited number of suggestions could be made to help you write better letters. The primary advice is to address your letter to the decision maker. That will result in faster action than by sending the letter to the department involved. It will end up there, but with direct instructions from the responsible person. With computers and word processors, form letters can be processed individually. The recommendations listed here will not fit every situation, but you will find a quick review of them beneficial when you start to write your collection letter.

1. Start collection procedures immediately after the account becomes delinquent.

2. Let your reader know in the first sentence that this is a collection letter.

3. Be persistent. Keep at it. "The squeaky wheel gets the grease."

4. Make collection letters brief, but not curt.

5. Avoid stilted language. Be clear. Be specific.

6. Be firm but reasonable.

7. Be kind, helpful, and respectful.

8. Be friendly and sympathetic.

9. Always retain your customer's goodwill.

10. Treat your reader as an honest person.

11. Appeal to the individual interests and feelings of your readers. Consider their points of view.

12. Never lower yourself by displaying anger, pity, contempt, or malice.

13. Never repeat an appeal made in a previous letter.

14. Provide a flexible collection plan.

15. Provide your debtor with a reason why it is to his or her advantage to pay promptly.

16. Make each successive letter stronger.

17. State the amount due in each letter.

18. Imply that the debtor will pay.

19. State how payment may be made.

20. Include the original due date.
21. Politely ask for payment—without apologizing.

Just what to include in a collection letter (to be added to or subtracted from the model letter chosen) will depend on various combinations of the following considerations:

- First delinquency
- Continuing delinquency
- New customer
- Longtime customer
- Small debt
- Large debt
- Urgency of need for cash flow
- Value of customer's future business
- Type of approach (humorous, serious, short, long, light, pleasant, or persistent) the writer believes the reader will respond to.

How to Do It

1. State the purpose of the letter clearly and in an interesting way.
2. Include data relevant to the situation: what the writer is asking for, how the reader can be helped, and reasons for paying now.
3. Restate the request for payment.

Series of Collection Letters

A delinquent customer or borrower often needs only a reminder that the last payment was not made. Because of this, many firms use a series of from three to six short collection letters. These can be form letters, updated on the computer, filling in the amount and due date. Each letter is more insistent than the previous one. This will save the time and cost required for composing personal letters.

Series One, Three Letters: Reminder

Letter One

Just a reminder . . .

of the amount written at the bottom of this note. It hasn't been paid. Will you mail your check today?

$72.90

Sincerely,

Letter Two

Has the mail been delayed again . . .

preventing your check from reaching us? Did you mail a payment on your account recently? If you did, please stop payment and send another check for $72.90. We are anxious to have your account on a current basis.

With hope,

Letter Three

There has to be a reason . . .

why we haven't heard from you after our previous reminders.

Will you let us know why? Or perhaps you would like to spread the balance over a longer period. Please let us know how we can help.

The amount due is $72.90.

Concerned,

Series Two, Three Letters: Past-Due Charge Account

Letter One

Dear Mr. Rowden:

Satisfying your personal needs is our prime concern. We hope you value our trust and friendship as much.

Recently your account has become overdue. Several notices making you aware of this were mailed with your monthly statements. Once again, you are being asked for immediate payment of $87.50.

Serving you and your family still remains our first desire. Please call us or stop by the store so we may discuss the easiest way for you to meet this obligation.

Sincerely,

Letter Two

Dear Mr. Rowden:

Sending another notice about your unpaid account upsets us greatly. Your credit was accepted because you had proved you were a trustworthy customer.

Your trust with us can still be kept by paying the full amount of $87.50. Pay today and avoid jeopardizing your credit reputation.

Very truly yours,

Letter Three

Dear Mr. Rowden:

We are in business to serve our customers and cannot afford to spend too much time trying to collect the $87.50 you owe us. One week from the above date, we will turn your account over to our lawyer. We hope you prefer to make your payment to us rather than to have our lawyer contact you.

Yours truly,

Series Three, Three Letters: Business-Invoice Past Due

Letter One

Dear Mr. Foltmer:

Enclosed is our invoice No. G-2971 in the amount of $199.80 for your order of May 21, and the bill of lading for shipment on May 22.

Terms are net 30 days.

Please mail your check to P. O. Box 0000, Sacramento, CA 00000.

Today, please.

Sincerely,

Letter Two

Dear Mr. Foltmer:

Your June statement is enclosed. Please note that $199.80 is 15 days past the 30-day due date.

We must request immediate payment of this past-due item.

If there is a question about the amount, please send us an explanation so we can clear your account.

A postpaid envelope is enclosed for your convenience. Please mail your check today.

Sincerely,

Letter Three

Dear Mr. Foltmer:

Re: Invoice No. G-2971
    Invoice Date May 22, _ _ _ _
    Balance Due $199.80

This is the last request we will make directly to you to pay the invoice shown here.

If no payment is received by September 29, we shall take whatever steps are necessary to collect the $199.80 due us. Why not mail your check today?

Sincerely,

Series Four, Three Letters: Past-Due Freight Bill

Letter One

Gentlemen:

Attached are copies of our freight bills that are past due. Just a reminder that our policy requires payment within ten days.

We would appreciate prompt payment.

Sincerely,

Letter Two

Gentlemen:

Although we sent you past-due reminder copies of the attached bills three weeks after our original billing date and again after five weeks, the charges remain unpaid and are now seriously past due.

Since we know you wish to pay your bills when due, we expect that these open items are just an oversight on your part.

As you know, our policy prohibits us from extending credit to customers who have past-due charges outstanding, and we have no alternative but to withdraw credit privileges in such instances.

We would very much like to continue extending you credit, and you will enable us to do so by sending us your remittance now.

Sincerely,

Letter Three

Gentlemen:

Two weeks ago we wrote to you with copies of the above freight-bill numbers advising you that they were seriously past due and in violation of our policy, even though we had sent you several past-due-reminder copies of the bills.

We assumed that failure to pay these open items was an oversight on your part and that our letter would bring a prompt response and enable us to continue extending credit. We regret to see that they are still unpaid, and the delinquent status of your account leaves us no alternative but to remove your company from our list of credit customers. Our terminal manager has been instructed to rescind your credit privilege and transact future business on a cash basis.

If the outstanding balance is not paid in ten days, our Collection Department will take whatever action is necessary to accomplish collection.

Sincerely,

Series Five, Four Letters: Overdue Charge Account

Letter One

Dear Mr. Cineros:

We're reminding you that your account is now 20 days overdue.

Please disregard this notice if you have already mailed us your check for $196.05.

Cordially,

Letter Two

Dear Mr. Cineros:

We would like to continue our friendship while doing business with you. However, we need to have you send us a check for $196.05 to cover your over-due account. Please mail your check today.

Sincerely,

Letter Three

Dear Mr. Cineros:

We have not heard from you regarding your long-standing past due account of $196.05. This account has been overdue since May 20.

You have been a reliable customer, and we would like to continue our friendly business relationship. Only if you pay your past-due account can we continue to offer you our quality merchandise and helpful service.

Please let us know if you have a problem in paying this. Otherwise we expect you to pay the $196.05 today.

Yours truly,

Letter Four

Dear Mr. Cineros:

We still have not heard from you regarding your overdue balance of $196.05. If this account is not paid within ten days, we will turn it over to our attorney. Please mail your check today to prevent our starting this legal action.

Very truly yours,

Series Six, Four Letters: Loan Past Due

Letter One

Dear Mr. Neel:

May we call your attention to your loan payment that you have no doubt overlooked? It is 30 days past due. The amount is $260.20. Please mail your check today.

Sincerely,

Letter Two

Dear Mr. Neel:

Your loan payment is now 45 days past due. Prompt payment of $260.20 would be appreciated. Please mail your check today.

Respectfully,

Letter Three

Dear Mr. Neel:

Again we call your attention to your loan payment due March 15. If there is some reason for the delay, please let us know.

We would appreciate receiving your check for $260.20 immediately.

Very truly yours,

Letter Four

Dear Mr. Neel:

It bothers us to have to say this, but we request that you pay the $260.20 owed to us. If we don't receive your check by November 30, we will by required to turn your account over to a collection agency.

Save yourself the embarrassment and loss of credit standing this would cause you. The enclosed envelope is for your payment. Please use it today.

Yours truly,

Series Seven, Four Letters: Patience

Letter One

Dear Mr. Koehl:

Just a reminder that your account is 15 days past due. If you have already sent your check for $429.97, we thank you for doing so.

Cordially,

Letter Two

Dear Mr. Koehl:

Patience is a virtue. We may sometimes seem lacking because we get a little impatient, but we try to be considerate of our friends and customers. Please accept this letter in that spirit.

Your account has become long past due (since March 15). Please mail your check for $429.97 today. We are expecting it.

Sincerely,

Letter Three

Dear Mr. Koehl:

You have been a customer of ours since 0000, a long time. I am sure the reason is not only because we carry merchandise you like but because of our helpful clerks, our easy-pay credit policy, our prompt service (at no extra charge), and our long-established reputation for quality.

We do all these things to please our customers and to cooperate with them. However, cooperation is a two-way street. By paying your bills on time, we have funds to replenish our supplies and to continue providing helpful service to our customers.

Your account has remained unpaid since March 15. If you are unable to make full payment now, please call or write so we can make other arrangements with you. Otherwise, would you please help us to continue helping you by mailing your check for $429.97 today? A postpaid envelope is enclosed for your convenience.

Sincerely,

Letter Four

Dear Mr. Koehl:

Your response to our letters about your long-overdue account has been completely negative. Not one word has been heard from you. We can be patient no longer.

We feel, therefore, that we must turn your account over to our attorney for collection. We dislike doing this, and in fairness to you we will postpone any action for ten days, giving you until June 27. Please mail us your check for $429.97 before that date to avoid the embarrassment of legal action.

Sincerely,

Series Eight, Five Letters: Credit Record

Letter One

Dear Ms. Sparacello:

No doubt you have overlooked payment of the enclosed statement. Your prompt remittance will be appreciated.

Account No.   _____

Date Due   _____

Payment Due   _____

Sincerely,

Letter Two

Dear Ms. Sparacello:

Your attention is again invited to your delinquent account. To avoid an unfavorable report of your credit records, we suggest an immediate payment of the amount due.

Account No.   _____

Date Due   _____

Payment Due   _____

Sincerely,

Letter Three

Dear Ms. Sparacello:

It is apparent that you have ignored our two previous reminders. Your account is now seriously delinquent.

We must insist that you pay this account immediately, or personally discuss this with us.

Account No.   _____

Date Due   _____

Payment Due   _____

Very Sincerely Yours,

Letter Four

Dear Ms. Sparacello:

There must be a reason for not paying your account. Whatever the reason, we would be happy to discuss it with you. We can make arrangements for smaller payments over a longer period of time if that would help you. We must hear from you or receive a check within the next 15 days. Your credit record is at stake.

Account No.   _____

Date Due   _____

Payment Due   _____

Sincerely yours,

Letter Five

Dear Ms. Sparacello:

Since you have apparently made no effort to pay the amount due us, we have no alternative to taking legal action. You may prevent this, however, by making payment by August 15.

Account No.   _____

Date Due   _____

Payment Due   _____

Very truly yours,

Series Nine, Five Letters: Installments

Letter One

Dear Mr. Rowan:

A friendly reminder that the first payment of $146.00 on your recent furniture installment was due five days ago.

If your check is in the mail, we send our sincere thanks. If not, please mail your check today.

Cordially,

Letter Two

Dear Mr. Rowan:

This is our second reminder about a late payment on your purchase contract.

Please mail us a check today for $146.00.

Sincerely,

Letter Three

Dear Mr. Rowan:

A third notice about the overdue payments on your furniture purchase contract is apparently necessary.

Is there a problem, either with the furniture or your ability to make monthly payments of $146.00? Please contact us by phone or letter or come in to our store to discuss this matter with us. You will find us fully cooperative with you in rewriting the contract if that will help you. Of course, payment is always appreciated, so please mail your check today if you can.

Sincerely,

Letter Four

Dear Mr. Rowan:

Is it possible that your circumstances have changed since we wrote your contract? Your credit at that time was sound, but we have received no payments.

Your first payment is now 45 days past due, and your second payment is 15 days overdue.

A good credit rating is essential if you are to continue making credit purchases. Your payment record is available to all merchants of the Fairview Retailer's Association. We expect a prompt payment of $292.00. Please mail it today.

Sincerely yours,

Letter Five

Dear Mr. Rowan:

We were happy when you purchased a new dining room set from us, and you appeared pleased with the furniture. We arranged a contract for easy monthly payments, which you agreed you could make on time.

Having received no payments or any indication of your interest in rescheduling payments, we have concluded that we can no longer carry your account.

This decision means that you will pay the full amount owed, $3,504.00, no later than November 17, or our attorney will be instructed to arrange for collection of the amount due.

A payment today will relieve you of concern about legal action.

Respectfully,

Series Ten, Six Letters: Future Credit Limited

Letter One

Dear Ms. Kashani:

Our records show the following amounts now due:

Current	$249.80
30 days	121.10
60 days	375.42
	$746.32

Please mail your check today to cover these amounts. If payment has already been mailed, you may disregard this letter.

Sincerely,

Letter Two

Dear Ms. Kashani:

There is a balance due on your account of $829.40, of which $746.32 is past due.

For us to continue serving you from our warehouse stocks and not limit your credit, you must mail your check today.

It is important that we receive your check by November 25.

Your cooperation would be appreciated.

Sincerely,

Letter Three

Dear Ms. Kashani:

Your account is considerably past due, $375.42 by more than 120 days. We are sorry, but we now must temporarily close your open-account credit.

Your lack of favorable response to our previous correspondence has left us no other choice.

Your prompt cooperation by mailing a payment will permit us to resume helping you. Please mail your check today.

Sincerely,

Letter Four

Dear Ms. Kashani:

Your account is still long past due, and we have not received any recent payments. Therefore, we have notified our warehouse to hold all your orders.

We want to open your account as soon as possible. To do this, we must receive your check mailed today for $746.32.

We will expect your check by December 20.

Your complete cooperation is anticipated.

Sincerely,

Letter Five

Dear Ms. Kashani:

Your past due account amounts to $829.40. We have asked for your cooperation, but have not received it, and you have thereby lost your credit standing with us.

We are now faced with the possibility of placing your account with our attorney for collection. We will, however, postpone that action for fifteen days, until January 29.

Fifteen days will allow you time to make financial arrangements so your debt to us can be cleared.

Sincerely,

Letter Six

Dear Ms. Kashani:

Our deadline of January 29, for receiving your check for $829.40 was yesterday. We received no response to our letter of January 14.

As indicated in that letter, we notified our attorney today to take any necessary action to collect your past-due account. You have 72 hours to stop the action. Why not mail your check today?

Yours truly,

Series Eleven, Six Letters: Credit Standing Jeopardized

Letter One

Dear Mr. Nussman:

Your check for our December 28, _ _ _ _, invoice No. 43211, in the amount of $529.80, has not been received by our office.

If it has been mailed, thank you. If not, please consider this just a reminder to mail your check today.

With regards,

Letter Two

Dear Mr. Nussman:

Our December 28, invoice for $529.80 is still unpaid. If you did mail your check, please let us know the date and your check number so we can review our records.

Otherwise, please mail your check today.

With regards,

Letter Three

Dear Mr. Nussman:

You have not acknowledged our previous two letters about our December invoice for $529.80. It is now 45 days past due.

Your credit rating is in jeopardy. To maintain your credit standing, please mail your check before you put this letter aside—today, please.

With regards,

Letter Four

Dear Mr. Nussman:

We are disturbed when we still see your $529.80 balance on our accounts-receivable computer printout.

When you ordered the electric motors from us, you expected prompt shipment, and you received prompt shipment. At the same time, we expected prompt payment but have not received any payment or even an explanation for your not paying.

Your credit rating can be restored, but only by mailing your check TODAY.

Regards,

Letter Five

Dear Mr. Nussman:

Let us be frank and strictly "business." You purchased electric motors from us in December of _ _ _ _. Your cost was $529.80. That was _ _ _ days prior to the date of this letter.

Your response has been zero. You have made no payments and you have not provided us with an explanation for delaying your payments.

What we can do is to allow you seven days from the date of this letter to make payment in full. On the eighth day, if we have not received your check, we will turn your account over to our attorney for whatever action he finds necessary to collect from you.

Regards,

Letter Six

Dear Mr. Nussman:

The final limit we gave you for paying your $529.80 bill has passed.

Any further correspondence or communication you receive about this overdue amount will be from our attorney. He will contact you soon. Why not avoid the additional expense by paying before he sues? Mail your check TODAY.

Very truly yours,

First Collection Letter Is a Reminder

Because the first collection letter is simply a reminder, it should be gentle. The purpose of the letter, however, should be presented in a positive and straightforward way. The reader should have no doubt, after reading the first sentence, that he or she is late in making a payment. A little sales pitch and an offer to discuss extended payments may be included. An enclosed envelope for customer convenience is recommended.

Dear Ms. Hibbard:

Have you forgotten the last payment on your loan?

The final payment is $65.20. Because your other payments were on time, I thought you would appreciate this reminder. Please use the enclosed envelope to send in your check for $65.20. May we have it today?

Sincerely,

Just a REMINDER Mr. Kollins:

that you may have overlooked making the last payment on your account. A copy of our bill for $37.98 is enclosed along with an envelope for your convenience.

Regards,

Dear Mr. Allo:

As you have always been one of our good customers, we feel sure that there must be a reason why your payments have gotten a little behind.

Is there anything we can do to help, or something we should correct? Please let us hear from you.

Sincerely,

Dear Mr. Danese:

We have not received your first payment, due two weeks ago. When you opened your account, I mentioned that I would be happy to answer any of your inquiries. Do you have any questions about your account? I am here to help. Please call or mail your check today.

Sincerely,

Dear Mr. Ezell:

We were pleased recently to open a charge account for you. Because your first payment is now overdue, we feel we may not have given you a clear explanation of our terms.

All purchases must be paid in full 25 days after the billing date.

Your unpaid balance is $546.20. Please mail your check today.

Sincerely,

Dear Mr. James:

Your check for $24.80 has not arrived.

This may be a small amount, but all overdue amounts are meaningful to us.

Won't you please help us serve you better by mailing your check for $24.80 today?

Sincerely,

Dear Ms Rovilla:

The year is almost over. Time seems to fly by unnoticed. Perhaps that is why you have not yet paid the $159.98 for your last purchase at Ender's.

Could you please mail your check today?

Sincerely,

Dear Mr. Leinhardt:

The second payment on your installment account is now overdue.

This may be because of a misunderstanding about the timing of your payments. Your initial payment was due two months after the purchase date, with monthly payments thereafter. It is understandable, however, if you assumed you were to pay at two-month intervals.

Please mail your second payment today and then plan to send regular monthly checks to arrive by the 5th of each month.

Sincerely,

Dear Ms. Carvajal:

Some people like a reminder that they may have forgotten to pay a bill. Our last invoice, No. 4442, in the amount of $1,120.47 was due 20 days ago. Please mail your payment today.

Sincerely,

Dear Mrs. Taccone:

We would appreciate receiving a check for $498.70. This will clear the balance on your statement, which you may have overlooked.

Thank you for your consideration.

Sincerely,

Accounts Payable:

Just a reminder that your invoice hasn't been paid. Perhaps the original was overlooked, or perhaps your payment of $_____ is in the mail. If not, please send your payment today or let us know now when we may expect it.

Sincerely,

Gentlemen:

A routine review of your account reveals the following past due balance:

Item Number	Date	Amount	Due Date
30.2233	2-4-_ _	$4,355.90	3-4-_ _

If your remittance is not already en route, your assistance in expediting payment would be truly appreciated.

Sincerely,

Dear Mr. Hughes:

We have not received your first payment due upon signing the Bidwell contract, which was signed July 30, _ _ _ _ .

Please clear this oversight by mailing your check today for $_____.

Sincerely,

Dear Mr. Glorioso:

Your attention is directed to the attached list of freight bills, which our records indicate are unpaid beyond the credit period permitted by our tariff.

You may have already made the payment, and it has simply not reached our accounting department. If these bills have not been paid, however, a prompt remittance would be appreciated. Please mail your check to West Transportation Co., P.O. Box 0000, Arlington, VA 00000.

Sincerely,

Dear Mr. Zamora,

We appreciate having you as our customer and hope you will appreciate this reminder that your account is slightly overdue.

Dealers are not allowed to accept credit cards on accounts owing charges two months in arrears, a condition your account is rapidly approaching.

If payment of the "new balance" shown on your most recent statement has not been mailed, do try to have it to us before your next statement date.

Thanks for your cooperation.

Sincerely,

(With permission of Judith A. Luff, Sun Company, Inc.)

Account No. 0000-0000-000-00
Amount Delinquent $77.94

Dear Mr. Wachtler:

Our records show that your credit card account is 30 days past due.

Please pay the amount shown above today. This will cover the past-due amount and your current monthly payment. Please use the enclosed postpaid envelope and include your account number on your check. If you have any questions please call the number listed below.

Sincerely,

Collection Department 1-000-000-0000

Middle Stages of Collection Letters

Second letters should still be reminders. They need be only variations from first letters, or slightly more irritating first letters.

Third or fourth letters become longer and more persuasive. The delinquent payer has ignored or given little importance to the short early letters, and now a change in tactics is required. An appeal is made to one of several human feelings; for example:

Sympathy: Your small amount due is only one of many accounts.

Pride or self-respect: We appreciate your past promptness, but now you are behind.

Justice: We have carried your account too long; be fair and pay now.

Self-Interest: It is in your own best interest to have a good credit rating.

Give the debtor an out by suggesting a longer payment period or at least the opportunity to discuss future payment arrangements.

Dear Mr. Needom:

We expected at least an answer to the last of several letters we sent you. As you know, you still owe us $1,403.58.

Truly, we are disappointed. I am sure you are not intentionally trying to make our work difficult, but that's what it amounts to. Is there some reason you have not paid? Some difficulty getting the money? Too many other bills to pay? Let's make this easier for both of us. Call us, and we can solve any problems together.

We have been fair with you, and now we believe you will be fair with us.

Sincerely yours,

Dear Mr. Revere:

This is somewhat embarrassing—embarrassing to us because you are a good friend and embarrassing to you because you owe this good friend some money—money that should have been repaid long before now.

Some time ago (April 16, _ _ _ _) you purchased a chair from us, and we were happy to accept your promise to pay within 30 days. You seemed pleased with the chair, and I am confident it has given you many hours of comfort. Isn't it only fair that you live up to your part of the agreement we made?

Let us be fair with each other. You have a comfortable chair. We would like our money. Since your payment is long past due, please make out your check now for $225.75 and mail it today in the enclosed postpaid envelope.

Sincerely,

Dear Mr. Tripplett:

You have not made a payment on your account during the last nine months. We realize that financial conditions in your area have not been good recently, and you have not been pressed for payment. By now, however, we feel you should be able to start paying again. We will be glad to work with you in making a reasonable payment arrangement.

Please call or write and let us discuss what can be done to get your payments started again.

Sincerely,

Dear Mrs. Vall:

You did not respond to our first reminder of your overdue account. Our new line of furniture started arriving yesterday, and we know you will love to browse through the wide selection.

To avoid having your credit limited, making this fine furniture unavailable to you, please mail your check for $362.48 today.

Sincerely,

Dear Mrs. Tucker:

Can we be of help to you in clearing the $205.47 you owe us? Your account is now 40 days past due. Because we did not receive a response to our statement and first letter, we believe there must be a reason for your not paying.

If there is a problem, please let us know so we can work together to clear your overdue amount. If there is no problem, your mailing your check today would be appreciated.

Sincerely,

Dear Mr. Vaughn:

For the second time we find it necessary to remind you of your obligation to make monthly payments on the contract you signed with us.

Please mail your check today to cover the November payment of $425.00. The December payment will become due in two weeks.

Sincerely,

Dear Mrs. Leinwar:

Have unforeseen circumstances kept you from paying your account at Warren's? If this is true, a moment of your time to explain the situation and to let us know when you can resume making payments will help us. Although we received no reply or payment following our first letter, we are understanding.

If this should be an item that has been overlooked, a prompt payment of $489.90 would be appreciated.

Mail your payment today, please.

Sincerely,

Dear Mr. Beamon:

Since our last reminder to you, an additional amount has become due. Are you aware of this?

No doubt you aren't, or you would have already sent a payment. While this is fresh in your mind, please mail your check for $397.20.

Cordially,

Dear Mr. Kase:

Doesn't the food taste better when your waitress greets you with a smile?

Here at Freeman and Stark we feel that collection letters should be presented with a smile. If our first effort was not successful, we will try again.

So, with smiles on our faces, we kindly ask for a reasonable payment today on your past due balance of $492.29.

Cordially,

Ladies/Gentlemen:

We again call your attention to the following invoices, which, according to our records, are still unpaid well beyond our normal terms:

Date	Invoice No.	Amount
7-17-_ _	78-458	$1,444.77
8-25-_ _	78-789	864.57
		$2,309.34

We would greatly appreciate your early remittance or informing us of the reason for further delay.

Sincerely,

Dear Mrs. Navo:

We have several times reminded you of your past-due account of $2,475. It is 90 days past due. Why have you not answered?

Simply, we are disappointed that our confidence in you was misplaced.

Not paying your bills on time can hurt your credit standing in the community. You can make time payments if you wish, and we will gladly work with you on a payment schedule you can afford.

Please restore our confidence in you and maintain your good credit rating by sending us a check now—even a partial payment will help.

Respectfully,

Dear Mr. Jules:

Payment of this overdue amount today will be appreciated:

Invoice No.	Due Date	Amount
A-445	4-3-_ _	$2,225.40

Please mail your check today.

Sincerely,

Dear Mr. Godfrey:

We again call your attention to your outstanding balance:

$1,512.47

Our records show that we have not received a payment since January 14, _ _.

Your remittance at this time will be appreciated. Should there be questions concerning the above amount, please contact us immediately. If not, please mail your check today.

Sincerely,

Dear Mr. Spears:

The attached statement shows a past due balance of $4,607.12 going back as much as 60 days.

Perhaps your check has already been mailed. If so, please accept our thanks.

If it hasn't been mailed, please send your check today.

Thank you,

Dear Mr. Pauls:

We have not received the balance due us of $500.50 or any response to our inquiries asking why you haven't paid.

Your two recent orders, No. 365 and now 372, and future orders will be held until your balance owing is paid. Do what is best for both of us by mailing your check today.

Sincerely,

Dear Mr. Ellerbe:

A statement was mailed to you on July 12, _ _ _ _. Perhaps you overlooked it. We are enclosing another copy.

Please mail your check for $1,132.40 today.

Sincerely,

Dear Mr. Deranger:

Your account with us has a past due balance of $2,257.00. With winter nearly over, you will soon be needing more building supplies.

To assure your getting them on short notice as you have in the past, please bring your account up to date by mailing us your check for $2,257.00 today.

Sincerely,

Dear Mr. Bruscato:

Recent payments of our invoices have been received long after the due date. Invoices appear to be paid in batches rather than individually when due.

Perhaps our terms are not clear, and I would like to take this opportunity to explain them.

Your credit terms are "Net 30 days," meaning that payment is due *here* 30 days after the date of our invoice. If you prefer to pay our invoices several at a time, we can change our terms to "15 Prox.," in which case payment is due here on the 15th day of the month following the date of our invoice. However, if the total amount of these groups of invoices exceeds your credit terms, more frequent payments will be necessary.

If you have any questions about your terms, or wish to change them to "15 Prox.," please call me at 000-000-0000. I will be happy to discuss this with you.

Please remember that continued delays in paying our invoices will result in our suspending shipments to you. We assume this will not be necessary and look forward to continued business with you.

Sincerely,

Appeals-Collection Letters

If a reminder or two and two letters haven't brought a positive response from your debtor, it is time to use the persuasion technique. This technique is to appeal to one of a person's normal motivations. These motivations include sympathy, fairness, friendship, justice, duty, honor, loyalty, pride, fear, and self-interest.

Persuasion letters tend to be longer than others because you are building a series of arguments rather than stating bare facts.

It is helpful to offer a solution to your customer's problem. Perhaps you can suggest installment payments, smaller monthly payments or delaying the date of the first payment.

Appeal to Fairness

Dear Mr. Dugas:

We expected an answer to the last of several letters we sent you. As you know, you still owe us $1,591.00.

Truly, we are disappointed. I am sure you are not intentionally trying to make our work difficult, but that's what it amounts to. Is there some reason you have not paid? Some difficulty getting money? Too many other bills to pay? Let's make this easier for both of us. Call us, and we can solve any problems together.

We have been fair with you, and now we believe you will be fair with us. Please call or mail your check today.

Sincerely yours,

Dear Ms. Judlin:

We try hard to be equally fair to all our customers, and I am sure you wish to be fair with us. Your account shows:

September 30	$1,452.78
October 31	2,475.91
November 30	<u>1,997.90</u>
	$5,926.59

Perhaps you have been putting off paying these past-due amounts. It would be only fair to pay them now. The enclosed postpaid envelope is for your convenience. Please mail your check today.

Sincerely,

Appeal to Friendship

Dear Mrs. Swain:

We think of you as a friend as well as a customer, and we hope you feel the same about us.

We feel obligated to tell you that your payment methods are not meeting our expectations.

For some reason your payments are getting farther and farther behind, and an explanation would be sincerely appreciated. The amount outstanding is $499.06.

Please contact us today so we can work together on this; even better, send us a check today.

Sincerely,

Dear Mr. Braddix:

You surely understand that we cannot permit your account in the amount of $7,744.55 to run indefinitely. We have tried to bring this matter to your attention in a friendly way, but such methods seem to bring no results.

We shall expect full payment within the next ten days. Your prompt attention to your past-due account will be appreciated.

Sincerely,

Appeal to Cooperation

Dear Ms. Mertz:

You have not responded to our previous notices about your account.

Your balance of $591.40 is considerably past due, and we ask that you give this overdue amount your immediate attention.

Your cooperation would be appreciated. Please mail your check today.

Sincerely,

Dear Mr. Lembo:

PLEASE GIVE YOUR IMMEDIATE ATTENTION TO THIS THIRD REMINDER of your past-due invoice in the amount of $1,121.05.

We have served you in good faith and hope to continue doing so, but now we must have your payment in full.

Please mail your check today.

Sincerely,

Appeal to Honor

Dear Mr. Mikimoto:

You will recall the recent letters we sent you on May 5 about your overdue account. Is a check for $379.80 on the way?

We allowed you the privilege of having an open account because you agreed to make regular monthly payments. We are asking now that you honor that commitment. If you haven't already done so, please mail your check today.

Sincerely,

Dear Mr. Zell:

It is our policy to help customers whenever possible. We allowed you an extra 45 days to pay for your last purchase, and you promised to pay within that period.

To date we have not received your check.

We now request immediate payment. Please mail your check today for $10,420.52.

Sincerely,

Appeal to Sympathy

Dear Mrs. Gsell:

Would you help us in our efforts to reduce costs? The reductions do get passed on to you. By sending your check for $579.90 now, we can eliminate the expense of writing additional letters and of carrying your past-due account.

We hope you will mail your check today.

Sincerely,

Dear Ms. Shimmer:

We are interested in and concerned about our customers. If there is a reason why we have not received a payment from you in several months, please let us know what it is. I am sure we can be of help by extending the time for payment. By working together, we can reach a solution that is right for both of us.

Please let us hear from you. Better still, why not mail your check today?

Sincerely,

Appeal to Loyalty

Dear Mr. Valenti:

PLEASE RETURN OUR CREDIT CARD.

There is no easy way to ask customers to return their credit cards. We regret making this request, but your account remains past due despite previous efforts to obtain payment.

You have been a valued customer for many years, since Feb. 2, _ _ _ _, and we feel that your loyalty deserves special consideration. If you can send payment of $822.46 today, please keep your credit card. This will assure continuation of your account. If there is a problem and you can't pay, call us and we will work it out together.

Sincerely,

Dear Mr. Polart:

You have been a customer of ours for over 20 years. Such loyalty cannot be pushed aside lightly. That is why we have permitted you to delay some of your payments well beyond our stated terms.

Two of our invoices are fourteen months past due. We have helped each other during many trying business slowdowns, but now we ask sincerely that you make at least a one-half payment of $368.33 today.

Sincerely,

Appeal to Duty

Dear Ms. Treen:

Your buying and our selling is a transaction of mutual benefit, providing, of course, that our merchandise is satisfactory with you and that you pay as agreed.

We feel we should not have to wait any longer for your payment that was due over two months ago.

We would appreciate a check for $391.57 today.

Sincerely,

Dear Mr. Lieder:

You received several reminders and letters since your account became due.

You have sent neither the payment nor an explanation for not paying.

The time has come, Mr. Lieder, for you to take a couple of minutes—today—either to tell us when we can expect your payment or to mail your check for $2,297.00.

Sincerely,

Appeal to Fear

Dear Mrs. Univax:

You have been sent several notices and two letters reminding you of your past due bill of $629.32, yet we have heard nothing from you.

We are asking that you take positive action now to clear your account. We do not wish to involve you in any financial difficulties, but we must have a payment this week.

Sincerely,

Dear Mrs. Abila:

In spite of the fact that we have sent you many reminders and letters about your past-due invoice No. 7229 of May 19, _ _ _ _, for $9,922.56, you have not responded in any way. Having received no explanation for your delay, we now urgently request an immediate payment.

It is not our intention to embarrass or harass you, but we must have action on your part. If you cannot pay the invoice in full, you may write a check for half of it today.

Sincerely,

Appeal to Patience

Dear Mrs. Oatis:

We have sent you numerous letters requesting payment of the $407 open on your account since October 23. We have heard nothing from you.

Therefore, we must now insist upon an immediate payment. Please mail your check today.

Very sincerely yours,

Dear Mr. Profumo:

You have not answered my previous letters requesting payment on your $823.50 purchase of brake linings. We have received neither a payment nor an explanation for not paying.

I am sure you would agree that we have been extremely patient.

Could you kindly make a payment of $200.00? Please do so today.

Sincerely,

Appeal to Justice

Dear Mr. Pallet:

Our previous two letters regarding your past due balance of $910.00 have brought no response. We have heard no objections or complaints and therefore assume you have no objections to the amount due.

We feel the only just course for you is to pay what you agree you owe.

We will look for a check before the end of this week.

Sincerely,

Dear Mrs. Stearns:

You are a new customer, and already your account is past due.

A continuing business relationship depends on a mutual agreement to comply with the stated terms of sale. We agree to provide quality merchandise and service. You agree to pay on time.

Your check for $749.50 should reach us within ten days.

Sincerely,

Appeal to Pride

Dear Mr. Kopp:

You have not replied to our two letters about your past due account of $1,432.70.

Also, our attempts to reach you by phone have been unsuccessful.

A check from you today would add to your pride in your reputation, and it will keep your credit rating intact.

Sincerely,

Dear Mr. Swaney:

Pride of workmanship is our first consideration. We are proud of the painting and sign work we did on your building, and we know you are proud of the results.

Pride should also extend to financial obligations. Our previous reminders that payment was due have been ignored. If there are circumstances of which we are not aware, please let us know so that we can work together in solving your payment problem.

May we suggest using the enclosed, postpaid envelope to mail a half payment today.

Sincerely,

Appeal to Courtesy

Dear Ms. Pradell:

We are at a loss to understand why we have not received payment on your past-due account or at least the courtesy of a reply to our several reminders.

You may have a good reason for your delay in paying, but we don't know what it is. We will try to work out an agreement for extending payments if that is what you need.

Please let us hear from you today. Your check for $302.40 would be most welcome today.

Sincerely,

Dear Mr. Cloino:

Thank you for your order of August 19, _ _ _ _. We appreciate your continued confidence in our lines of quality builder's hardware.

As a courtesy to you, we will ship your order September 3, as requested.

There is, however, the problem of a past-due amount of $4,412.93, about which you have received previous letters.

We hope you will respond to our faith in you by mailing a check today for the overdue amount.

Sincerely,

Appeal to Credit Standing

Dear Mr. Odom:

On February 3 we mailed you a detailed statement of all unpaid billings, as you had requested.

We were expecting a prompt reply or a check from you. That was three weeks ago, and we still have no reply.

Your account is seriously past due, and that is adversely affecting your credit rating.

We are asking for full payment of $1,478.94 today.

Sincerely,

Dear Mr. Price:

You have been sent several letters regarding your overdue account in the amount of $6,991.45. We have had no reply from you.

Your credit rating may suffer because when other suppliers ask us for our credit experience with you, we have no choice but to report your slowness in paying.

We strongly suggest immediate payment in full or partial payment with a statement of when you will pay the balance.

Please contact us today.

Sincerely,

Final Collection Letters

The final collection letter is the last step prior to turning the account over to a collection agency (which normally takes up to 50 percent of anything collected) or to an attorney for whatever legal action he or she thinks will open the delinquent's pocket book.

However exasperated the creditor is, the goodwill of the debtor must be retained. Do not demean the delinquent payer or use any foul language. Care is required to avoid writing anything libelous or even halfway libelous. Tact must be the watchword.

Dear Mr. Abrahms:

I would like to talk to you in person about your delinquent account. Since this is not feasible, let me talk frankly in this letter.

Your payments were on time until the beginning of this year, but since then we have received no payments. During this time you have continued to buy from us. You have ignored our past reminders. Something is wrong. Can we help? Please phone or drop in to visit so we can get together on a payment plan.

At this time we must insist on hearing from you within the next ten days. After that, we will have no choice but to cancel your credit and turn your account over to a collection agency. We don't want to do this because it may harm your credit rating. We must hear from you by November 20.

Very truly yours,

REGISTERED MAIL
Re: Unpaid $24,000

Dear Mr. Sorrell:

Contacts by Bethlehem personnel attempting to secure payment of the captioned have been to no avail.

Consider this as our formal demand for full and immediate payment of the outstanding balance. If your payment is not received within 10 days of this letter we will begin litigation proceedings.

It is our hope that you will provide an acceptable response to this demand in order for both of us to avoid additional cost.

Sincerely,

(With permission of R. H. Dietrich, collection manager, Bethlehem Steel Corp.)

Dear Mr. Kirchberg:

Because of the extreme slowness of your payments over the past two years, we can no longer extend credit to you. We have discussed this time and time again, but to no avail. Starting today all sales will be cash-with-order.

We will be happy to continue serving you under these conditions. You can expect the same quality of merchandise and the same fast service—and our super-fast emergency service.

We do expect you to make regular payments on your present balance. Appropriate collection or legal action will be taken if your delinquency continues.

Sincerely,

Dear Mr. Bermudez:

We have had no response from you in answer to our many phone calls and letters during the past twelve months. Our invoice No. 4447H of March 12 in the amount of $14,217.90 remains unpaid.

Our next step is to take legal action to collect the money due us. This is unpleasant for both of us and is damaging to your credit rating. However, you may avoid legal action by making payment within ten days: on or before March 30, 0000.

Whether or not we take legal action is now your decision.

Sincerely,

Dear Ms. Flisciuk:

When credit privileges were extended to you, we expressed our confidence in your ability and willingness to pay your obligations promptly.

In accepting our credit card, you agreed to pay by the due date of your monthly statement.

The balance shown above must be paid immediately.

Credit privileges are temporarily suspended until payment is received.

Sincerely,

(With permission of Judith A. Luff, Sun Company, Inc.)

Dear Mr. Danart:

On May 25, _ _ _ _, our legal department is scheduled to file a suit to collect our claim against you.

The decision to do this comes only after all other methods of persuasion have failed. To us it is a distasteful procedure, and to you it is a black mark against your reputation.

We want to give you one last opportunity to avoid litigation. You may do so by paying us in full no later than May 13.

Sincerely,

Dear Mrs. Claiborne:

May we get serious for a moment? This is about your past-due account, with a current balance of $696.53. Your last payment was received in May, and now it is November.

All our previous reminders, notices, letters, and phone calls have not succeeded in getting a payment from you.

We are now making our final appeal: Please mail your check for $696.53 by November 22. If we do not receive it by then, your account will be turned over to a collection agency. The resulting decline of your credit rating can be serious.

Mail your check no later than November 22 in the postage-paid envelope enclosed.

Sincerely yours,

Dear Mr. Fontana:

The balance due Marmon Company of $9,928.00 is now due and payable. Your inability to live up to your commitments and frequent misrepresentation of information is very disheartening. Therefore, I will set a deadline of June 30 for receipt of the entire balance.

If the balance is not received by that date, I will request the assistance of a local collection agency or hire counsel for the resolution of this matter. Please be aware that Marmon Company reports credit experience to credit gathering agencies.

Sincerely,

Dear Mr. Elfert:

It is difficult to write an old friend a letter that may not end up being considered friendly.

That is because of the several invoices (copies attached) that have been past due for many months.

We have sent numerous reminders and letters requesting payment or an explanation for not paying, and we have offered methods of paying in easy installments.

We are very patient with old friends, but we also have to consider our own financial responsibilities.

Therefore, following a grace period of 15 days, your overdue invoices will be sent to our attorney for the necessary collection procedures. Please consider the consequences and mail your check today.

Sincerely,

Dear Mr. Bazley:

I would like to talk to you in person about your past-due account. Since that is not feasible, let us talk frankly in this letter.

Your payments were on time until the beginning of this year, but since then we have received no payments. During this time you have continued to buy from us. You have ignored our past reminders. Something is wrong. Can we help? Please phone or drop in to visit so we can get together on a payment plan.

At this time we urgently request that you contact us within the next ten days. After that, we will have no choice but to cancel your credit and turn your account over to a collection agency. We don't want to do that because it may harm your credit rating. We must hear from you by November 20. The amount outstanding is $6,142.29.

Very truly yours,

Dear Ms. Dufrene:

We have used every reasonable means available to persuade you to pay the $2,129.47 you owe us. Your refusal to cooperate makes legal action necessary.

Action by the courts becomes a matter of public record, destroying your credit standing. Court procedures are inconvenient and costly to you. You are then left to wonder why you didn't avoid all that notoriety by making an honest effort to pay an honest debt.

This is our last attempt to help you. We will allow you ten days, until August 24 to make a mutually satisfactory arrangement for payment of your debt. After that date, our attorney will proceed with court action.

Very truly yours,

Dear Mr. Breewood:

You haven't made a single payment, a single reply to our letters, or a single return of our phone calls about our invoice No. 47-222 of July 1 for $22,733.34.

This invoice is now more than 120 days old, and you must agree we can no longer extend the time for payment. We are writing you this FINAL plea for payment to avoid unpleasantness.

We must let you know that unless we receive your check by November 12 we shall have to request that our attorney begin the litigation process. That can be more costly than paying your debt.

Please send your check for $22,733.34 today to avoid further action.

For your convenience, please use the enclosed, postpaid envelope.

Sincerely,

Dear Mr. Arcana:

This is your FINAL NOTICE before our auditing firm closes your account.

Our last of many efforts to obtain payment will be to turn your account over to the Credit Bureau for collection. This will complicate further service from us and limit your credit with other retailers.

To forestall this action, mail your check for $722.40 by January 30. Remember, this is your final notice.

Sincerely yours,

WARNING

This is our FINAL NOTICE, Mrs Golden, regarding the total amount owing on your account. If we do not hear from you within fifteen days from the date of this letter, your account may be referred to a collection agency.

You don't want this to happen, and we don't want to take this kind of drastic action. It's up to you.

Make a payment today.

Minimum Payment Due $3,200
Total Amount Owing $32,000

Sincerely,

Mrs Irma Golden
00 Fairview Drive
Old Oak, MN 00000
Account #724-368

CHAPTER 6

Information: Providing and Requesting

Providing Information

The basis of a successful letter providing information is clarity, and the key to clarity is brevity. Too often, adding supposedly clarifying details becomes a distraction to the reader. If you wish to say, "Starting in April, send the FICA report to J. C. Henning rather than to A. M. Mondale," an explanation of when Henning replaced Mondale, whether this is temporary or permanent, Henning's background and qualifications, whether Mondale has quit, retired, been promoted, or shuffled sideways, and your regrets or congratulations are of no importance in getting the report rerouted.

Repetition should be eliminated. To write, "We would appreciate your taking the $188.50 credit we issued so that it can be cleared from our books and your account brought up to date," is stating the purpose twice. Eliminate either "it can be cleared from our books," or "your account brought up to date."

The second paragraph of the following informational letter illustrates the confusion resulting from disorganized thinking:

> General availability of railroad freight cars throughout the country improved slightly during the week as the weather moderated in the Northeast.
>
> We have shortages of high-roof box cars in the Northwest. In addition, the South Bend mill has been short of box cars throughout the week. We expect to clear up the South Bend shortage by Saturday, and we are using standard box cars in lieu of high-roof cars to avoid delays in customer shipments from the Northwest.

What the author has done is to organize the second paragraph this way:

Problem A, Problem B, Solution B, Solution A

Going from solution B to solution A causes an awkward twist in the reader's thinking because he or she has to jump backward three steps to relate solution A to problem A.

The second paragraph should be reorganized as follows:

We have a shortage of high-roof box cars in the Northwest. We are replacing these with standard box cars to avoid delays in customer shipments. In addition, the South Bend mill has been short of box cars throughout the week. We expect to clear up this shortage by Saturday.

The rewritten paragraph is easier to follow and can be outlined as follows:

Problem A, Solution A, Problem B, Solution B

Because the ending of a letter is its most emphatic part, a courteous note that offers additional assistance is helpful in eliciting the reader's cooperation. Following are examples of simple but effective ending paragraphs:

If you have any questions about this subject, please let me know.

If you require additional information, please let me know.

Any questions should be addressed to me (to this department).

If you have any questions, please do not hesitate to call.

If you have any questions or comments, please let me know.

If you have any questions about this information, please do not hesitate to call me at 000-000-0000.

If you wish further details, please call me at 000-000-0000.

If you have any questions, please call me at 000-000-0000.

For further details, please contact me at 000-000-0000.

For further information, please call me at 000-000-0000.

Should you have any questions, or require additional information, please do not hesitate to contact me.

Please let me know if you need additional information.

Please call me if you have any questions.

If you have any questions, please call me.

How to Do It

1. State the topic in the first sentence.
2. Be precise.
3. Omit unnecessary details.
4. Offer cooperation.

Shipping Instructions

Dear Mr. Thomas:

When we place orders for aluminum wheels with you, either for our account or to be billed to one of our customers, please be sure they are shipped prepaid and the freight is included on your invoice to us.

We would appreciate your not making any collect shipments.

Sincerely,

Procedural Change

Dear Sales Manager:

Attached are three requests for credits from customers who state that they did not agree to pay for the molds used in making their aluminum castings. They understood that the mold cost was included in our sales price.

This has been a problem, and we will solve it.

We must have a clear understanding with our customers as well as a definite commitment if our customer is to pay. The commitment must be obtained before we buy the molds. This is the responsibility of the sales representative.

Until further notice, all purchase orders for molds will be sent to me for approval. The purchase order must state whether we pay or the customer pays.

If you have any questions about this, please let me know.

Sincerely,

Price Increase

Dear Customer:

Due to the rapid rise in labor and operating costs, Ames Fast Maintenance finds it necessary to increase service charges on September 1, _ _ _ _.

Service-charge increases will vary, depending upon the type of service your company uses: on call, when needed, or monthly preventative maintenance.

We appreciate your past business and look forward to a continuing friendly relationship.

Should you have any questions, Please call us at 000-000-0000.

Sincerely,

Purchasing Policy

Dear Mr. Greene:

In order to do the best purchasing job possible, the responsibility for control of major raw materials, process chemicals, maintenance, and capital equipment is vested in the Headquarters Purchasing Department.

We are committed to a policy of buying materials and services at the division, mill, plant, or office closest to the point of ultimate use, commensurate with sound purchasing practice. This is a system of decentralized buying with centralized control.

Purchasing by Headquarters will be done only in two instances.

1. For those divisions that do not have a purchasing unit.
2. In cases where such a procedure will save our company money.

Although the purchasing function is decentralized, the basic responsibility for policies and procedures remains the function of Headquarters Purchasing Department. Good two-way communication is essential.

Best regards,

Bid Price

Dear Mr. Crown:

This is to notify you that our bid price is $4,500 for each electric motor, to disassemble, replace worn parts, rewind, and reassemble. These are the six motors we discussed and looked at on April 7.

Sincerely,

Complying with Request

Dear Mr. and Mrs. Heurtley:

Enclosed is a sample of the paint we mixed for you at your request. Please look at the sample to make sure it is the color you wanted.

Then sign the sample and mail it to me in the enclosed envelope.

To expedite the process, please call me with your approval before returning the sample.

Thank you again for choosing Damon Interiors.

Sincerely,

Data No Longer Required

Dear Mr. Jose:

For the foreseeable future it will not be necessary to submit the quarterly tax information reports to Lawrence & Lawrence as you did in the years _ _ _ _ and _ _ _ _.

You should, however, continue to accumulate the data monthly so that your preparation of the annual tax reports can be done quickly.

Regards,

Lease Instructions

Dear Mr. and Mrs. McLennen:

Regarding the lease at 422 San Carlos Way, Mr. Wells has asked me to send you the enclosed new lease for your house. The lease is for a three-year term beginning the first of July _ _ _ _, with monthly payment of $630 which should be mailed to Mr. Wells at this office.

If the terms are satisfactory to you, please sign both copies where indicated and return them to me with your check for $630, after which I will send you a copy signed by Mr. Wells.

A return envelope is enclosed for your convenience. If you have any questions, please call me.

Sincerely,

Action Taken

Dear Tom:

I received a copy of the letter sent to you by the chief accounting officer of the division of corporate finance of the SEC commenting on one of the financial items on the last 10-K report filed by Ace Manufacturing Co. This is not serious, and I think it can be clarified by a short amendment to your 10-K report.

I am sending a copy of this letter to your accountants with a request that they prepare the amendment.

Sincerely,

Dear Mrs. Metover:

You sent a letter to all separate clubs in the Association requesting that we establish safety committees to meet requirements of the insurance carrier.

We have established such a committee, which will provide safety suggestions to members at our monthly meetings and at other times as necessary. Also, a written monthly report of violations and incidents will be made.

Sincerely,

Payment Instructions

Dear Mr. Fussell:

Because of our revised computer procedures, our accounts-receivable system now requires that each customer location be identified by a customer number.

The customer number, located on the above mailing label, has been assigned to identify all payments sent to this location. Your assistance in showing this customer number on all checks is requested.

Invoice numbers being paid must continue to be listed on your check.

This, together with your customer number, will permit us to promptly record the receipt of your payment.

Sincerely,

Confirmation

Dear Mr. and Mrs. Homer:

This is to confirm the closing date of June 30 at 9:00 A.M. in our office.

Mr. Wilson has requested that you bring tax papers, fuel bills, insurance policies, and other papers you have that apply to the house when you come for the closing.

Sincerely yours,

Dear Mr. Dixon:

Confirming our telephone conversation of May 20, please cancel our purchase order number 000-0000.

Sincerely,

Payment Delay

Dear Mr. Trasatti:

I was astounded to receive your billing, copy enclosed, for $98,010. Your bid, copy also enclosed, was for $85,000.

We discussed your finding that additional foundation work was necessary and a steeper roof pitch was required by last month's change in the State building code.

When you mentioned these additional requirements and costs, you gave no indication that they would amount to anywhere near $13,010.

As a building contractor, you do excellent work, and I'm not disputing the $13,010 upcharge. But there are two things we must straighten out. First, any contracts in the future must be written before work is started. I can't take these huge surprises. Second, we don't have the cash to pay the entire billing now. The additional $13,010 will have to be spread over the next six months.

We will be working together in the future, but remember: no more oral agreements, only written contracts.

Sincerely,

Continue Procedure

Dear Ms. Michales:

Over the past few months, significant progress has been made in controlling late payments. Your monthly report analyzing the late payments has brought much helpful attention to the problem.

Please continue sending this report to the headquarters Accounts Payable Department.

Sincerely,

Number Code Changes

Dear Mr. Chalbon:

In order to obtain more detailed information from our computer printouts, please make the following changes, effective May 1, _ _ _ _.

Old Number	*New Number*
8000-1200-1722-01	8000-1200-1721
8000-1200-1722-02	8000-1200-1722
8000-1200-1722-03	8000-1200-1723

Because of limited spacing in the computer program, the last two digits of the old number do not show on the printout.

We will appreciate your cooperation in making the changes.

Sincerely,

Repeated Instructions

Ladies/Gentlemen:

As I have previously requested, all dividends and capital gains for my account should be in cash rather than in shares. I was surprised, therefore, to learn that the gains of December 1, _ _ _ _, were being held in shares.

Please forward the capital gain, in the amount of $492.10, in the form of a check.

Sincerely,

Distribution of Reports

Dear Ms. Greene:

The following will be mailed to you in several packages within the next few days for distribution to all salaried employees at your location:

1. A summary description of the new health-benefit package and a cover letter from the chairman of the board. (Please staple the cover letter to the description before distributing.)
2. A blue pamphlet describing medical benefits.
3. An orange pamphlet describing dental benefits.
4. A report and cover letter from Vice President A. B. Walker on Safety Performance by location for the year _ _ _ _. (Please attach the cover letter to the report.)

If any of these is not received by April 30, please call me at 000-0000.

Sincerely,

Claim Against City

Dear Mr. Martin:

It is a pleasure to assist you in your claim against Stewart City for the inadvertent damage to your property. The enclosed form is for your use in filing the claim. It is IMPORTANT that you read and follow the instructions on the back of the form.

My staff will be most willing to provide any assistance. Please feel free to call 000-0000 and ask for Claims Assistance. Your cooperation in returning the claim form as soon as possible will help us to complete the processing with a minimum of error and delay.

Before sealing the envelope, make sure you have filled in your CORRECT street address and phone number.

Sincerely,

Effect of Strike

Dear Customer:

Because of a failure to agree on terms, the union has called a strike which may affect our operations. Despite this, our company intends to do everything possible to maintain normal shipping operations from our warehouse.

Our priority will be to minimize disruptions that might inconvenience our customers.

Your cooperation during this period is appreciated.

Sincerely,

Layoff

Dear Joe Arvella:

This is to notify you that you are being laid off in compliance with Article XX, Section 3, of our current labor agreement. We hope you will be available for recall in the near future.

Please check with Human Resources to verify that your current address and phone number are on file.

Sincerely,

Statement of Future Occurrence

Dear Jim:

Effective July 1 we will close our welding shop. Any work in progress will be transferred to:

Amos Welding
0000 Third Avenue
Phone 000-0000

Our machine shop will remain open and will be expanded to handle larger steel rollers.

We appreciate your past welding business, and after July 30 will be able to take care of your machining needs.

Sincerely,

Dear Mr. Atwood:

A new 1000 KVA Electric transformer will be installed in the Sitcom Plant during May _ _ _ _.

Preparatory to the installation, General Electric requires eight hours of downtime on all existing electrical systems.

The downtime has been scheduled for Saturday, March 13. There will be *no electrical power* in the Sitcom Plant on that day.

Sincerely,

Policy Change

Dear Mr. Rosen:

The Company announced in the news release on August 15 that certain divisions will change their fiscal year-end from December 31 to September 30.

This will not change the monthly accounting procedures currently used by the Western manufacturing branches. Adjustments will be made at Headquarters.

Sincerely,

Dear Mrs. Clement:

We have changed our credit policy to make buying easier for all our customers.

You now have 60 days in which to pay for your purchases without an additional interest penalty.

This may be bucking the current trend of shortening payment periods, but we feel our extended no-interest policy will be welcomed by our regular customers.

We thank you for your past business and hope to see you soon.

Sincerely,

Change in Items Used

H. R. Baker:

As of April 1, we will discontinue using motor housing numbers 400-500 and use only the substitute numbers 800-900.

Please sell as scrap any remaining housings numbered 400-500.

Best regards,

Address Change

Dear Customer:

Our address for receiving your payments is changed to:

000 Industrial Avenue
Montview, IL 00000-0000

This change is for your payment of invoices and statements only.

Other correspondence and purchase orders should still be sent to the address shown at the top of this letter.

Your cooperation in changing your records will be appreciated.

Sincerely,

Billing Department

Dear Ms. Ortenberg:

Until further notice please send my monthly statements to my office address:

000 West Elm Street, Suite 102
San Francisco, CA 00000-0000

Please change your records.

Sincerely,

Will Contact You Again

Dear Mr. Franks:

We have received your claim forms for the transit damage sustained in your recent shipment form Watson Co., San Diego.

One of our representatives will phone you within a few days to arrange an appointment to inspect the damage.

Sincerely yours,

Reason for Cooperation

To All Houseparents:

The daily Milk and Meal Sheets must be turned in to Jean Overland on the first working day of each month.

These sheets are part of a report that must be mailed to the State by the seventh day of each month.

A timely turn-in of the Meal Sheets is money in our pockets.

Sincerely,

Send Records Elsewhere

Dear Dr. Dandry:

I have moved to another city. Please send my medical records to:

Dr. J. D. Huggit
0000 South Main Street
City, State, Zip Code

I thank you for the care you gave me and wish you the best.

Sincerely,

Too Busy

Dear Mr. Gondrella:

My business workload has increased dramatically these past three months and shows no signs of letting up.

Therefore, with regrets, I can no longer spend Saturdays helping your son, Kevin, with his math studies. He has improved greatly, and I enjoy working with him, but I can no longer spend the time. I'm sure you can find another tutor for Kevin. His school can probably make a recommendation.

The best,

New Paint Required

Dear Mrs. Grundy,

As I said I would, I got a painting contractor to examine the outside of your house.

He said he could touch up the bare spots for a reasonable charge—he said that would be $150. Then he went on to explain that he couldn't match perfectly the surrounding areas because they had faded, and then the whole house would look spotty. As I was afraid, he said no reliable painter would do that.

The painter said his lowest price for a fairly good paint job would be $400. He understands your financial situation and doubts that any painter would bid lower.

He then suggested that you could (I can help you here) contact the Elderly Helpers Association. They would not charge for labor and might be able to get donated paint. He then warned that the workers would be amateurs.

If you would be satisfied with that, the expense would be minimal. The choice is up to you.

Cordially,

REQUESTING INFORMATION

A request for information can be short and direct. For example:

> Send me an analysis of steel tubing sales, by customer, for the month of October.

This is brief and functional, but the tone is unnecessarily commanding. The simple addition of the word *please* to start the request would increase the recipient's willingness to help. A word or two of explanation would also improve the reader's willingness by making him or her feel a part of the project. Two examples:

> For our annual purchasing department study, please send me a list of the minority vendors from whom you made purchases during the last six months of _ _ _ _.

> Mr. Holmes has asked that we provide him with an analysis of steel tubing sales, by customer, during October. Please send this data to my attention.

Long requests should be separated into items that can be listed and numbered. This clarifies the request and simplifies the answering. Here is an example:

> Please send us quotes on the following:
> 1. 24,000 B22, 16 oz. cans
> 2. 5,000 A22, 1-gallon cans
> 3. 17,000 AA4B, size 14 plastic lids

Because the ending of a letter is the part having strongest emphasis, the last paragraph should be a polite but persuasive punch line in your effort to obtain the information requested. The following are suggested ideas for the closing paragraph.

> We look forward to receiving your reply.
>
> Your cooperation will be appreciated.
>
> Your cooperation will be truly (greatly) appreciated.
>
> Your cooperation and understanding will be appreciated.
>
> Your prompt reply will be appreciated.
>
> We will appreciate receiving this information as soon as possible.
>
> We will appreciate receiving this data by September 25.

A quote from you would be appreciated.

Thank you for your anticipated cooperation.

Your prompt attention will be appreciated.

Thank you. (This is a common ending for a letter either requesting or providing information. Some authorities object to a thank you in advance because it seemingly implies an end to communication on the subject.) An expression of appreciation is preferable.

How to Do It

1. Make the request specific.
2. State or imply a reason.
3. Show appreciation for the expected cooperation.

Accounting System

Ladies/Gentlemen:

Do you recommend a particular system or set of forms for bookkeeping for automotive shops? If you do, I would appreciate knowing what the system is and receiving a copy of the forms.

Also, many trade associations collect data related to production and financial activities from members and summarize these. I would appreciate receiving your latest available data.

Sincerely,

Acknowledgment of Gift

Dear Ansel:

I know this is a busy season for you, but I wanted to ask if the parcel I mailed you on the twelfth of last month has arrived. If it hasn't, I'll have the post office put a tracer on it.

The parcel is a leather portfolio case and is a thank-you gift for the time you took from your busy schedule to show Harry Longworth some of the interesting parts of Denver. Both Harry and I appreciate your kind hospitality.

Sincerely,

City Information

Dear City Manager:

Auburn, California, is one of the locations my wife and I are considering for retirement, which will be in six years.

Please send us general information about Auburn, especially data that would be of interest to a retired couple. We may wish to buy residential property in Auburn before retirement.

Receiving this information would be greatly appreciated.

Sincerely,

Recent Sales Activity

Dear Ms. Rosenthal:

Once again we are at the time of the year when Mr. Keith Monte of Monte-Atlanta Corp. will wish to discuss can purchases for their Tampa Cannery.

Please let me know what their sales activity has been this past year and what you see for the coming year. This would include prices, quantities, delivery schedules, and other data you think pertinent.

It is Mr. Monte's plan to be in Miami Beach next month from the fifteenth through the nineteenth prior to calling on a supplier in Ohio. Could the company boat be available in Miami on the nineteenth, before his trip to Ohio?

May I hear from you soon?

Sincerely,

Order Information

Dear Mr. Portofino:

We are ready to add floor lamps to our small-furniture store. Please send us pictures—in color if possible—of your line of floor lamps. Because this is a conservative, working-class neighborhood, we are not interested in far-out, modernistic designs, but would like new and interesting styling.

We want to have floor lamps available for our fall promotion in October. A prompt reply will be appreciated.

Sincerely,

Ames Blouses
Attn: Order Department:

I would like to order your blouse No. A727A in yellow. First, because stated sizes vary so much from one manufacturer to another, could you please send me two measurements from your small and medium sizes of this blouse:

With the blouse spread flat (1) the chest width at the lower part of the arm seams and (2) the length from the shoulder top to the blouse bottom.

From those measurements I can tell whether to order a small or a medium blouse.

Sincerely,

Data for Newsletter

Dear Mr. Robinson:

Our personnel manager has requested that we provide statistical data for the monthly Newsletter, as is done at other divisions.

Below is a suggested format. Please discuss it with your division manager and provide me with your suggested changes by May 1st.

	June This Year	*June Last Year*
Bbls produced		
Bbls shipped		
Production efficiency %		

Your cooperation will be appreciated.

Sincerely,

Dear Mrs. Deroche:

As the leader of the group that visited several Native American churches recently, could you write a report or summary of your trip for our monthly newsletter?

Our whole congregation will be interested in what you saw and discovered as well as your suggestions for helping these churches. This help could be one of our Mission projects this coming year.

Phone me if you need any assistance with what to say or how to write the article.

All the best,

Credit Information

Ladies/Gentlemen:

We have the name of your organization as a credit reference for

August Mann, Inc.
00 Second Street
Holloway, FL 00000

It will be appreciated if you will give us the benefit of your credit experience with this company, as well as any other comments concerning its management and general reputation, which would assist us in extending an appropriate line of credit.

The information you share with us will be held in strict confidence and will be used for credit purposes only. We will welcome an opportunity to reciprocate at any time.

Year of first sale   _____

Highest credit last 12 months   _____

Amount now owing_____

Amount past due _____

Terms of sale_____

Promptness of payment _____

Special comments   _____

Enclosed for your convenience is a self-addressed return envelope. Your early reply will be appreciated.

Cordially yours,

Here is a short version of the above letter (it is advisable to enclose a postpaid envelope):

Would you please submit the following credit information on the above-named firm. We appreciate your cooperation and will gladly reciprocate at any time.

Then list the information required from the model letter above. Additional facts that could be requested include the following:

Date of last sale   Number of days slow

Average credit extended   Prompt in payment

Recent high extended

Unearned cash discounts

Discount period

Unjust claims

Referred to collectors

Written off to expense

Credit Application

Dear Mr. Harkins:

We were pleased with the quality and prices of your line of Champion hardware you exhibited recently at the Cleveland Hardware Show. We believe the Champion line would improve our retail sales.

With this in mind, we wish to apply for an open credit line of $5,000 until our experience suggests a higher amount.

As soon as possible, please let us know that our credit has been approved.

Sincerely,

Credit Card

Dear Mr. Henry:

Please arrange to secure a telephone credit card for John Hamilton, who has transferred to our administrative staff. Please forward the credit card to my attention.

Sincerely,

Warranty Questions

Dear Mr. Donaldson:

We are delaying payment of the attached invoice for service work performed by you to make our second cooler operable.

Even though the cooler has been installed for several months. It was not operated until last month. The adjustments you made were adjustments I feel should be covered by the warranty. Additionally, I was under the impression that when you volunteered your help, it was covered by the warranty.

Please look into this, and let me know what will be done.

Cordially,

Making an Appointment

Dear Harry:

I have looked over the proposed agreement for the sale of your heavy equipment. It meets all the normal requirements, but I do have a few questions and want to go over the payment schedule.

We can discuss the questions over the phone or you can phone for an appointment before May 25, when it will be necessary to sign the final document.

Sincerely,

Dear Antoin,

My son Peter wants to write a high-school report on the shipping industry as it relates to Seattle. Because you have been working for the Dollar lines as an accountant for many years, I thought you could provide him with some useful data.

Will it be all right for him to call you some evening soon to make an appointment to talk to you? We would both appreciate it.

Sincerely,

Old Equipment

Branch Managers:

The Johnson hoists at many branches have fallen into disrepair and many are no longer used for a variety of reasons.

I would like to evaluate the status of this equipment at each branch to determine the cost of repair, how much help you may need from Central Engineering, and what performance and saving opportunities are available.

By Monday, July 7, I would like replies to these questions from each of you:

1. Are the hoists operational? If not, why not?
2. When were attempts last made to repair them?
3. What repair work will be necessary to make the hoists operational?
4. What savings are possible compared with your present hoisting system?

John Harvey is available at Central Engineering to help you answer the above questions. Feel free to call him at 000-0000.

Sincerely,

Corporate Name

Dear Mr. Davidson:

I will proceed to clear the proposed name of your new corporation and arrange to set it up as soon as you notify me to go ahead. When you call me, I will also need the following information:

1. Names and addresses of directors to be elected at the first meeting
2. Names and addresses of officers of the corporation
3. The fiscal year to be selected by the corporation

I enjoyed meeting you yesterday and look forward to meeting the other principals as soon as they are all back in town.

Sincerely,

Please Investigate

Dear Joanne:

Thank you for your letter of November 10 about Sanders Company complaints.

Although your letter refers to four complaints from them, we have received only two written complaints as of the first of November. As explained to you over the phone, the complaint on service did not exist. I wonder, therefore, who or what has caused the sudden rash of excuses to cease buying our belting.

I would be interested in hearing if you are able to determine who is really the culprit who is trying to instigate our removal as their supplier.

Sincerely,

Office Furniture

To the Sales Department:

Please send us a catalog of your office furniture and supplies. We are planning to purchase new furniture and file cabinets.

Sincerely,

Life-Insurance Questions

Dear Mr. Thomas:

Can you help me find the answers to a few questions about my life insurance policy No. 5320116? The questions are these:

1. What is the present death benefit?
2. What is the present cash value?
3. What is the current loan against the cash value?
4. What will the death benefits be at March 30, _ _ _ _?

Your reply will be appreciated.

Sincerely,

Procedural Change

Dear Mr. Sharper:

Your current practice of mailing two copies of your invoices to A. C. Corporation, Milwaukee branch—one marked *original*—and also mailing two copies of the same invoice to the A. C. Corporation headquarters office, Detroit—one marked *original*—is confusing. This has resulted in duplicate payments because two copies are marked *original*.

In the future, please mail your invoices, one *original* and three copies to A. C. Corporation, Milwaukee only.

Your cooperation is appreciated.

Sincerely,

Dear Mr. Hiller:

Last year we received a number of product complaints that could not be tied down to specific dates and crews. I would like to suggest that we stamp or print the factory job number on each item. This would also separate the jobs we have manufactured for us by outside firms.

I would appreciate your comments and any suggestions.

With regards,

Confirming a Conversation

Dear Ms. Wong:

I would like to confirm my understanding of our phone conversation yesterday. You mentioned an upcoming sale of Branson white-leather walking shoes with a nonskid sole. You gave me order number 568294, which I understand entitles me to order a selection of these shoes now rather than having to wait until the sale is publicly announced next month.

This would be of great help to our—and your—fall shoe sales.

Would you please confirm in writing that I can order now at the sale price using order number 568294. A prompt reply will be appreciated.

Sincerely,

Personnel Evaluation

Dear Sandy:

Please make a brief written evaluation of each of your fork truck drivers, covering the following points:

1. Description of duties
2. Performance rating for each of the duties
3. Outstanding weaknesses and strengths

Rank performance from a high of 4 to a low of 1. Number 4 is consistent performance above the position's requirements.

Please have these ready for my review by October 14. We will discuss the ratings on October 16 and set up a program for performance improvement.

Sincerely,

School Courses

Dear Dean Ramirez:

I will start my engineering training at Arbor College in October.

My present plans are to specialize in electronics. Perhaps you can help me select the courses and their sequence to ensure that I take the necessary ones. We might also discuss my understanding of my goals.

I would appreciate an appointment with you—at your convenience. Please write to the above address or phone me after 6 P.M. at 000-0000.

Sincerely,

Dear Registrar:

Please send me the information I need to enroll in Jordan's Trade School.

I plan to start this coming fall in your computer-repair class.

Sincerely,

Price Quote

Dear Mr. Harrison:

As part of our program for developing vendor sources,* a quote from you on the items listed below would be appreciated.

_____

_____

_____

Please return your quote in the enclosed postpaid envelope.

Sincerely,

*The words *vendor sources* can be changed to *alternate suppliers* if applicable.

Report Request

Attn: Investor Relations:

Please send me a copy of your 10-K report as filed with the Securities and Exchange Commission for your fiscal year ending September 30, _ _ _ _.

Sincerely,

Attn: Public Relations:

Please mail me a copy of your Annual Report for operations during the year _ _ _ _.

Sincerely,

Dear Al,

I am still looking for:

1. Supplies inventory changes you recommended
2. Purchase-order study
3. Standard costs for ink usage

Please let me know when you expect to have these ready for my review.

Best regards,

Dear Bob,

What happened to the report comparing manufacturing and purchasing costs of tie-downs?

Sincerely,

Chemical Hazards

Dear Supplier:

In order to ensure the safety and health of all our employees, protect the environment, better serve our customers, and comply with current Government regulations, we must identify any hazards associated with the chemicals you supply us.

All of the questions on the enclosed SAFETY ADVICE are important. We would like a response that leaves no spaces blank. Answer each question as completely as possible.

Upon receipt of your response, it will be reviewed in light of our use of the chemical. If further information is required, we will phone or write for the specific data needed.

Any future changes in composition of the chemicals from that currently used should be reported promptly with a revised SAFETY ADVICE.

Your assistance is greatly appreciated, and we look forward to continuing our friendly relationship.

Sincerely,

Physical Inventory

Ladies/Gentlemen:

We request that you take a physical inventory on September 30 of all merchandise held by you for the account of A. C. Corporation. This inventory is necessary due to our fiscal year closing on December 31, _ _ _ _.

Please prepare your inventory report in triplicate and attach an Inventory Certificate to each copy of your report. Copies of Certificates are enclosed.

Please mail all three copies to my attention.

Please be certain that the cutoff is as of the end of business on September 30 and that all receipts and shipments or deliveries of merchandise up to the time of taking the physical count are properly recorded.

Sincerely,

Opinions Asked

Dear Concerned Citizen:

The Concerned Citizens Legislative Committee needs your help in identifying concerns in this state that should be brought to the attention of the state Legislature. Your fears, frustrations, and comments will be tabulated and presented by the Committee to the state Legislature during its _ _ _ _ session.

Your views are important to the welfare of this state. We will make sure the Legislature becomes aware of matters that are important to *you*.

Please complete the enclosed short questionnaire and return it in the enclosed envelope. *Please mail it by April 30.*

Sincerely,

Survey of Consumption

Ladies/Gentlemen:

The State of California Department of Water Resources would like to ask your help in an important survey of industrial water use. Our objective is to obtain information on the specific nature, location, and amount of water use that will enable us to develop plans for effective water management and development. Your plant water data will help us estimate future water needs and the need for supplemental water supplies.

Our last survey, in 19_ _, revealed a total industrial water requirement of about 500,000 acre-feet, or about 20 percent of total urban use. We believe that percentage figure has changed because of increased awareness of the need for water conservation and because of the increased water recycling and reuse by industries such as yours. The 19_ _ drought emphasized the potential economic threat of a water shortage. Today's demands on our existing supplies emphasize that shortages could occur unless we plan for the future now.

We believe the information we need will be readily available from your _ _ _ _ year-end reports. We will of course treat your plant data as confidential, privileged information and will not publish individual plant data.

We would appreciate your returning the enclosed form by May 15. Please direct any calls you may wish to make regarding this survey to the nearest Department office as indicated on the back of the questionnaire.

Sincerely,

(With thanks to Superior Court Judge Ronald B. Robie, former director, California Department of Water Resources.)

Suggestions

Ladies/Gentlemen:

To help me update our commodity-file index, I need your input in the form of suggestions for items that should be added to or deleted from the present index.

In order for your responses to be incorporated into the revised index, your input is needed by February 27. If no response is received by that date, I will assume that the present index is satisfactory.

Your suggestions will be appreciated.

Sincerely,

Transfer

Dear Mr. Jordes:

For three years I have worked in general accounting, and I believe that has provided me with a sound background for a beginning position in our Tax Department. Tax work has been my interest and aim, and my goal is to become an expert in corporate tax accounting.

I would like to transfer to our Tax Department when an opportunity becomes available. Would you let the appropriate people know of my interest? Your help will be appreciated.

Regards,

Travel Plans

Evans Travel Agency:

We would like to spend about a week in New Orleans during the first half of May. My wife and I will be first-time visitors.

We would fly from and return to Oakland, California, and stay in a first-class hotel. Would a rental car be helpful? What side trips should we take? Would a paid guide be worthwhile?

Please send what information you can with a suggested itinerary and an estimate of the cost.

Sincerely,

Maintenance Agreement

Dear Mr. Leingar:

I understand you offer a homeowner's appliance-maintenance service. Please send me a brochure or list of your services, including any restrictions, and the costs for various appliances covered.

Do you cover other house repairs such as plumbing and electric wiring?

A prompt reply will be appreciated.

Sincerely,

Historical Question

Kimberly Clark
Legal Department

I am writing an article about events during the Great Depression of the 1930s. Were sanitary napkins used before 1934?

Your answer will be appreciated.

Sincerely,

(Answer: Yes, first used in 1919.)

Claims Service Evaluation

Dear Mrs. Davis:

You recently contacted our claims office by phone. We are striving to provide our customers with timely and clearly explained replies.

To help us evaluate and improve our service, would you please take a moment to complete the enclosed postpaid card and return it to us.

Your assistance is greatly appreciated.

Sincerely,

Medical Facility Evaluation

Dear Mr. Segal:

Regional Medical Center is conducting a survey of patients to determine their satisfaction with our service. The study seeks to determine how our system can provide better care to those who visit us.

The study includes a telephone survey of a number of patients to discuss their most recent clinic visit. An individual from the Medical Research Bureau, an opinion-research firm, *may* be calling you soon regarding your participation. Your response will be strictly confidential.

We sincerely hope that you would be willing to give us your valued thoughts. Please contact Andrea Wilson at 000-000-0000 before June 12 if you do *not* wish to be called.

We appreciate your cooperation.

Sincerely,

CHAPTER 7

Complaints: Making and Answering

MAKING COMPLAINTS

Some people love to complain. Most people don't, but at times writing a complaint letter is necessary. A consumer writing a long, rambling complaint about a product or service can expect a return letter outlining a method of correction that is more troublesome than helpful:

> Please fill in the enclosed form and mail it to us. Under separate cover send the clock to our Central Service Center. After we have received both, we will examine the clock and then send you an estimate of the repair cost if the damage is not covered by our limited warranty. If you accept our estimate, you can notify us by mail. We will then repair the clock, send you the bill, and return the clock when payment has been received.

Perhaps you will receive a form letter that hardly touches the issue:

> Please accept the four boxes of Super Soap we are sending you. Super Soap makes your clothes whiter and brighter.

To get a proper response, the complaint letter must be brief and clear. The items of complaint must be specified or listed. Acceptable solutions to the problem or the requested action must be spelled out or listed.

The following complaint is short, direct, positive, and insistent—but still polite. The politeness is emphasized by the use of the phrases "will you please" and "we would appreciate." The most derogatory statement is a mild "so far we have heard nothing from you." The insistence is shown by the phrases "it is imperative" and "your doing this immediately."

The situation has been made easy for the receiver of the letter by enclosing copies of the original request and the original inventory certificate. Both the purpose of the letter and the requested action are stated clearly.

> On September 12, we mailed you a letter requesting that you take a physical inventory on September 30. A copy of this letter is enclosed.

So far we have heard nothing from you, and it is imperative that we receive the inventory certificate, copies of which are also enclosed.

Will you please follow through on this request and return the certificates to the locations shown in our letter. We would appreciate your doing this immediately.

How to Do It

1. State specifically what is wrong.
2. Explain your viewpoint in a reasonable manner.
3. Suggest specific adjustments or corrections.

Transit Damage

Dear Mr. Baldwin:

Attached are some photos of a truck shipment of cereal boxes that arrived at Des Moines this morning on our order No. 7771.

As you can see in the pictures, there was a space of about three feet between the last stack of boxes and the truck door. This space was not braced or filled with dunnage, allowing the boxes in the rear of the truck to shift and fall over.

Please call this to the attention of those in charge of loading trucks. Reasonable effort must be made to minimize damage while in transit.

Sincerely,

Dear Mr. Beach:

I am returning the gas-exhaust fan with attached motor I ordered for a customer's boat on March 1. My phone order was taken by Bill Wasser. He assured me the fan would arrive before March 15 when my customer would leave this area. My customer left March 15, but the fan didn't arrive until March 22.

In addition, as you will see when you examine the fan, the stem and motor bearings are jammed so the fan blades don't rotate easily.

Your service in the past has been good, but please don't let this incident start a trend.

Please cancel any charge you have made to my account.

Sincerely,

Customer Service:

Your company gives such excellent service that I regret having to make a complaint. On February 4, however, I received my order of grass seed, which arrived with the carton broken and most of the seed gone. The local post office people say the seed was not packaged properly and was not insured.

Please refill my order.

Sincerely,

Cost of Purchases

Dear Jim:

During recent months there has been a substantial increase in the dollar amount of rollers purchased rather than manufactured. This has led to a variety of problems. Internal paper work has left much to be desired. Our controller, working with the Sales Department, has this aspect of the problem under study.

Second, the effect of purchased rollers on profit forecasting has contributed to great variances in two of the last three months. This part of the problem will be brought under control through an improved flow of information from the Sales Department to the Administrative Department. Again, our controller will be calling on the Sales Department to assist him with this part of the problem.

In the future, before a commitment to purchase rollers is made, I want to review the cost, price, and profit relationships. It appears that in some cases we are not breaking even as planned, but are actually losing money.

My review will continue until I have satisfied myself that these outside purchases are contributing to our profits.

Sincerely,

Messy Work Area

Dear Ms. Warren:

I pointed out three weeks ago that the finish polishing area is a filthy mess. I expect immediate action from everyone to clear the area and to keep it clean on a daily basis.

This is one area that should be kept as clean as a kitchen.

Sincerely,

Low Sales

Dear Gordon:

As of your March 31 report to Tony Andrews of Willow Pass Co., we are running far behind last year's sales to them.

It was my understanding with our salesman, Bill Boyd, that he and Tony agreed on 4 to 5 million units per month this year. At the rate we are going, it looks as if we will average only 3 million units per month.

Being Bill's sales manager, find out how he and Tony explain this.

Sincerely,

Sales Forecast

Dear Rowena:

After reviewing the sales forecast for the next four months, I can see trouble ahead. Each month our salespeople are forecasting a decrease in sales from our budget. When you had the opportunity to change the budget, you elected to stay with the one put together by our previous sales manager.

The real problem will be in March. The salespeople have forecast a reduction from the budget of 190M units, which is less than February, although March has three more working days.

Is your March forecast realistic? If it is, we must cut back from our normal two-shift operation.

Sincerely,

Manufacturing Errors

Dear Jim:

A. J. Token is one of our more profitable accounts. Until recently, we served them 100 percent. During our recent strike and immediately after when we were having printing problems, Token gave a trial order to our competitor, Smith Manufacturing. Now Smith has 30 percent of Token's can business.

Two problems are contributing to this:

1. While it is not economical to run volume orders to precise quantities, Token has repeatedly asked us *not* to underrun orders because they must fill specific orders with our cans. We are consistently shipping both under and overruns.

2. Token picks up most of their own cans from us. Too often they will make an appointment to pick up at a specific hour and then have to wait as long as four hours to be loaded. Idle driver time costs Token as much as on-the-road time.

Although these may seem like minor items, unless they are corrected, they will lose this business for us.

What can you do to correct these problems? What can I do to help you? I would like a reply by July 20.

Sincerely,

Manufacturing Problem

Dear Mr. Elkart:

We are having a problem with the Boro Air Hammer, manufactured by your company. The problem has caused a drastic decline in our production rate.

Dust is being drawn into the lubricating system, activating the machine's emergency cutoff. After a great deal of investigation, we find that we can operate the hammer if the speed is reduced.

It appears that one of two steps could be taken to correct the problem:

1. Take measures to prevent dust from entering the lubricating system.
2. Install a filtering system sufficient to remove the dust.

I would appreciate having someone from your company take an in-depth look at this problem. May I hear from you soon?

Sincerely,

Shipping Errors

Dear Nancy:

We are having a lot of problems with sales to Adam-Sloop Co., and these seem to stem from your shipping department.

Here is a sampling:

1. On 11-12-_ _, our dray tag 3300 indicated Adam-Sloop's order 1221 "complete" with a quantity of 5000. Adam-Sloop recorded receipts of 15,000. There were probably three units per package, but the quantity should be stated correctly.

2. Dray tag 3322 of 11-15-_ _ indicated "various" for Adam-Sloop's purchase order number. They had to unravel which orders this shipment applied to.

3. On 12-18-_ _, a load was received on dray tag 4412, four weeks *after* they received our invoice.

Nancy, these are only a few of the current problems. Adam-Sloop has about had it untangling our sloppy shipping procedures. We don't want to lose this customer.

Will you please check into this problem and let me know if you need more information.

Sincerely,

Billing Error

Dear Ms. Danzig:

In reply to your letter of August 11, please, please, please! try to get your computer-billing and receivable departments together. We are developing a large correspondence file because of errors on your invoices.

The invoices mentioned in your letter, numbers 8-1-4949, 4950, and 4951, are internally inconsistent: They state "freight allowed" but do not allow the freight that should have been allowed because we paid the freight bills. (See paid copies attached.)

Please correct your records.

Sincerely yours,

Computer Error

Dear Mr. Lucas:

As you requested, this is why we had to rerun your branch's payroll for the week ending August 21.

The payroll-card transmission from your terminal for August 19 was dated August 18. The error report we sent to your branch indicated the error, but it was apparently ignored. Thus, the computer automatically paid overtime rates for the hours worked on August 19 but reported as August 18.

We reran the weekly report correctly on August 24 for an additional cost to you of $840.

This situation points out the necessity of checking all input data and any error reports from our center.

If I can be of further help, please call me.

Sincerely,

Catalog Order

Dear Catalog Shipper:

The enclosed dress was not what the catalog photo made it appear to be, so I am returning it.

Not only was the style different but the color sent to me was not the one I ordered.

I'm enclosing the catalog page. If you can send me the dress pictured in the proper color, please do. If this is not possible, I would like a refund.

Sincerely,

No Follow-up

Dear Mrs. Simons:

Your representative, Barry Langston, was here and gave us an estimate on two shutters on October 26.

On October 27 we realized there was a problem of an obstruction that might hinder opening the shutters.

Barry Langston was called on October 27. He said he would call back on October 30 or 31 to give us a date when he could return. No call back. We called the Detroit office on November 1. Barry was not in, but called back November 2. He said he would notify us on November 6 or 7 when he could return to check the shutter-opening problem. Again, no call back. It is now November 14.

We had wanted the shutters installed by December 23, and will have more installed at a later date.

We are returning the estimate: We have ordered the shutters from a company that solved our obstruction problem.

Sincerely,

Labor-Law Violation

To The Board of Directors:

This is a formal complaint concerning wages and hours.

I am in the process of filing a formal report to the Labor Commission under Section 3, paragraphs A and D, of the Industrial Welfare Commission Order No. 5-80. According to this code, my income is at least $200 per month under the allowed minimum wage and overtime amount.

The response of your manager, Mr. Williams, was, "Mentioning your action to anyone in this organization will result in your immediate termination."

I hope that your concern about this situation will make it possible for you to resolve it without any further action on my part.

Respectfully yours,

Misrepresentation

Dear Mr. Randall:

It isn't often that I become upset enough with sales personnel in a store to write a letter to the manager. However, a recent incident occurred in your sporting goods department that left me both angry and frustrated—and more than a little disappointed.

As a novice camper, I am far from knowledgeable about the types and quality of equipment required. Because of this, I relied upon your clerk, Harley Stolman, to provide me with accurate information when I needed a lantern. My original intention was to buy a Coleman, a well-known brand, even to me. The department clerk persuaded me that the store brand, on sale at the time, was a better buy in the long run and of equal quality to the Coleman. When I used the lantern this last week, it failed to provide adequate light and was difficult to operate. I am thoroughly dissatisfied with it. I realize now that I should have refused to give in to the clerks persuasive tactics.

I would like to return the lantern and apply the price to the purchase of a Coleman lantern. The original receipts are enclosed, and the lantern is being returned by parcel post. Please let me know the additional amount of money required. Please ship it to the above address via UPS.

Sincerely,

Noisy Driver

Dear Mrs. Frames:

I don't like being a wet blanket, but I feel it is necessary to say something about the noise outside my window each morning at 4 A.M.

Everyone's schedule is different, but since I work and your son doesn't, I'm usually sound asleep when he zooms in from a party or whatever. The shouting and screeching of tires have left me bleary-eyed.

I would appreciate it if you would speak with him and ask him to be a little quieter at that hour of the morning. Some of us need our sleep.

Sincerely,

Meetings Out of Control

Dear Mr. Swanson:

The town meetings need to be better structured if any effective business is to be carried out.

Last week's meeting required over three hours to do what could have been completed in five minutes. Everyone in the audience seemed to be talking, and the speakers went unheard.

Perhaps following *Robert's Rules of Orders* would help to better organize future meetings.

Sincerely,

Barking and Biting Dogs

Dear Ms. McDowell:

The barking of your dog all night has kept me from sleeping for the past week. I realize that in this part of town a dog is required for protection. However, he seems to be spending half the night howling to get in.

I don't mind when I don't have to work the next day, but getting up at 6 A.M. is hard after losing half a night's sleep.

Is the entrance where the dog scratches and barks to get in at the opposite side of the house from where you sleep, making it hard to hear him? If that's the case, would you mind if I would call you each night just as a reminder that he's out there? I'd appreciate it greatly.

Sincerely,

Dear Mr. Walton,

I am sorry to have to report that your dog nipped at our baby yesterday. I'm sure it was the baby's fault because the dog is normally quite friendly, but your children do bring him here unleashed, and it isn't possible to keep an eye on him all the time. I wonder if you would ask your boys to leave Fido at home—at least until the baby is old enough to understand that he shouldn't pull the dog's tail.

Kindest regards to you and Mrs. Walton,

No Stop Light

Dear Council Members:

The lack of a stoplight or a sign at the corner of East St. and West St. has created a dangerous situation for both motorists and pedestrians.

In the past six months, seven accidents (two of them serious) have occurred. Schoolchildren must cross East St. at that point to get to school and often have to dodge cars to do so.

In order to prevent further accidents and to save our children's lives, it is absolutely imperative to place a traffic control at that point.

Sincerely,

Delayed Phone Service

California Public Utility District

Ladies/Gentlemen:

Can you tell me when I can expect my phone to be in service?

Three months ago, July 12, _ _, I moved into my new apartment at 24th Street and Kingley Drive. This is a new apartment complex. The building contractor is using one garage for his office, which has a working telephone. Friends who call me say my phone rings but no one answers. The phone in my *apartment* does *not* ring, although the instrument has been checked by the city telephone company. The city says the connection will be made "sometime."

I am losing my patience with fumbling excuses from the builder and the local phone company. The telephone here is a public utility and should be operational.

Please respond with action.

Sincerely,

Slow Response

Dear Mr. Bader:

I realize large corporations must be thorough when arranging legal contracts, but taking three months to change a name, and meanwhile cutting me off from one and a half month's interest on my October 1, 0000, receipts is unreasonable. Some banks accomplished this change in fifteen minutes.

Here is what happened:

1. 8-14-_ _   Phoned your disbursement department asking what data was needed to put my account into a trust. Left a message with the phone operator.
2. 8-21-_ _   Bob Johnson returned my call stating what data I should send.
3. 8-22-_ _   Sent letter to Bob Johnson with data he requested.
4. 9-4-_ _   Arron Walvoord sent me a letter requesting additional notarized data and suggesting it be reviewed by an attorney.
5. 9-10-_ _   Mailed notarized data to Arron Walvoord.
6. 10-10-_ _   I phoned Arron Walvoord. He said the name change had been approved and another two weeks would be required to complete the paperwork because of details required by the computer system.
7. 10-31-_ _   Arron Walvoord wrote me a letter that my records had been changed.
8. 11-15-_ _   I received payment due me on October 1.

There must be some way your company can change your computer programs to expedite what should be a simple operation.

Sincerely,

Gardener Problem

Dear Mr. Balenchine:

About the gardening here at the house we are renting from you: The tree near the driveway and the walk from the front porch had pale-green leaves when we moved in but now it appears to be dying, possibly from lack of water. The gardener has not been good about checking the sprinkler-system coverage, and we haven't been able to figure out how it is controlled. We have discussed this situation with the gardener, but nothing has changed. Mr. Hayes spends under ten minutes a week mowing the lawn and does no more unless we are home to question him. This fall we plan to do quite a bit of traveling. We suggest you consider hiring a different gardener.

Sincerely,

Improper Installation

Dear Mr. Short:

The air conditioner/heat pump your company installed seven months ago, on July 22 (see copy of your invoice enclosed), was blown off my roof this morning. True, there was an unusually strong windstorm for a few minutes, but none of my neighbors lost a heat pump.

I suspect the unit was improperly bolted to the roof structure. You will need to reinstall the heat pump, properly this time, at your expense.

Sincerely,

P. S. I am enclosing a newspaper photo of the air conditioner lying on the ground.

Dear Mr. Santana:

The rug you installed in our new house is stretching loose *again*. On May 4 we told you about the living room rug stretching and bunching up near the entrance into the front hall.

You sent a man to tighten the rug, which he did, but it was then June 12, over a month later.

Now the rug needs to be stretched again. Please send a carpet man *before* November 30, because as I understand, your one-year installation warranty expires then.

You are being notified well within the warranty period, and therefore this second repair is also at your expense.

Sincerely,

ANSWERING COMPLAINTS

If we were all perfect, adjustment letters would be unnecessary. But such letters are necessary, and the writer answering a complaint can grasp this opportunity to write what is in reality a sales letter. The writer is selling goodwill.

Answer promptly or the goodwill will melt away as the complainer begins to boil. If no answer is possible immediately, at least let the complainer know you are working on the problem. The problem may seem a slight irritant to you, but to the complainer it is important or it would not have been mentioned. The complainer's viewpoint must be recognized because he or she is your customer or perhaps your neighbor. The friendship of neither should be jeopardized.

There are, however, times when the complainer is out-and-out wrong. Don't say that in your letter, but remain calm and polite and thank the writer for bringing the problem to your attention. Give convincing reasons for your position and, when possible, offer some help or an alternative. End on a friendly note.

Adjustment letters must use positive statements—positive from the complainer's point of view. For example:

Negative—We can't make the adjustment.

Positive—We suggest you talk to your local dealer.

Negative—Your complaint arrived today.

Positive—Thank you for bringing this problem to our attention.

Negative—We don't know what is wrong.

Positive—We are investigating the problem and will let you know as soon as possible.

Remember: you are selling goodwill.

Opening Sentences

Start with this thought in mind: *my customer is the one who keeps me in business.*

> We are shipping you a new vase today to replace the broken one you received.

> Thank you for your letter of May 23 pointing out a problem with your new washer.

> We appreciate the concern you felt when your new vacuum cleaner began to smoke.

> Your replacement motor will be shipped tomorrow.

> Yes, we certainly will honor our guarantee.

> You were absolutely right in feeling cheated.

> Thank you for bringing our billing error to our attention.

Closing Sentences

The closing thought for a letter adjusting a complaint is this: *if I am going to keep this customer, I must keep his or her goodwill.*

> We shall always appreciate your business and your confidence in us.

> We appreciate your telling us this problem and giving us the opportunity to correct it.

> We appreciate your business and will continue to do our best to earn your confidence.

> We are always ready and willing to help a customer with a problem.

> If you ever have problems again, please let us know. We are ready to help.

> We service what we sell. Call us at any time.

> We are sorry for the inconvenience we caused, and we will make every effort to prevent a recurrence.

> Above all, we want our customers happy.

How to Do It

1. Agree with the complainer on some point or thank him or her for bringing the problem to your attention.
2. Tell what action has been taken.
3. End with a goodwill-building statement.

Disturbed Retail Customer

Dear Mrs. Lincoln:

Your letter of May 14 really took us down a few pegs. I will admit that we were partly to blame for the mix-up, but surely our whole organization can't be as bad as you picture it.

We are sorry for the confusion with your order, and we are sending you a new sofa with the pillows and seats upholstered as you requested. Please come in for a visit before deciding to quit us completely. We have served you well in the past, and we know we can do so in the future.

Sincerely,

Misrepresentation Reply

Dear Mr. Venti:

We are sorry our Clarkston lantern did not meet your needs. In most cases they have performed well. We have received no more complaints than about the better-known brands.

When we receive the lantern you have returned by parcel post, we will ship you a Coleman replacement via UPS as you requested.

Due to the inconvenience you have experienced, we will make no additional charge for the Coleman lantern. We are sure you will be pleased with it, and we apologize for the inconvenience the Clarkston model caused you.

Sincerely,

Convenient Hours

Dear Customers and Friends:

Our bank will open at 8:00 A.M. weekdays and Saturdays starting March 1.

Since operating branches in this area, we have heard many complaints about banking hours being for the convenience of bankers, not customers. We are correcting that situation.

Starting March 1, our hours will be:

> Monday–Friday 8:00 A.M.–5:00 P.M.
> Saturday 8:00 A.M.–Noon

We hope you like the added convenience.

Sincerely,

Extended Payments

Dear Mr. Evers:

You are absolutely right in not liking the way we handled your proposal for extending payments on your account.

Please accept my apologies for sending you a letter that should never have left our office. It was a form letter to delinquent customers and was sent because somehow your letter proposing an extended payment plan did not reach our credit department when it should have. Communications between our own departments failed at a crucial time.

As we discussed on the phone, we are happy to cooperate in making your payments easier. If you will sign the enclosed agreement and mail it to us with your first payment we will again be working together.

We are sorry for the inconvenience this has caused you, and if you wish to discuss any details furthers please call me personally.

Sincerely,

Employee Rudeness

Dear Ms. Mentris:

You are right that a rude employee should not be working at Bascom's. The employee who made discourteous remarks to you when you wanted information about our fur coats has been transferred to a nonselling department. She has many good qualities not related to customer contacts. When you shop here again you will not see her.

If you find any of our salespeople who cannot answer your questions, you may ask for me, and I will find the answers.

Please accept my apology.

Sincerely,

Misdirected Mail

Dear Mr. Fife:

The purpose of this letter is to follow up on our phone conversation of July 11 and your letter of June 28.

The problem referred to in your June 28 letter appears to have started earlier this year when some operations were discontinued at San Jose. At that time, we were requested to route *some* reports to San Mateo that previously had gone to San Jose. These instruction changes obviously did not result in proper routing of all reports affected.

We have issued report-distribution instructions to correct the problem pointed out in your letter; we believe this will correct the mailing problem.

I would like to mention, however, that members of my group have found it extremely difficult to acquire and verify proper mailing instructions for reports. Letters such as the one you initiated on June 28 are helpful in assuring correct distribution, and we appreciate your notification of the problem.

I encourage you to continue calling our attention to any problem of this nature. Please call Linda Arnette at 000-0000, extension 0000, to expedite the notification process.

I am sorry for the inconvenience caused by the erroneous mailing instructions.

Sincerely,

Late Delivery

Dear Mrs. Polk:

Your annoyance at not having received the engraved silver cups you ordered March 4 is understandable.

Orders requiring engraving work need from four to six weeks for delivery. Our salesperson apparently did not make that clear, and we are sorry for the misunderstanding.

Your order will be shipped on Tuesday of next week and should arrive within four days. Please forgive the delay. I am sure you will like the fine workmanship in the engraving.

Sincerely,

Dear Mr. Carmbs:

You have complained recently about late deliveries from our warehouse and your consequent lost sales.

We took your complaints seriously. We hired a new warehouse manager with several years' experience and the highest recommendations from two previous employers. He is new in this area and won't be bogged down by following our past operating procedures and practices.

Our new manager, Bert Watson, knows his job depends on prompt deliveries. We would appreciate your notifying us of any late or unsatisfactory delivery experiences in the future.

Best regards,

Low-Sales Reply

Dear Mr. Tross:

As you requested, I contacted our salesman Bill Boyd and Tony Andrews of Willow Pass Co. about our lower-than-expected sales so far this year to Willow Pass Co.

The 4 to 5 million units per month budgeted by Willow Pass for this year is a monthly average of the 12-month period. Willow Pass did expect each month's consumption to be near that, but their customers had a slow start this year due to the severe winter in Kansas and Nebraska. The balance of this year looks promising. Our sales to Willow Pass Co. are expected to increase starting in May, and their total purchases for this year should average over 4 million units a month.

Regards,

Meeting Control

Dear Ms. Destefano:

You are right to point out that our town meetings have been somewhat out of control.

The Council has appointed Mr. Pate as the new moderator. He is a man of strong character, strong discipline, and strict impartiality.

Rest assured that future town meetings will be controlled and productive.

Sincerely,

Damaged Merchandise

Dear Mr. Chen:

Thank you for your letter of July 17 describing damage to the coffee makers you received July 14.

A replacement order was shipped today.

We are sorry about the damage and the inconvenience it is causing you. We have installed a new conveyor loading system and although the product-damage problem is nearly licked, we have an occasional setback. We will try harder next time.

Sincerely,

Dear Mrs. Shawner:

This is to thank you for your letter of July 7 and the five dollars for handling expenses.

I am very sorry to learn that the Abrim lamp shade we sent you arrived damaged.

I am sending you a new shade and am requesting our Accounting Department to issue a refund check for five dollars.

Thank you for bringing this to our attention. If we can be of help at any time, please do not hesitate to call us.

Sincerely,

Dear Ms. Walden:

Thank you for returning the model L502 printer that no longer works properly. We have examined it carefully and we are sorry to report that it has been badly mishandled. The large dent at the upper left side indicates that it was either dropped or hit severely. This type of damage is not covered by our warranty, but the machine can be repaired and returned for $136.00. The printer is well worth that expenditure.

If you wish us to make the necessary repairs, please send a check for $136.00.

Sincerely,

Dear Mr. Freitas:

We really blew your order for the exhaust fan and motor for your boat. The motor and fan will be replaced, and I'm sorry we didn't meet your requested delivery date.

At this point all I can do is apologize and promise that we will work harder to take care of the needs of our customers.

Regards,

Dear Mr. Guthrie:

We are sending our salesperson, Jane Hatton, to look at the damaged boxes you received on September 27. She will be able to determine if it is a manufacturing error or shipping damage, and she will want to get a count of the damaged boxes. In either case, we will give you credit or rerun the order. Please discuss your preference with Ms. Hatton when she arrives Tuesday afternoon.

We are sorry for the inconvenience to you, but Jane Hatton will set things straight. We value your business and friendship.

Sincerely,

Merchandise Guarantee

Dear Mrs. Wells:

Yes, we certainly will honor our guarantee. If you wish, we will refund your money or send you a replacement for your new convection oven that does not heat properly.

We would like to suggest, however, that our serviceperson for your area first check your oven. The problem may be small and could be fixed in your home. Our service representative, Harold Bentley, will phone you to make an appointment at your convenience.

We are sorry for the trouble the oven has caused you, but we are confident it can be fixed to your complete satisfaction.

Sincerely,

Unsatisfactory Chair

Dear Ms. Brooks:

We were disturbed to learn that the chair you recently purchased from us did not hold up. We want our customers to be happy, and that is why we have a policy of guaranteed satisfaction.

There are three ways we can handle this situation: (1) we can replace the chair, (2) we can give you a full refund, or (3) you can apply the amount to any other merchandise in our store—you may decide that a different chair will suit you better.

Please indicate your preference on the enclosed postcard and also write in the date we can pick up the chair. Pickups are made in the afternoons.

We are sorry for the inconvenience and do appreciate your calling the problem to our attention.

Sincerely,

Unsatisfactory Television

Dear Mr. Abbot:

Thanks for your letter of July 8 calling your dissatisfaction with our Nicord television to my attention.

I'm investigating the problem personally and hope to have an explanation for you shortly. I intend to straighten it out—we want our customers to be satisfied customers.

In the meantime, could you please send me a copy of the sales slip. This will help by giving me the model number, serial number, and date of purchase.

You will hear from me immediately after I receive the sales slip.

Sincerely,

Foreign Object in Food

Dear Mr. Dennison:

I was shocked to learn that you found a tack in one of our Krispy Kookies, but we are grateful that you suffered no injury. You can rest assured that we will take every step necessary to ensure that no similar incident will ever occur again.

We thank you for bringing this to our attention. Please accept our sincerest apologies for the concern this incident caused you.

Sincerely,

Declining Responsibility

Dear Mr. Bishop:

We regret that our frozen dinner did not meet your expectations, but we doubt that the problem is in the processing. We carefully control the quality of our products up to the time they leave the processing plant. Sometimes, during their handling in the retail stores, they are allowed to thaw and are then refrozen. This may cause problems when customers prepare them.

Because we feel we cannot accept responsibility for handling damage after the product leaves our plant, we suggest you check with your local store for a possible refund.

We appreciate your interest in Jamieson's frozen foods.

Sincerely,

Dear Mrs. Utterberg:

To answer your complaint about our hired gardener, Jim Hayes, we had great difficulty getting any part-time gardener for the house you are renting from us. The gardeners hired before Mr. Hayes were not dependable, and those who seem dependable didn't want a part-time job. We felt lucky to get Mr. Hayes, a local high school teacher.

If you wish, you may attempt to hire someone else, and I will arrange to pay him or her. If this is not feasible, my only suggestion is that you could water the trees and shrubs that are now underwatered.

Sincerely,

Editing of Newsletter

Dear Mr. Walsh:

You have asked why I severely edited your submitted material about our new church organ. There are reasons for the statement in each issue that "Editors have the right to edit all submissions."

First is the limited space available. The Board of Directors has limited the size to twelve pages, the primary reason being the costs of paper and postage.

Second, a detailed, scientific explanation of the manufacturing history, backgrounds of current manufacturing and sales personnel, other current installations of similar organs, and chip designs for electronic organs are of no interest to the majority of our readers.

A letter sent to each large donor who is interested in these technical details would be a better way to inform them.

Sincerely,

Paint Work

Dear Ms. Tannen:

I agree with some of your assertions that our paint job on the inside of your office is sloppy. True, some of the edging work is not as precise as it should be, and the paint drops on the floor were not thoroughly cleaned up.

Next week, at a time convenient for your office staff, we will correct these shortcomings.

But about the paint being too thin on some areas, you recall that I discussed this possibility with you when you said you could afford only one coat of paint. We use the best covering paint available, and in most cases one coat will cover adequately. As I stated, however, when the color is changed even slightly, complete coverage using only one coat cannot be guaranteed. We can repaint any of the areas needing better coverage, but there will be a minimum charge.

Please let me know your decision.

Sincerely,

Pricing Error

Dear Mr. Helverson:

Your check for $12.50 is enclosed. You were right in discovering that our Arctic electric blanket was advertised at a price higher than in other stores in this area.

We have built a large-volume business on the basis of quality at the lowest price. We are proud of our reputation.

Upon investigation, we found an error in the advertisement. We are happy to send you—and the others who bought a blanket in response to our ad—the difference between our advertised price and our competitor's price.

We are sorry for the inconvenience we caused you and look forward to serving you for many years to come.

Sincerely,

Shipping Error

Dear Mrs. Montez:

You are certainly justified in being angry about our blunder in returning the unordered merchandise you had returned to us. Please let me apologize. The error was ours, but it would help us when you return merchandise if you would enclose a note to me or our sales representative stating why it is being returned. This will ensure proper credit to you.

You will receive immediate credit for this returned merchandise and all shipping charges.

Again, I am sorry for the inconvenience to you. We do value your business and your friendship.

Cordially,

Billing Error

Dear Mr. Mapes:

You are correct. We did make an error on our invoice No. 42772 of January 10. You are entitled to the 7 percent discount that we unintentionally overlooked. We will mail you a corrected invoice today. I am sorry for the trouble this error caused you and thank you for calling it to our attention.

Sincerely,

Dear Mr. Watson:

We are sorry for our error that made it necessary for you to return our last bill.

You are correct that we omitted the normal 10 percent discount. The $32 freight charge, however, is for air express that you requested on the shipment of diaphragms from our Cleveland plant.

A corrected bill will be sent today.

We are sorry for the inconvenience to you and we assure you we will make a special effort to prevent future billing errors.

Sincerely,

Dear Mrs. Tardiff:

Your letter dated September 13, in reply to my letter of August 11, resulted in an investigation of procedures in our billing department.

We discovered some carelessness in checking facts prior to the actual billing. This fault has been corrected, and we thank you for calling it to out attention.

Sincerely,

Dear Dr. Casey,

It's easy enough to understand your disturbed frame of mind about Sport Center's repeatedly billing you for the baseball shoes you returned on May 29. Our billing department is certainly throwing you a curve. Please accept our apologies.

We finally got the data into our new computer correctly, and you will no longer be bothered with the erroneous charge.

Cordially,

Statement Error

Dear Mr. Mayer:

The error in your October statement showing a charge of $329.99 for a shipment of batteries was due to a billing error.

We are sorry for the inconvenience, and a credit memo to cancel the billing is enclosed.

Sincerely,

Biting Dog

Dear Mr. and Mrs. Tasker:

Thank you for telling us about our dog, Fido, nipping at your baby. Fido has started doing that lately, and we have now taken him to the animal shelter with instructions to warn any future owner of his recent behavior.

This will lighten our responsibility and eliminate your concern about Fido's biting.

Cordially,

Complaint-Handling Procedure

Dear Mr. Kowalski:

In reply to your letter asking for our procedures for handling complaints, you must have had some problem with the plastic shrink-wrap machine you purchased from us, or you suspect you may have problems in the future. Let me assure you that any problems occurring during our two-year warranty period will be resolved at our expense.

We do have a procedure we follow closely.

First, we ask you to have your own maintenance department try to locate and correct the problem. You may submit a schedule of labor hours and costs, parts replaced and their costs, and a short explanation of what was checked and what was changed. Our engineers will evaluate this data, and if it is reasonable, you will be reimbursed.

Second, if that procedure does not produce satisfactory results, we will send the nearest qualified mechanic to your plant to make the necessary repairs. This service is at no cost to you.

Third if our mechanic cannot correct the defect, he or she will report his or her finding to us, and we will send a person or crew from our factory.

Fourth—and this should never occur—we will replace the machine.

We honor our two-year warranty, and we sincerely hope you will not have the opportunity to test us on this point.

I appreciate this occasion to explain our complaint procedure to you.

Sincerely,

Dear (Customer):

File No. #____

Thank you for taking the time to contact Ford Motor Company to explain the concerns you are experiencing with your vehicle. We regret any inconvenience you have experienced and assure you that we are anxious to retain you as a satisfied customer.

A summary of your concern has been sent to your dealer. Please contact the service manager at your dealership within three days after you receive this letter and provide him with the above file number.

If you need further assistance, you may recontact us at 1 800-000-0000. To help us serve you more quickly, any future contacts should reference the above file number.

Thank you for giving us the opportunity to assist you.

Sincerely,

Owner Relations Operations
Ford Customer Assistance Center

(With thanks to Ford Motor Company)

Dear Mr. Arlington:

As one of our new customers, you will be interested in our complaint procedure. We hope you never need this information—but just in case . . .

If one of our small tools or appliances should fail, please return it freight collect with the packing slip (don't forget this detail) and a short statement of the problem as you see it. We will check the tool or appliance and either repair or replace it. We will also honor your request for a refund, although we think our merchandise is too dependable for you to want that.

Customer satisfaction is FIRST. Only after that do we get on with our other business.

Best regards,

CHAPTER 8

Employment

Both employees and employers find matching the person to the job a difficult and frustrating experience. As an applicant, a good letter or résumé won't guarantee that you'll get the job, but it can help open the door. As an employer, you'll find yourself called upon to write a wide variety of letters ranging from rejections to acceptances, from references to reprimands, and how you do it reflects not only on you and your company, but may also have legal ramifications. In both cases, carefully written letters are essential.

Section I contains letters to be written by applicants; Section II, letters by employers; and Section III, letters by third parties. This series of letters does not comprise a job-hunting or employee-search program, but is an aid to these undertakings. It will be helpful to both employers and applicants.

Section 1—Letters Written by Job Applicants

Cover Letters for Résumés

Résumés and job-application letters may be mailed to employers with or without a cover letter: Opinions of human-resources managers vary as to which is more effective. The key to a result-getting cover letter is brevity, because the purpose of the letter is to save the reader time. People reviewing résumés usually do this infrequently and are busy with their regular work.

Although the cover letter should be short, it must also be long enough to persuade the reader to turn to the résumé itself. Mention the job you are applying for and one or two of your strongest selling points.

How to Do It

1. Indicate what job you are applying for.
2. Provide one or two items of experience.
3. Mention that the résumé is enclosed.

Advertising Executive

Dear Mr. Schuron:

I am applying for a position as an advertising executive. I have 15 years' experience in marketing, research, supervision, and program creation and development. The majority of my work has been with New York agencies. My résumé is enclosed.

Sincerely,

Accounting Manager

I am applying for the position of accounting manager advertised in the *Seattle Times* on April 12, _ _ _ _.

I have 20 years' experience as a senior accountant for a paper manufacturer. That position included closing the accounting books monthly, preparing the monthly and annual financial statements, analyzing costs, training employees, and approving vendor invoices with a check-signing authority of $10,000. Other responsibilities are shown on my résumé.

Sincerely,

Staff Manager—Telephone Company

Dear Mr. Troska:

After 25 years of increasing responsibility with Mountain Bell, I feel qualified for your opening as staff manager of revenue and engineering. I have advanced from phone operator and trainer through office-management-equipment installation, cost studies of engineering changes, property investments, and land purchases. My résumé is enclosed.

Sincerely,

Management-Information Systems

Dear Mrs. Varea:

I am ready for a position as management-information-systems supervisor. During the past ten years I have advanced steadily in computer-administration supervision, learning to operate and training others to operate each new program. I have installed computer systems for inventory control, desktop publishing, and management control. My enclosed résumé provides more details.

Sincerely,

Writer of Sales Letters

Apex Advertising Agency

Dear Mr. Woodward:

I am qualified to write sales letters for your agency. Twenty years as a salesperson on the road for a steel company, a greeting-card company, and an envelope maker has taught me what appeals to customers. An auto accident has made me incapable of continuing to sell on the road, but I have written sales-oriented articles for several trade publications and can put my selling abilities on paper. My résumé is enclosed.

Sincerely,

Cover Letters for Job Applications

Job application cover letters are similar to résumé cover letters, but should be even briefer. Mention what job or position you seek, only one or two strong qualifications for the position, and that your job-application letter is enclosed. Your objective is to get the human-resource manager to read your application letter immediately.

Use the same three-step How to Do It outline suggested for résumé cover letters.

Secretary

Dear Mr. Finkelstein:

My eleven years as a private and legal secretary, added to two years of teaching office procedures, should meet the requirements for a private secretary in your busy office.

I am interested in such a position with your company.

The enclosed letter explains my qualifications further.

Sincerely,

Market-Research Trainee

Dear Mr. Kalil:

My schooling and job experience have prepared me for your opening for a research trainee. I have a 4.0 grade-point average in my marketing major at the University of Southern California and worked two years part time doing market research for Anderson Sheet Metal Company. The enclosed letter provides details.

Sincerely,

Retail-Department Manager

Dear Ms. Apollo:

In response to your newspaper ad for a menswear department manager, I am qualified and interested. I increased the sales volume by 20 and 30 percent in the two previous menswear departments I managed.

The enclosed letter details my previous experience.

Sincerely,

Résumés

Résumés are a form of advertising. Their purpose is to get an employer to call you for an interview.

Because your résumé represents you, keep it neat, specific, and accurate. Remember the old but true cliché, "You will never have a second chance to make a first impression."

The ideal length is open to question, but most agree that it should be no more than two pages. Emphasize your strengths and omit your shortcomings rather than trying to explain them. Mention your education. The employer is interested in your highest level of schooling, and in any courses that are directly applicable to the job you are seeking.

Two styles of presentation are recommended. First, what might be called an "impersonal past tense," for example, supervised twenty-four clerks, designed machine tools, sold women's clothing. Second, the " impersonal present tense." For example, supervising twenty-four clerks, designing machine tools, selling women's clothing.

Even if you don't send out your résumé—you may choose instead to write a job-application letter—writing a résumé requires that you review your experience and organize it logically and clearly. You'll learn about yourself while going through this exercise and be better prepared to make a good presentation at your interview.

Advertising Executive

RONALD WALKER
0000 Bedford Ave.
Brooklyn, NY 11226
(718)000-0000

OBJECTIVE: A position in advertising where I can maximize my advertising, supervisory, research, estimating, and buyer skills in both print and media.

SUMMARY: Offering over 15 years experience, an A.A. degree in Business, and a comprehensive background in all areas of advertising marketing: display, media, and outdoor. Ability to thoroughly research, analyze situations, propose creative solutions, develop good rapport, and bring projects to completion under budget deadlines.

EMPLOYMENT HISTORY

Print Advertising/Sales Director
United Media, Phoenix, AZ 1994–Present

Responsible to publisher of Equal Opportunity Employment journal for selling and placing advertising in the *1995—Recruitment and Education Publication*, for equal-opportunity employment.

- Brought in major new accounts, including American West Airlines, TRW, and Acme Printing Company.
- Won opportunity to attend California training seminar in telemarketing/sales for being one of the two highest ranking salespeople.

HBE, Inc., Brooklyn, NY 1990–1994
Media Supervisor/Public Relations/Sales Supervisor

Responsible to manager for billing, account activities, office management, client entertainment, and advertising.

- Supervised production of eight sales representatives.
- Increased sales advertising of present accounts 30%.
- Computerized billing procedures from manual operation to IBM system.

Grey Advertising, Inc., New York, NY 1988–1990
Media & Print Estimator

Responsible to supervisor for invoices, estimates, media placement, and client/agency communications.

- Responsible for over two million dollars of account estimating.
- Responsible for print and media advertising for Revlon Cosmetics.
- Increased Revlon account 25%.

Media Corporation of America, New York, NY 1983–1988
Print Media Supervisor

Responsible to vice president for invoices, schedules, and coordination of client services.

- Instituted telemarketing program to determine placement of effective advertising.
- Managed research-development projects.
- Increased sales production over 25%.
- Acted as troubleshooter for major accounts.

Atwood Richards, Inc., New York, NY 1977–1983
Media Coordinator/Public Relations Administrator

Responsible to Account Executive for media layouts and client functions on the *Daily News* (newspaper) account.

- Coordinated advertising promotions of barter products for TV shows.
- Managed marketing and sales of house accounts.
- As supervisor of outdoor display advertising, increased sales 25%.

ADDITIONAL EMPLOYMENT

Time, Inc., New York, NY
Biller/Payer/Estimator

Responsible for invoices, schedules, and sales communications for public accounts.

B.B.D.O. Advertising Agency, New York, NY
Media Print Biller/Estimator

Responsible for invoicing and payments for Dodge Motors and General Foods accounts.

ADDITIONAL INFORMATION

Education
Associate Arts degree, Kingsborough Community College, Brooklyn, NY.

Continuing Education
Accounting, Brooklyn College; Sales/Marketing, Pace University

Affiliations
Society of the Arts, Sales Professionals

Senior Accountant

February 2, _ _ _ _

ADAM VILBERT
7122 Yorktown Lane
City, California 00000 000-000-0000

Education

University of Washington, Seattle, Washington
B.A. degree in business
Additional accounting courses

Business Experience

Senior Accountant, Riverside Paper Corporation, manufacturer of forest products

January 1977–Present

Accounting Responsibilities:

Closing the accounting books monthly.

Completing monthly profit-and-loss statement and balance sheet.

Preparing journal entries and supervising preparation by others.

Making detailed analyses of General Ledger balances.

Preparing monthly cost statements for Materials, Labor, Plant Operations, Selling, Administrative, and selected cost centers.

Assembling detailed reports of costs and variances from the budget.

Some examples:

Feedback report that compared actual and standard costs of products shipped.

Month-by-month comparison of fixed overhead costs by categories.

Status of construction projects in progress.

Detail of each element of cost of pallets used.

Travel and entertainment costs by categories and salespeople.

Maintenance costs categorized by labor, material, and cost centers.

Calculating a mid-month estimate of profit for the current month.

Reconciling bank statements.

Preparing annual report of SEC data.

Preparing year-end tax-data reports.

Completing Federal Census of Manufacturers report.

Making monthly and quarterly sales and use-tax reports.

Writing workflow procedures: e.g., accounting for printing die costs; obtaining cost of raw materials used.

Approving vendor invoices for payment, with check-signing authority of $10,000.

Training and supervising accounts-payable clerks, billing clerks, and junior accountants.

Supervising statistical and production clerks.

Assisting in preparation of annual budget.

Controlling inventory by using card systems and usage reports to reconcile actual material usages to standards. Explaining variances.

Cost Accountant and Purchasing Agent for Reliance Trailer & Truck Company, San Francisco, manufacturer of trailers and truck bodies. January 1973 to December 1976.

Establishing procedures for analyzing project costs. Preparing cost estimates. Installing a card system for control of purchases and inventories.

Cost Accountant and Work Order Clerk for Fruehauf Trailer Company, San Francisco, manufacturer of truck trailers and truck bodies. July 1971 to January 1973

Having responsibility for job costs of manufactured truck bodies and repair work. Billing customers. Assisting with purchasing. Making card systems of inventory control operate effectively.

Further Experience

Preparing business and personal income taxes for two CPA firms. Doing the accounting and tax returns for a small corporate manufacturer.

Assistant Staff Manager

ELIZABETH TOLLIVER
0000 Jewel Drive
City, Colorado 00000
(303) 000-0000

Work Experience

1966–Present MOUNTAIN BELL, Denver, Colorado

1995–Present Assistant Staff Manager—Division of Revenue

- Managed and directed the development and completion of land and building-investment studies, space-analysis studies, and operating-rent studies for a seven-state area.
- Verified studies for accuracy and integrity to ensure correct revenue income from interstate toll within the Bell System.
- Negotiated with AT&T Long Lines to establish rental arrangements and originated new methods to expedite billing corrections.

1990–1995 Facilities Planner—Engineering

- Originated special studies for AT&T involving circuit analysis, video channels, and embedded costs.
- Implemented a quality-control system along with job aids for a staff of eight engaged in separation of interstate telephone toll revenues.
- Analyzed and compiled costs of outside facilities for sale to and purchase from independent telephone companies, the U. S. Government and other common carriers.

1989 Engineering Technician

- Analyzed and scheduled central-office equipment installation.

1984–1989 Technical Assistant

- Coordinated pole-attachment agreements with cable Antenna Television Companies and Power Companies.
- Conducted field audits and authorized billing.

1974–1984 Service Representative—Commercial

- Performed all customer-contact functions in a small public office; this included order writing, bill collecting, banking, and public relations.

1966–1974 Operator/Instructor—Operator Services

- Conducted training classes.

- Operated switchboard handling emergency, long distance, overseas, and special-assistance calls.

Education

BELL SYSTEM TECHNICAL AND MANAGEMENT TRAINING, UNIVERSITY OF COLORADO, Denver, Colorado.

Curriculum: Real Estate

Systems Administrator

ELLEN CREIGHTON
2252 Mariposa Street
City, CA 00000
000/000-0000-home   000/000-0000-office

8/93 to Present
SYSTEMS ADMINISTRATOR
Newport Harbor Art Museum, Newport Beach, CA

Manage the implementation of the museum's computer system: accounting, capital campaign, art inventory, and desktop publishing. This encompasses project management, system design and programming development of administration of system policies and procedures, training, and troubleshooting.

Systems knowledge includes IBM compatibles, Windows 95, Corel-WordPerfect 8, Microsoft Word, various application packages, and networking.

11/91 to 8/93
SYSTEMS SUPPORT SPECIALIST
Imperial Corporation of America, San Diego, CA

Supported the 120 PCs (IBM compatibles) and the McCormack and Dodge mainframe system for the Finance Division. Support for both areas consisted of application development, training-class development, and instruction, and user assistance/troubleshooting.

7/90 to 11/91
MARKET RESEARCH COORDINATOR
Cushman & Wakefield of California, San Jose, CA

Researched and maintained a data base on the condition of the Silicon Valley real-estate market. Generated statistical reports from this data base, which were used by the company's brokers and published locally to substantiate Cushman & Wakefield's reputation as a source of reliable market information. dBase and Lotus 1-2-3 were used in the development of these reports.

7/86 to 7/90
ADMINISTRATIVE ASSISTANT
PERSONNEL CLERK/RECEPTIONIST
Coordinated the 1984 and 1990 sales meetings, planned and implemented all activities involved in the production of the sales newsletter, and worked as the editor of the corporate newsletter.

Education:

B.S. in Business Administration/Marketing.
San Jose State University, 1988.
GPA: 3.7/4.0

Job-Application Letters

A job-application letter is basically a sales letter; therefore, present yourself with confidence. This type of letter is sent instead of a résumé—do not send both. It is another approach to obtaining an interview.

Before writing a job-application letter, however, it is wise to complete a résumé. Doing so requires that you review in detail your job experience and organize it in a rational way. Having done that, you have the facts for your application letter.

The model letters that follow are suggestions, and none will fit you exactly because your letter must reflect your personality as well as your qualifications. Emphasize your strongest ability, then describe two or three others, but don't get carried away trying to mention all the applicable experience you have. Rely on your highlights. The purpose of this letter is to obtain an interview. It is there that you can add details.

Application letters should be sent to the president or highest company officer of the department to which you are applying.

How to Do It

1. Specify the job you are seeking.
2. State your accomplishments and abilities.
3. Ask for action from the employer.

Answering Ad for Accounting Manager

Dear Mr. Franklin:

This is in reply to your advertisement in the *Chicago Tribune* for an Accounting Manager.

I have twenty-five years' experience, the last twenty with one corporation, in all phases of plant accounting. My responsibilities included, closing the accounting books monthly, followed by preparing the profit-and-loss statement and the balance sheet; preparing journal entries and supervising their preparation by others; preparing monthly cost statements for materials, labor, administration, selling, and selected cost centers; making detailed reports of costs and their variances from budget for top management.

Additional responsibilities were calculating a midmonth estimate of profit for the current month; reconciling bank statements; furnishing annual reports of SEC data; year-end tax data, Federal Census of Manufacturers, and sales-and-use tax reports; writing accounting and workflow procedures: training and supervising accounts payable and billing clerks and junior accountants; overseeing inventory records and control systems; approving vendor invoices for payment, with check-signing authority to $10,000.

My accounting experience was preceded by two years of stock control and ordering, and three years as a combination purchasing agent and cost accountant.

I am available for an interview at your convenience to discuss these accomplishments and how my experience will help you. I will call you next week to arrange a meeting.

Sincerely,

Cold-Call Application Letter for Museum Director

Dear Ms. Lindstrom:

This is an application for the position of museum director at your new art museum. I understand the museum will be small, but monetary considerations are not a factor to my employment now.

I have a Bachelor's degree in Interior Design from Bradley University, a Master's in Art from Farnsworth Art College, and a Master's in Business Administration with a major in Accounting from the Riverside Finance School of Armstrong University.

My work experience includes eight years in several levels including director of the Johnson Art Museum, six years as Administrator of the Zella Sculptors Museum, and three years as curator of the Westin Museum of Modern Art.

You may reach me at the above address or phone number.

Sincerely,

Cold-Call Application Letter for Administrative Assistant

Dear Mr. Finkenstein:

When you are ready for a new administrative assistant, I am interested in that position.

In your busy office, speed, accuracy, and broad-based competence are paramount. During my secretarial career, I have developed expertise in all business-oriented computer programs. My five years in good standing as a legal secretary for Smith, Alexander & Wingate vouches for my capability.

During my six years as an administrative assistant with Waterford Manufacturers, I handled many responsibilities in addition to typing and taking dictation. My statistical and accounting training from the ABC Technical School helped with the preparation of seven monthly reports and a comprehensive annual report. My English skills helped in the proofreading of approximately thirty letters sent out weekly. My two years' experience teaching office procedures at ABC also proved invaluable when training new and temporary personnel.

Mr. Finkenstein, I look forward to applying my skills, energy, and enthusiasm to the challenge of a busy office such as yours. Can we arrange an interview at your convenience?

Sincerely,

Cold-Call Application Letter for Computer Systems Manager

Dear Ms. Kowalski:

I am seeking an opportunity to work with World Destiny as a Computer Systems Manager. My professional experience and my awareness of your unparalleled reputation and accomplishments have led me to want to work for World Destiny.

Since 19_ _ I have focused on computer-system design, implementation, maintenance and training. As Systems Administrator for Newport Harbor Art Museum for the past two years, I have directed accounting, capital campaign, inventory, and publication production. We designed the system from scratch, developing all applications, policies, procedures, and training programs. I was well prepared for such a challenge by my previous positions as a Systems Support Specialist and MicroComputer Assistant for the Imperial Corporation of America.

Over the years, I have worked with Novell networks, IBM PC compatibles, and McCormack and Dodge mainframes, using programs including dBase, Clipper, Lotus 1-2-3, Corel WordPerfect suite 8, Wordstar, Sympathy, Windows 95, and Microsoft Word. This familiarity with a variety of hardware and software has helped me to get up to speed on nearly any computer with a minimum training period.

Additional experience in other fields also reinforces my value to World Destiny. As a Market Research Coordinator for Cushman & Wakefield of California, I not only researched and maintained a comprehensive database of Silicon Valley properties, but also generated statistical and written reports that substantiated Cushman & Wakefield's reputation. Previously, I coordinated companywide annual sales meetings and publication production for Qualogy, Inc.

Ms. Kowalski, while this experience more than qualifies me to join any number of successful companies, it is my personal goals that spark my interest in being part of the World Destiny team. I believe my computer, promotional, and organizational skills, fueled by my convictions, make World Destiny and me right for each other. Can we arrange an interview at your earliest convenience? I will call within the next week to arrange a meeting.

Sincerely,

Application Letter for Job Suggested by a Present Employee

Dear Mr. Cibron:

Mr. Ralph Andrews, production manager of your Los Angeles plant, suggested that I contact you about an upcoming opening in your Redwood City plant for an assistant plant manager.

I have seventeen years' experience with corrugated-box-making operations, including manufacturing, assembling, installing and repairing the machinery, as well as supervising machine operators, scheduling orders, and computing costs of major machine installations.

Five years' experience selling boxes has acquainted me with the customer's viewpoint.

One day's notice is all I need to arrange an interview at your convenience.

Sincerely,

Dear Ms. Wang:

Ms. Ellen Hobert of your customer-service department, finding that I was interested in customer-service work, said I should write to you to apply for the opening when Janice Larson leaves.

I have a year of experience as a customer service representative in an electronics store. Prior to that I sold electronic appliances for two years. I have learned how to balance store policies and customer satisfaction (not always easy). I enjoy working with people, and my employers consider me a team player.

Sincerely,

Thanking an Employer

The five categories of letters that follow: Accepting Offer of an Interview, Thank You for the Interview, Thank You for Your Recommendation, Accepting Job Offer, and Rejecting Job Offer, are basically thank-you letters. Even when rejecting a job offer, you are thanking the employer for having accepted you.

The basic outline for all these letters is the same.

How to Do It

1. State what the thank you is for.
2. Mention the appropriateness of what you have received or been offered.
3. Be sincere, brief, and pleasant.
4. When appropriate offer something in return.

Accepting Offer of an Interview

Dear Ms. Apollo:

Thank you for calling and scheduling an interview to discuss my qualifications as manager of your menswear department. I will be at your office at 9:00 A.M. Friday, May 4.

I am looking forward to our meeting and am interested in helping increase your store's sales.

Sincerely,

Dear Mr. Rose:

Thank you for scheduling an interview on January 16 at 10:30 A.M. I look forward to reviewing your Industrial Engineering opening with you at that time in your Detroit office.

I feel sure you will find my twelve years experience definitely applicable to your needs.

Sincerely,

Thank-You for the Interview

A follow-up letter after a job interview can often be the extra push that gets you the job. Indeed, some human-resource managers consider the thank-you note an essential step in the job-hunting process. A letter received two or three days after the interview will keep your name in front of the employer. The letter also provides an opportunity to add what you wish you had thought of during the interview.

A short thank-you for the interview is sufficient for the introductory pleasantries. Then mention the main topic of the interview—the main topic from the *interviewer's* point of view—and what you can contribute to that situation. Follow this with helpful information that you may not have included in the first discussion. You can then add reminders of your strong qualifications and abilities. End with a statement of when you will contact the company to schedule a second interview.

Keep in mind throughout the letter that you are selling your ability to help the company you wish to work for.

Dear Mr. Jumpiere:

Thank you for the interview on the 22nd. I am confident I can fill the position of purchasing assistant. I agree that with your expanded activities, you need someone who can devote time to comparing prices and researching alternate sources of supply, and I have a program in mind that has been used successfully by other firms. Because it could easily be adapted to your operation, I would like to present this procedure for your consideration.

In my previous job we purchased from several of the same suppliers that you use. I believe I can adapt quickly to your purchasing procedures.

I will phone your office on the 30th to see if we can set a time to continue our discussion.

Sincerely,

Dear Ms. Apollo:

Thank you for the interview on May 4. The challenge you presented intrigues me. I am sure I can improve the mix of merchandise offered to your particular customers. That was the primary reason for increased sales in my two previous positions. My experience will be an important influence in enhancing the appearance and total sales volume of your store.

I will call you next Wednesday to see when we can arrange another meeting. At that time I can provide a more structured outline of my suggested changes in your menswear department.

Sincerely,

Dear Ms. Edwards:

Thank you for explaining the changes you wish to make in ladies' business suits and dresses. I have been alert to regional changes and trends over the past few years, and this awareness will be a great help to that department. My work in fashion design will also be helpful.

Thank you, too, for introducing me to your buyer under whose direction I would be working. We would be completely compatible.

As you suggested, I will call you on September 12 about continuing our interview.

Sincerely,

Dear Mr. Becker:

Thank you for the interesting interview on Monday, April 14. We did find an amazing number of similarities between the accounting operations of your company and the one I am now involved in, although the two industries are shipbuilding and paper finishing.

You mentioned several difficulties in getting data necessary for accurate cost controls. Most of the same difficulties were experienced where I work. Several problems were solved, and others are being solved. I would like to present these solutions in more detail when we meet again. I am sure that many can be adapted without any changes in your accounting procedures, merely changes in details.

I will phone you Wednesday, the 30th to see what we can arrange.

Sincerely,

Dear Mr. Hokimoto:

Thank you for the interview yesterday. I certainly appreciate your evaluation of my education and experience.

I will enroll in the two courses you suggested at the Ace Technical Academy and also obtain a couple years of practical experience in electrical assembly. You may expect at that time for me to ask for another interview.

Again, thank you for your helpful suggestions.

Sincerely,

Thank-You for Your Recommendation

Dear Mrs. Marconi:

Thank you for the letter of recommendation you wrote to Ms. Edwards at Marlene's Fashions. Your comments about my fashion-design work, and my energy and dedication, struck a responsive cord with her. You made a great contribution to my being hired. I start work there next week and can hardly wait. Thank you again for your help.

Cordially,

Dear Mrs. Howell:

I deeply appreciate the letter of recommendation you wrote to Westminister Clothiers. I am sure it was a determining factor in their hiring me as their office manager, a wide-scope management position.

I am sure they will be pleased with my work, as you were. I learned a great deal from you that will be applicable here, and I approach this opportunity fully confident of success.

Sincerely,

Accepting Job Offer

Although accepting a job is usually done verbally and the acceptance formalized when personnel records are completed, it is a polite gesture to mail a letter of acceptance. Adhere to any deadlines suggested by the employment offer.

Dear Mrs. Chang:

Thank you for offering me the position of branch manager of the Regan Department Store in Marquette. Your confidence in my ability is gratifying.

The decision to grant me full control of all the facets of the store operations will provide the means of initiating needed changes in both merchandising and advertising. These two areas will become my first priorities in improving the image of the store.

I am eager to begin work as soon as possible.

Sincerely,

Dear Ms. Walters:

How can I thank you for the joy your letter gave me? I checked the mail daily for the last month, eager to know if you had found a way of utilizing my talents and experience. Your response justified every moment of anticipation.

Although employment with *Bank* magazine will only be part time, I intend to involve myself fully in the operation of the magazine. As I mentioned in the interview, the position is of great value to me as a means of reentering the job market after taking time out to raise my children. Therefore, you will find me willing to accept all manner of assignments.

I will report to your office at 9:00 A.M. Monday, July 16.

I look forward to beginning work.

Sincerely,

Dear Mr. Priori:

I am happy to accept your offer to join Litton Department Store as menswear department manager. I will report to your human-resources office Monday, May 21.

You will find that my knowledge and experience in the menswear field is reinforced by my dedication and hard work. I am eager to get started.

Sincerely,

Dear Mrs. Varea:

I was pleased that you accepted me for your supervisor of management-information systems. I will make sure that your decision is the right one. You will find that I work hard and learn fast. I have always gotten along well with subordinates while improving their output. I will report next Tuesday morning as we agreed. Again, thank you.

Sincerely,

Rejecting Job Offer

As a job applicant, you may find yourself in the position of having to reject a good job offer, either because you don't want the job or because another offer is more attractive. You may at that time be inconsiderate of the employer's viewpoint, thinking that your unfavorable response is just one of the trials employers must put up with until you realize that your refusal may be only temporary. A few years hence you may want to apply again or find that you have to work closely with the firm you are now rejecting. A polite letter stating a plausible reason for your declination is the accepted way to end the negotiations.

Dear Ms. Urban:

Thank you for offering me the position of accounting manager. I am sure I would have enjoyed working with you, but two days ago I accepted an opportunity with another company.

Sincerely,

Dear Mr. Schumacher:

I appreciate your asking me to come in for a second interview for your industrial engineering position, but on June 2 I was offered another position, which I accepted.

Sincerely,

Dear Mr. Chun:

It was a pleasure discussing your marketing opportunities. I thank you for your insights into the range of possibilities at Jones & Johnson.

However, as I indicated, my primary interest is in production, and although I recognize the connection between the two fields. I prefer to start with a production job.

Thank you for your consideration.

Sincerely,

Resignation

See Chapter 9, Termination and Resignation.

Section II—Letters Written by Employers

How to Do It

1. If the subject, from the reader's viewpoint, is positive or neutral, state the purpose of the letter in the first sentence.
2. If the subject, from the reader's viewpoint, is negative, make a related, positive statement in the first sentence. State the negative fact near the middle of the letter.

Tentatively Accepting Applicant

With this type of letter, the employer is hedging his or her bets and buying time. The applicant is not an ideal choice, but may be acceptable if the first or second selected employee doesn't work out. Also, the interest of the applicant is retained while the employer searches for a better candidate.

> Dear Miss Terres:
>
> Thank you for your job application letter. It indicates that you are qualified for our opening for a fry cook, a fast-paced job.
>
> We need to review a few more letters and résumés before asking you to come in for an interview and demonstration of your abilities in the kitchen. That may take us a week or two.
>
> Sincerely,

> Dear Ms. Schroll:
>
> Thank you for your résumé and list of references. Your application for our accounts-payable supervisory position is now being considered by our controller.
>
> Due to the number of qualified applicants who responded to our advertisements and notices, it will be three to four weeks before we can reply.
>
> Sincerely,

Dear Mr. Gilbert:

Thank you for your job application letter (for your résumé) (for returning our job application form).

Because we review each one in detail, we will need up to three weeks to set up a timetable for interviews. We will let you know as soon as possible if you will be invited to discuss your qualifications.

We apologize for the delay necessitated by the large number of applicants.

Sincerely,

Requesting Data from References

To avoid possible legal complications, some companies decline to provide any information other than dates of employment about former employees. Sometimes, however, you may receive helpful information, especially if it is complimentary to your applicant. Often a letter requesting, "Any details that may be helpful in our decision to hire John Jones will be sincerely appreciated," may get better results than a prepared questionnaire. Also, a person other than an employer may be more willing to share his or her personal observations and to provide details than a business concern might be.

Dear Mr. Wheadon:

Your name has been given us by <u>Maria Costanza</u> as an employment reference. We would appreciate an early response because <u>her</u> continued employment depends in part upon the receipt of appropriate recommendations from former employers.

Our company has employed <u>Ms. Costanza</u> in the position of <u>psychiatric social worker</u>, which requires skill in dealing with the day-to-day behavior of mildly disturbed adolescents.

We would appreciate receiving a straight-forward appraisal of her ability to provide professional quality social-work services to such children in a residential group-home setting.

Would your company be willing to hire <u>her</u> again?

We greatly appreciate your assistance.

Sincerely,

Dear Mr. Vergara:

James A. Blowden has applied for a job as senior maintenance mechanic at our Westland trailer-body shop. Repairs and preventative maintenance of various light and heavy machinery is required.

Could you provide us with the exact dates of his employment and other details that would apply?

Sincerely,

Requesting Data from Applicants

Dear Mr. Terry:

Thank you for your reply to our advertisement and for your résumé.

We wish to learn more about your abilities and how you might fit into our organization.

Please complete the enclosed application form. If the answers to some questions repeat what you have already sent us, please repeat the data.

The enclosed pamphlet will help you become better acquainted with our company.

We look forward to your prompt reply.

Sincerely,

Dear Mr. Hezeau:

Your application letter details an interesting background for the position of industrial electrician. Your educational and work qualifications are excellent.

However, we would like a few additional details. Please fill out the enclosed application form and explain the lack of activity during the 1990–95 period. We will show no bias but wish to be informed. A prompt reply will be appreciated.

Sincerely,

Providing References to Another Employer

You may be asked to provide a reference about a former employee. Often this presents no problem, but occasionally compliments cannot honestly be given. When this occurs, be especially careful about what you write. Because recent federal laws permit people to examine their personal files, precautions are necessary to prevent a legal suit against your company. An attorney or your company's legal department should be consulted before you put anything derogatory about a person in writing.

Some human-resources departments give references by phone only. Uncomplimentary statements should be vague. Such mild words as, "John Allison has worked here for seven years, and except for some personal problems his work has been satisfactory," could be the basis for a legal suit by John Allison, and, although true, the "personal problems" statement would have to be proven in court. Litigation could be avoided by writing, "John Allison was employed here from January 15, 19_ _ to March 31, 19_ _," ignoring any reference to character or performance. If you feel you can write only a negative recommendation, don't write any.

Examples of a wide variety of letters are included in the section that follows.

Dear Mr. Heiman:

I am sorry we cannot provide any information on Alice Wooden except that she was employed here from October 14, 19 _ _ until December 31, 19 _ _. We treat personal data about our employees as confidential material.

Sincerely,

Dear Mr. Hansen:

I am happy to recommend Norma Bellson, who has worked under my supervision for the past four years as a billing clerk. She does her work on schedule and is more accurate than most billers. In addition, her work is neat and thorough. She is always on the job a little ahead of time and her absenteeism is nearly zero.

Norma grasps new ideas and instructions quickly. She has a bookkeeping background and would be excellent as a billing clerk or junior accountant.

Sincerely,

Dear Ms. Wiles:

Theresa Anderson receives my hearty recommendation as an accounts-payable clerk. She did excellent work under my supervision during the last six years. She got the bills paid on time, was cooperative, and was willing to do other assignments, mostly in the area of accounting reports. She has no accounting background but was extremely helpful with routine reports. Her computer skills are top quality. She was on time and had a better-than-average attendance record.

I wish I had her back.

Sincerely,

Dear Mrs. Amos:

Arlene Goldin is a precise statistical clerk; her work is fast and accurate. She is consistently pleasant, tackling all assignments with a smile. She usually comes to work early, and she was absent only five days in the four years she worked here.

She learns quickly but is not really analytical or research minded. On the other hand, after being shown step by step how to do a report or assignment, few can better her performance.

I recommend her highly for a position working with numbers.

Sincerely,

Dear Mr. Cunningham:

As vice president of this bank for eight years, I have overseen John Sands in his capacity as loan officer. He is a serious and dedicated worker, and his reliability and integrity are above question. He is well respected in local banking and real-estate circles.

I highly recommend John Sands to you. He is a man who will help your organization grow.

Sincerely,

Invitation to an Interview

Dear Mr. McConnell:

Thank you for returning your completed application form.

We have scheduled an appointment for you at 10:00 A.M., Monday, March 20, at our Wilmington office. Transportation, meals, and lodging will be reimbursed to a maximum of $550.

We look forward to a pleasant and informative discussion with you.

Sincerely,

Dear Ms. Won:

Our fashion designer, Miss Warner, would like to discuss your application further at 1:00 P.M., Wednesday, April 22.

If you cannot keep the appointment, please call her at 000-0000.

Sincerely,

Dear Mr. Abdul:

We have scheduled an interview with you for 1:00 P.M. Monday, March 3, to discuss your application for our research-trainee position. Please ask for Mr. Neal.

Sincerely,

Rejecting Tentatively Accepted Applicants

Dear Mr. Fritz:

To keep you up to date on the status of your résumé, it has been further reviewed by managers directly interested in your specific abilities.

Although our needs are constantly changing, we have not been able to identify an appropriate opportunity for you at this time.

We thank you for your interest in the ABC Corporation, and wish you well in locating a position.

Sincerely,

Dear Ms. Bokeman:

Your application has been carefully considered again by our corporate management team.

Your qualifications are impressive; however, we have made an offer to a candidate who has a background in this industry and whose recent experience is directly related to the available position.

Thank you for your time and interest in pursuing employment with our company.

Sincerely,

Rejecting Applicant

Dear Mr. Gallatin:

Just a short note of thanks for visiting me in regard to our present opening.

You have a fine business experience with Jansen Manufacturing, of which you should be proud. However, comparing the business we have here at Walkup Corporation and your overall capabilities with a much larger firm, I think this would be the wrong place for you.

Thank you for taking the time to come in, and the best of luck in finding just the opening you want.

Sincerely,

Dear Mr. Guiterez:

Thank you for considering our opening for a junior accountant. Although your qualifications are good, we have accepted another candidate. We will keep your application on file for future consideration.

Best wishes for finding another position that suits your qualifications.

Sincerely,

Dear Mr. Pappas:

We have received your recent inquiry concerning employment with Winston Developers and appreciate your interest in our company.

We have reviewed your experience and education against our current requirements. Although your qualifications are impressive, we feel that our current opening does not offer a close match to your background.

As you might imagine, our operations and employment requirements are continually expanding and changing. We have placed your résumé in our future-reference file where it will be reviewed again as openings in your area of interest become available.

We sincerely appreciate your interest in becoming associated with our organization. We regret that this response cannot be more favorable, and we wish you well in locating the opportunity you desire.

Thank you for considering Winston Developers as a potential employer.

Sincerely,

Dear Mr. Berge:

Thank you for your recent letter and résumé for the position of first reader for our publishing house. Your background will get you a job with a publisher you can be sure, but right now we have no opening for your special expertise. We wish you quick success in finding the right publishing house.

Sincerely,

Dear Ms. Lattler:

Thank you for sending your résumé and giving us the opportunity to consider you for the accounting-manager's position.

Our financial officers have thoroughly reviewed your qualifications. They are excellent, but do not quite fit the position we have in mind at the present time. Your technical experience is notable, especially in the area of tax accounting, but right now we need someone who is stronger in supervisory experience.

We will keep your file active, and when promotions create an opening to fit your qualifications, we will write or call you.

Yours sincerely,

Accepting Applicant

A written record of being accepted for a job is appreciated by the applicant. The letter eliminates doubt and confusion and clarifies details such as where and when to report. Information about lodging availability and what to expect the first day will be of help in some situations.

This type of letter affords a great opportunity for a sentence or two (no more) of good impression building. Make the new employee glad to have accepted a position with your firm.

Include a congratulatory statement.

One word of warning, however. Do not lead the employee to believe his or her acceptance is a "contract" for employment by using such words as "guaranteed employment," "permanent employment," or "tenure." Do not use such phrases as, "you can stay and grow," "as long as you do your job," or "a long and successful career." A mere hint that a contract exists could put future attempts to terminate the employee into a tangle of legal difficulties.

How to Do It

1. Make a congratulatory statement.
2. State or imply that selection was made from many applicants.
3. Present a low-key sales pitch for the employer.
4. List any special conditions: when, where, and to whom to report; temporary lodging; first assignment; or other.

Dear Miss Garcia:

Your recent application for office clerk has been approved by the Human Resources Department. Your abilities appear suitable to the needs of J. P. Sundstrom, and we offer you a position beginning immediately at the salary discussed.

At J. P. Sundstrom, every employee is an important member of the firm. Even entry-level employees are selected with great care.

Congratulations on being selected. If you accept our offer, please let me know and report to the Human Resources Department on Wednesday, September 17, at 8:00 A.M.

Sincerely,

Dear Ms. Rhymer:

I am happy to inform you that Burns School can offer you the position of instructor for the ____–____ school year. Selection from among so many qualified applicants was difficult. However, the results of your interview, coupled with the fine recommendation we received, led us to decide in your favor.

You should arrive the Saturday before classes resume. Temporary lodging will be available at Beogan Hall. Just call ahead or ask at the gate. We can also help you to locate an apartment in the area. Our classes begin September 7, and the first few days will be rather hectic. Be prepared. I will assume that you accept our offer unless I hear from you in the next week. Once again, congratulations on your selection.

Sincerely,

Dear Mr. Bluelake:

Congratulations on being accepted by Dover Corporation as our assistant human resources administrator.

This letter confirms our acceptance of you for this full-time position. The starting salary is $35,000 annually. Normal hours are from 8 A.M. to 5 P.M. five days a week. You will, however, be expected to work some extended hours when required.

A brochure is being mailed separately outlining our personnel policies, fringe benefits, retirement policy, current payroll taxes withheld, our savings plan, and other details of employment.

When you report for work on August 1, you must bring a driver's license or other identification with your picture, your social-security card, and your birth certificate or proof-of-resident–alien status.

To accept this offer, please sign the enclosed copy of this letter and mail it in the postpaid envelope.

Sincerely,

Dear Mr. Berg:

Congratulations on being selected as our new Parson store manager. I hope that you will accept our offer and that the salary offer is commensurate with your expectations.

The decision was a tough one since many qualified people were being considered. However, your creativity and enthusiasm won out over the others. I personally feel that the right choice was made.

We're a difficult store to work for since the public eye is always on the image projected by both our fashions and our employees, but you should have no problem in these areas.

Try to arrive in town by September 2, so you can get settled before the big season really begins and your duties multiply by the hundreds. Call when you're ready to begin work. My best to you in this new undertaking.

Sincerely,

Welcome to New Employee

A welcome letter sent to an employee shortly after he or she starts work projects a positive image. It also displays courtesy, consideration, and, of most importance, friendliness.

Say something nice about your organization and that you are proud to belong. This will help the new employee feel the same way.

Give your assurance that the reader has become a member of a strong team. Tell how you will assist in his or her orientation or what the employee can do to get off to a good start.

Dear Mr. Lopez:

We at Aatel are glad to welcome you to our financial staff. We admire the work you did at Pierce Tractor and believe you can do as much for us. You will find a professional and cooperative staff here, and I am sure you will enjoy working with them.

I will arrange to have lunch with you soon to discuss some aspects of your work. In the meantime you will find Mr. Bond most willing to answer your questions.

Welcome aboard,

Dear Miss Yim:

With great pleasure we welcome you to the nursing staff of Bowden Hospital. I know you will enjoy working with our team of skilled nurses.

If you wish additional help with your orientation or with your settling into this community, please give me a call.

Cordially,

Dear Mr. Yost:

Welcome to Phillip Door Company. You will find your dual positions as cost analyst and purchasing agent interesting and often busy. Your background will be helpful in both these jobs.

We will soon introduce you to your fellow employees—think of them as teammates. They are a congenial group, and you can rely on them for help when you need it.

Best regards,

Dear Mr. Reilly:

We at Rowell Manufacturing Corp. are pleased that you have agreed to join us as our advertising manager. We are confident that your years of experience will meet the needs of our company and of this position.

If you have any questions about your employment, please feel free to ask me.

Sincerely,

Performance Appraisal

It might be more accurate to describe a job-performance evaluation as a memo rather than a letter. The evaluation is written by a supervisor who reviews it verbally with his or her superior and then with the employee.

How to Do It

1. Summarize the appraisal in the first paragraph.
2. Include a statement of advancement potential.
3. Make judgments based on relevant data, not broad, general statements.
4. Use positive statements. Negative performance should be stated in a way that suggests improvement is possible.
5. Make suggestions for ways to improve.
6. Include the employee's reaction to your evaluation.

Performance Evaluation

If Martin Willard continues his present rate of on-the-job learning, he will be ready for promotion from production foreman to production superintendent in one year.

Positive Aspects: He has a clear grasp of production scheduling, its planning and follow-through from operation to operation as well as the importance of timing in meeting scheduled deadlines.

He understands the function of each machine and how to make adjustments to control the scheduled flow of the product and how to maintain quality.

Negative Aspects: He needs more training in cost control. Schedules and quality are well controlled but the cost of supplies and labor to do so is sometimes excessive. Separate seminars are to be arranged with the purchasing and accounting departments to broaden his awareness of these two factors. His use of this education will be monitored by the production manager.

Some subordinates complain of his harshness, while admitting his effectiveness as a supervisor. The corporate director of labor relations will assist Willard in how to use a more tactful approach when instructing machine operators.

_____	_____
Michael Rosen	Martin Willard
Production Manager	Production Foreman

Job Performance Review

Another approach to job evaluation is to use a list of qualities. Each one is given a grade, 1 through 5 (highest being 1), followed by a brief comment if appropriate.

Date:

Name:

Present job:

Years at present job:

Evaluator:

Job Duties

Accuracy

Knowledge

Understanding

Meets deadlines

Attitude

Initiative

Analytical ability

Judgment

Planning

Flexible to change

Ability to present facts or ideas

Cost awareness

Accept responsibility

Safety awareness

Telephone etiquette

Housekeeping of work area

Leadership

Enthusiasm
Drive to "get it done"
Self-confidence
Willingness to make decisions
Follow-up
Ambition
Delegates authority
Ability to organize work load
Training subordinates
Motivating people
Supervisory ability
Ability to assist supervisor

Personal Characteristics

Work habits
Judgments made calmly
Contacts with others
Punctuality
Appearance
Dependability
Personal habits

Overall Grade

__ 1. Outstanding   __ 4. Marginal
__ 2. Good   __ 5. Unsatisfactory
__ 3. Acceptable

General Comments

_____   _____
Evaluator   Subordinate

Recommendation for Promotion

Dear Mr. Human:

Robert Winslow has developed at an accelerated pace during the past two years. In his capacity as sales service manager, he has displayed much decision-making ability. Leadership is one of his strongest qualities.

Although the youngest person in the Sales Service Department, both in age and seniority, Robert was able to assume command upon promotion to his present position. He is rated as a No. 1 performer.

Robert has indicated a desire for line management and is willing to relocate. He is capable at this time of functioning as a field sales manager.

Sincerely,

Dear Mr. Chan:

Rosa Ramada is ready for a promotion to laboratory manager.

She has worked under my supervision for five years as a laboratory technician, many times assuming my responsibilities when I was away. She is quite capable in that position. Her technical knowledge in both chemical and physical testing fields is without peer.

Ramada has received excellent training in cost control and administrative management. She is ready to move upward.

Sincerely,

Promotion Notice

NOTICE

We are happy to announce that Arlene Britton has been promoted to finance manager. She has been our accounting manager for the past four years in charge of all accounting and statistical reports.

In her new position she will assume the additional responsibilities of corporate banking, capital structure, and stockholder relations.

Congratulations, Arlene. You have our full support.

(signed)

Congratulations on Your Promotion

Dear Alice:

Congratulations on your promotion. It has always been a pleasure working with someone as competent as you.

We look forward to more of the same fine work in the future.

Sincerely,

Dear Bud:

It was great to hear of your recent promotion. There is no doubt you have earned it, and I am confident it will not be the last.

I have always felt you handled the problems we sent you exceptionally well.

We look forward to working with you in the future.

Sincerely,

Dear Ted,

What a pleasure to have watched you move up rapidly from sales service trainee to sales service supervisor to salesman to sales manager to production manager—and now to the TOP at this plant: resident manager.

I could see that you had the ability, and I am glad that headquarters management was aware of your accomplishments. It has been a pleasure working with you through all these promotions, and I hope you continue to climb the corporate ladder. Congratulations, Ted.

Best regards,

Promotion Denied

Dear George Veith:

We here, and also the staff accountants at headquarters, recognize the accurate and timely reports you turn in. You are learning quickly and show promise for future advancement.

At the present time, however, we feel you need more experience and a fuller knowledge of corporate procedures and policies before we can advance you to an assistant-controller position.

Do not become discouraged. Promotions always seem to take more time than they should. You are on the right track. Stay there and keep learning.

Best regards,

Reprimand

Begin a reprimand with a compliment. A statement such as, "Your work record in the past has been excellent," or, "Your attitude is commendable," will put the person being addressed in a more receptive frame of mind than it would if reacting to a caustic remark.

Make the letter short: That will eliminate unrelated ramblings. Make negative statements in a positive way. For example, rather than saying, "You are making too many mistakes," say, "We believe a little more effort will improve your work."

Suggest specific corrective action, goals the person can accomplish, such as 95 percent attendance, 200 units per hour, or report 57A completed by the 11th of each month.

When one employee's performance improves, his or her accompanying new attitude often carries over to other workers.

Dear Jim:

Cintex plant reports sent to Headquarters during the past six months have been on time and have raised no significant problems, with one notable exception: The sales-invoice processing has steadily deteriorated. This has delayed our receipts of data for the Sales Statistical Reports. It is also delaying our cash receipts because customers are getting their invoices late.

While some of the problems can be attributed to the Headquarters Data Center, the major problems are being created by the Cintex plant. The problems at Headquarters will be resolved, and I am confident that the future support from the Data Center will meet our standards.

The problems being created by the plant are in three categories: (1) late receipts past-cutoff date, (2) month-end bunching of sales invoices, and (3) illegible documents and invalid data.

The attached schedule details the receipts in the Data Center for the month of February. As you will note, 22 percent of February's invoice volume was apparently billed on the last two days of the month. With 20 billing days, the expected percentage of billings on the last two days should not have exceeded 10–12 percent. Additionally, over 3 percent of the month's invoices were received after the cutoff date.

I am going to monitor future closings more diligently. Each month we will publish a report on the prior month's closing to highlight problems and take corrective action as necessary.

Please give this your personal attention. We must resolve this problem.

Sincerely,

Dear Howard:

Your work during the past four years has been excellent, but lately that is being offset by your absentee record. I am aware that your health has not been the best, but regular attendance is one requirement of your job. Something must be done to improve your attendance, because we cannot schedule our work-loads efficiently when we cannot depend on you to be here.

If you need to see a doctor, we can easily schedule time from work for you to do that. Please give this serious thought; we need you on our team.

Sincerely,

Memo to Wendell Rodgers, salesman
        from J. C. Alward, president, Ace Interior Decorators

Please carefully read the complaint letter I received this morning from Mrs. Vicari, a potentially profitable customer.

Note the many dates you said you would call back or make a return visit. The customer looks upon these unkept promises as lies. One failed contact may be excusable, but not seven in only three weeks.

This morning, call Mrs. Vicari and apologize, and remember the importance courtesy plays in persuasive selling.

Dear Dave:

I know you have been trying, but upon reviewing the first three months of _ _ _ _, we find ourselves running 20MM units behind our budget, and your short-range forecast shows no improvement in the next few months. Last January, I suggested you consider 19_0 costs for _ _ _ _ rather than your bud-geted figures, since your volume for _ _ _ _ and _ _ _ _ are similar. For the first three months of _ _ _ _ you are behind _ _ _ _ by 6MM units; therefore your costs should be as low or lower than _ _ _ _.

If you will evaluate your Profit Analysis Report, you will see how the loss of volume has lowered your profit. Besides the loss of profit resulting from loss of volume, your salespeople are not obtaining last year's average price level, let alone the price they projected for this year.

Comparing the first three months of _ _ _ _ with the first three months of _ _ _ _, you have spent $7,000 more for printing, $19,000 more for cutting tools, and $18,000 more for packing—all of these are higher expenses with lower volume.

The only area in which you have reduced costs is wrappings, to the tune of only $930. This is the only sales-controlled item in which any improvements have been realized.

I would like to know by May 7 what steps you have taken to:

1. Bring your sales volume up to your _ _ _ _ budget level.
2. Bring up your depressed average price level.
3. Decrease your printing costs and bring them in line with _ _ _ _ costs.
4. Decrease your cutting tool costs and bring them in line with _ _ _ _ costs.
5. Decrease your packaging costs and bring them in line with _ _ _ _ costs.

Also please advise me by May 7 when these objectives will be accomplished.

Sincerely,

Termination Warning

See Chapter 9, Termination and Resignation.

Termination

See Chapter 9, Termination and Resignation.

Accepting Resignation

See Chapter 9, Termination and Resignation.

Notice of Employee Leaving

The occasion will arise when a company terminates an employee but wishes the real reason hidden. This may be prompted by controversy that would affect employee morale if brought into the open. These notices are brief, noncommittal, and pleasant. All signs of irritation, disgust, or "serves-them-right" feelings are omitted.

NOTICE

Mr. Albert Johnson, manager of our Arlington plant, has left the company to pursue other business interests. He will be replaced by Mr. Gerald Norgard, currently manager of the Sutherland plant. This will be effective July 1st.

(signed)

NOTICE

Ms. Georgia Hayes had chosen to take early retirement. She preferred not to transfer with us when we move to Willows in August. She joined James & James in 19_ _ as secretary to Mr. Arnold James.

We will miss Georgia, and I am sure all of you join me in wishing her a pleasant retirement.

(signed)

NOTICE

Mr. Thomas Tassin has resigned effective July 31 to return to private law practice. We will miss Tom and the contributions he has made to this firm. We wish him success in his new venture.

(signed)

Retirement Congratulations

Dear Tony,

I want to congratulate you and extend my best wishes for your retirement next month. You are to be commended for forty-seven years of productive and innovative work. Many of the procedures you established will continue for years to come.

You should have all the time you want now to play golf with your buddy, Charlie; no more waiting for the weekend.

We will miss your smiling presence. Enjoy your leisure.

Sincerely,

Dear Ms. Landers:

It will seem strange here without your cheery "good morning" each day. Our customers will miss you too (but I hope not enough to forget us).

Let me say once again how much you have done to give our store its reputation for friendly service. After thirty years of being so helpful, I doubt that anyone can replace you.

Please accept my personal gratitude for your devoted service and my best wishes for an enjoyable retirement. Come to visit us as often as you can; we think of you as one of our family.

Sincerely,

Dear Rozanne:

Your approaching retirement, I am sure, will not mean idling and relaxing. You have been too active in too many projects for that, and I believe that the only way to retire is to stay as active as ever, but restrict the activity to pleasurable things.

I am sure you will enjoy yourself, and let me add my congratulations to the many others you receive. You deserve them all.

Sincerely,

Dear Employees:

Alfred Parton, general manager of the Western Core Division, will retire June 30 after a long and distinguished career with Antelope Machine Corporation

I know you will join me in extending to Alfred our appreciation for the leadership he has provided in developing the West Core Division into the strong organization it is today. Our best wishes go with him in his retirement.

Sincerely,

SECTION III—LETTERS INVOLVING THIRD PARTIES

Thanks for Helping Me Get a Job

Dear Ms. Mitchell,

I want to thank you for all you did for me in your legal secretary class. I followed your suggestion and registered with Temporary Service. With the help of your recommendations, I was employed by the District Attorney's office for five weeks, by the trust office of Bank of California for two weeks, and by Marsh & Marsh for four weeks. The experience could not have been better. Next week I start a full-time job as a legal secretary for the law firm of Moyan, Lane & Watson.

Sincerely,

Dear Mr. Mapes:

Thank you for your most helpful suggestions about my entering the field of financial planning. Recent publicity about that profession has been mixed, with many firms emphasizing sale of securities rather than planning for the future.

By following your guidelines, I have established a business that helps others in the way I had hoped.

Again, thanks for your professional approach and your personal courtesy.

Best regards,

Recommending a Job Applicant

Dear Mr. Arbani:

This is in response to your letter of March 4 requesting a personal letter of referral on Robert R. Riley.

I have personally known Robert for a number of years. He is a good friend of my son. I also know his family well because his father is my wife's doctor.

Robert is a tenacious young man and seems to be a determined, straightforward individual who knows where he is headed.

If you need further information, please write or phone.

Sincerely,

Dear Mrs. Apolo:

Gary Lindstrom is a dedicated worker who has received his master's in library science and is studying for his doctorate. He worked here for seven years and completely reorganized the fiction and business departments. He also tripled the size and usefulness of our business-reference section. Business students and managers now use it daily.

His library knowledge and empathy with people makes Mr. Lindstrom a strong candidate for head librarian.

Please let me know if you would like additional details.

Regards,

Dear Mr. Callas:

Mrs. Lee Andry has been with us as secretary for three engineering managers for five years. For personal reasons she has found it necessary to move to Atlanta. Because she is a highly qualified secretary and administrative assistant, I thought you might be able to use her in your company. If not, perhaps you could offer her some suggestions for continuing her career in the Atlanta area.

I will be happy to return the favor anytime. If you or any of your staff should be coming to the Northwest, please call me; we can set up a business dinner

Cordially,

Rejecting Applicant Recommended by a Third Party

Because this is a "bad-news" letter, couch the decision in the middle. Courtesy and goodwill suggest that this is a letter that *should* be written, even if it seems to be an annoying obligation.

Dear Mr. Fenwick:

I thank you for recommending that Ms. Allison Walters see me about our computer opening. Your interest in our company is appreciated.

At the present time, in spite of her excellent academic training, we require someone with more on-the-job experience.

Thanks again for your interest in our operation.

Cordially,

Dear Mr. Thurber:

We appreciate your sending Mr. Edward Todd to see me about employment here. I can understand why you recommended him. He would be a great addition to our team, but right now we just don't have a place for him.

But I thank you for considering our company as a place to work for someone you obviously regard highly.

Sincerely,

Congratulations on Promotion

Dear Mr. Mosk:

Our entire family cheered when we learned of your advancement to regional manager. Congratulations! It is a good feeling when a former neighbor—and such a friendly one—is given a big promotion.

Sincerely,

Dear Ms. Bonfiglio:

I'm delighted to hear that you have been appointed to the Board of Directors. Perhaps I should also congratulate Lenkurt Co. for recognizing such a good person.

Regards,

Dear Chuck:

It was great to hear of your recent promotion. There is no doubt you have earned this promotion, and I am confident it will not be the last.

I have always felt you handled the problems we sent you exceptionally well.

We look forward to working with you in the future.

Sincerely,

Dear Tom,

We were thrilled when we heard of your promotion. Congratulations! We hope the added responsibility will not keep you too tied down. When you are more settled, please call us, so we can congratulate you in person.

Sincerely,

Dear Jim:

The good news of your appointment as president of Saxxon Company came to me today from our friend Bob Anslowf. Hearty congratulations, and may I wish you every success. I agree that you are the best one to keep the company on its profitable course. The work, I'm sure, will be hard enough to be interesting and let's hope light enough not to be a burden.

Cordially,

Congratulations on Retirement

Dear David,

Congratulations on your retirement! I recall when you started work for Bullwright Construction, over 40 years ago. I even remember your first day: You complained about your sore arms from pushing a heavy wheelbarrow all day. Must seem like ancient history to the immediate past president.

Regards,

Dear Anne,

I learned yesterday from Joan Bartlett of Computer Supplies of your recent retirement from Woodstock & Sons. Congratulations!

You worked long and hard for them for too many years and certainly deserve a few months at the beach. I say a few months because I know you won't stay idle long, but perhaps you can work in a more relaxed atmosphere. You're entitled to that.

The best to you,

Dear Mary,

It pleased me so much to learn you had finally retired from Wellsworth Construction Company. Forty-two years is a long time to wait for retirement wishes from your long time friend. At last I can say it: CONGRATULATIONS.

Now you can join our Wednesday afternoon bridge and discussion group between your relaxation periods.

Always the best,

CHAPTER 9

Termination and Resignation

TERMINATION

A letter announcing termination of employment should be a model of fairness. No matter how angry the writer is with the employee, it should be remembered that a letter is a written record that can come back to plague the writer if it is not reasonable and polite. The company needs complete documentation of the reasons for the dismissal because some dissatisfied employees take their cases to the National Labor Relations Board, the Equal Employment Opportunity Commission, or to their attorneys. The letter should also be brief in order to eliminate a tendency to present the sad news slowly, and thus painfully, to the recipient.

Here are a few "just causes" for terminating an employee:

- The employee has been forewarned of disciplinary measures for actions or lack of actions.
- The company's requirements are reasonable.
- All employees are treated equally.
- The employee's performance justifies termination.

The letter, however, must be positive. Leave no doubt in the reader's mind that he or she is being fired. The first question that comes to the reader's mind is, "Why me?" This must be explained in order to make the letter complete. The explanation must sound reasonable and plausible, as well as being true, so the employer's goodwill (as much as possible under the circumstances) is retained. Terminating an employee is an integral part of any business, but it is also a painful experience for both parties. Treat the situation as even-handedly as possible. This can be done by including all the following points in the termination letter.

How to Do It

1. State regrets at having to terminate the employee.
2. State the fact of termination.

3. Explain why the decision to terminate was made.

4. Make a comment that will retain the employee's goodwill.

5. End on a note of encouragement.

Plant Closed

Dear Mr. Perez:

The recent reorganization and increasing inflation have forced AZE Corporation to close down several of its operations. Your department will cease operation effective January 10.

I regret having to terminate your association with AZE, as I believe that your work and enthusiasm have made you an asset to the company.

Rest assured that I will recommend you highly to potential employers as a most competent individual.

Sincerely,

Company Cutbacks

Dear Jean:

I regret having to tell you this, but due to a corporate program of cutbacks, your services will have to be terminated. The effective date will be May 31.

This cutback is being made companywide and will affect about 150 salaried employees. Seven or eight will be laid off in this branch. When deciding whom to let go seniority was the primary factor. However, headquarters management has determined that certain occupations will be affected more than others.

We are sorry to see you leave and will certainly provide a good reference when you need it.

Sincerely,

Temporary Layoff

Dear Mike:

You have been aware that for the past six months our sales have dropped considerably.

We regret to announce that because of this several salaried employees will be placed on temporary layoff starting Monday, February 3. We anticipate that the layoff period will last from three to four months. By that time we expect the start of the vegetable-canning season to stimulate sales sufficiently to call you back to work.

Meanwhile job duties will be redistributed among those remaining so there will not be a lot of catching-up work when you return.

Best regards,

Company Merger

Dear Carol:

The recent merger of Gordon and BFG Shoe companies has created a large pool of employee talents, many of which duplicate each other.

It is unfortunate, but many faithful employees of Gordon will have to be released by the end of the fiscal year—September 30, _ _ _ _ —in order that a more efficient, cost-effective operation be established.

It is my sad duty to inform you that your position is one that will be terminated.

This unhappy occurrence is not meant to reflect upon either your competence or productivity, both of which I would personally vouch for.

If there is any way in which I can be of assistance, please let me hear from you.

Sincerely,

Financial Problems

Dear James Calabar:

It is with deep regret that I must inform you of the recent decision to terminate your association with J. Alcove, Inc., as of December 30, _ _ _ _. Recent financial problems have forced us to scrutinize our manpower resources carefully, and several employees have, unfortunately, suffered in the process.

Your work here has been admirable, and I will certainly provide you with the highest of recommendations if called upon to do so.

With your skills and abilities to work with people, I have no doubt that you will soon secure a position with another organization.

Sincerely,

Office Consolidation

Dear Eloise Madden:

The closing of this plant and office and its consolidation with the Emerville plant and office was announced last month.

Unfortunately, you are among the office workers who will be let go on September 30. The consolidation will eliminate the need for duplicate positions.

We have enjoyed you and your work here and wish you the best in future employment.

Sincerely,

Indiscretions

Dear Mr. Ludding:

The decision has been made to request your resignation effective June 5, _ _ _ _.

Recent publicity regarding alleged indiscretions with several of our members has made effective functioning in your position close to impossible.

Although individual board members maintain a belief in your innocence, public opinion has made our decision inevitable.

You are highly competent in your field, and we trust that several new positions will open for you.

Sincerely,

Personal Friend

Dear Tommy:

We have been personal friends for several years now, which makes this the most painful thing I have been asked to do in my business career. After long discussions with Ron Alyn, he has concluded that the best thing for all concerned is that you leave the company.

I know you will be leaving many friends, but conditions are such that this seems the best thing to do. Your severance pay will allow you time to locate new opportunities and I'll be glad to help you in any way I can, now and in the future.

Sincerely,

Temporary Assignment Declined

Dear Mr. Odin:

It is with regrets that I must tell you that your employment with Cancon Corp. will be terminated as of June 15, _ _ _ _.

We asked that you help out temporarily at the Raleigh plant during their labor strike, and you refused to go. The reason for your refusal is not important, but the fact of refusal is. We feel we can no longer depend on you.

Your termination is no reflection on the quality of your office work here.

Sincerely,

Performance

Dear Allan:

I am sorry to be the one to tell you this, but your service will no longer be required. However, your pay will continue for two full months. The time is based on your years of service.

We have repeatedly asked you to put more effort and willingness into your work. We believe you have the potential to do a competent job, but your last three reports were late, incomplete, and inaccurate, and therefore useless to our managers who rely on these reports for operating decisions.

Perhaps you should seek a job that is less demanding and has less critical deadlines. I am confident you will soon find work more suited to your abilities.

Sincerely,

Classroom Procedures

Dear Mr. Weeks:

The school board has recently received several strongly voiced complaints regarding your procedure in the classroom. After a thorough investigation into the charges, the board has voted not to renew your contract for the coming academic year.

Admittedly, Milltown is not an avant-garde town, and many unusual approaches to education are not fully appreciated by the parents of the schoolchildren.

I trust that you will locate a position in a school system that is more receptive to your techniques, and we wish you well in your endeavor.

Sincerely,

UNWANTED EMPLOYEE

An unwanted employee is not necessarily one who is incompetent. The employee may be overly aggressive or chronically late with reports and assignments. He or she may come to work late, interrupt or annoy fellow workers, be uncooperative, or perhaps be lacking maturity or educational background.

The common solution (I've witnessed this a great many times) is to seek or create a transfer to another department or location for the employee. By all means make it seem to be a promotion or an opportunity for future promotions. Give the employee a high recommendation.

MEMO to: Joe Kass
   from: Andrew Golemi

It is time, Joe, to consider a transfer from this plant to Headquarters for our Tim Waley. Tim has done exceptionally fine work here for three years, he knows the job area thoroughly and he is an ambitious go-getter.

Tim is ready for exposure into a new area of purchasing, which he can get only by moving on. Headquarters is the best place for broadening his skills.

I would like to suggest that you approach Lester Leehams of corporate purchasing about this. I can furnish whatever supporting data you need about Tim, and I can interest him in the possibilities for future promotions.

Sincerely,

Dear Arthur Janacek,

I have an ideal candidate for the Box Plant accounting opening that has been announced throughout the corporation. I understand Walt Karukonda is taking early retirement.

Jeanne Leflor has done similar accounting work here for five years. She is extremely precise in her numbers work, catches on to new ideas quickly, is willing to do any task asked of her, is pleasant, and has the lowest absentee record in this office.

She has mentioned a few times that she would like to explore accounting work further afield. I have supervised the type of job she would be going into, and she is well qualified.

When you decide on a date for an interview, I can get her a flight to Ontario, California, if you can have someone meet her at the airport.

Whether interested or not, please let me hear from you soon.

Best regards,

TERMINATION WARNING

Some adults retain the childhood characteristic of needing a superior to restate their limits. A child may extend his or her limit of walking one block from home to two blocks unless constantly reminded. A teenager will stay out until midnight unless reminded often that the limit is 11:00 P.M. An adult employee will arrive at work later and later unless occasionally reminded that work starts at 8:00 A.M. Coffee breaks increase from 15 minutes to 20 or 25 minutes. Reports will be completed late unless the deadlines are restated each month. Employees overcome by these habits often respond to a less subtle reminder. The direct approach is required.

When these employees reach the line requiring a warning of possible termination, skip over the calm, subtle tones and state directly the reason for the warning letter, the potential consequences of the employee's actions (or lack of actions), and how the employee can avoid termination.

How to Do It

1. State regrets at having to consider termination.
2. Give reasons for considering termination. Mention *specific* reasons or actions or lack of actions or instances or examples.
3. Make clear that the reader is in a probationary situation.
4. End on a note of encouragement.

Personal Problems

Dear Mr. Bowen:

Termination of an employee is never a happy duty, and we make all possible efforts to avoid that situation. However, unless your work performance shows substantial improvement, Elko Corp. will be forced to terminate our association.

Personal problems affect all of us periodically. When these occur, help should be sought so that such problems do not affect work performance to the point that an individual is unable to function effectively.

Unless you seek professional help and make the effort to perform well once again, we will have no choice left but to sever the relationship.

The excellence of your past record cannot be overlooked, and I trust that your future efforts can be equally successful.

Sincerely,

Below-Standard Performance

Dear Ms. Mesa:

We dislike very much having to acknowledge your continuing poor performance. But you should be aware that it could lead to termination of your employment.

Not only has your individual sales volume declined recently, but customers are complaining about your rudeness, your careless appearance, and your reluctance to answer questions.

We hope and anticipate that you can soon overcome these negative impressions. Your attempts to improve your sales and attitude will be watched.

Sincerely,

Dear Mr. Sobert:

It is with reluctance I inform you that unless conditions improve measurably, Bradford's will have to terminate your association with this company.

Personnel performance and productivity rates have shown steady declines in the past twelve-month period. Frankly, unless improvement is observed, the department will have to be revamped and several other employees released in order to make up our losses.

To be realistic, we estimate that such improvement will take a minimum of six months to become visible. Given your excellent performance record in the past, there is no reason to assume anything but success.

Sincerely,

Dear Mr. Phillips:

This is a written record of our discussion following the accounting audit by the Sano Company on May 22. You have a copy of the 52 errors in accounting procedures and policies noted by the Sano Company auditors.

We discussed with you our concern and disappointment with these errors as well as your performance as an office supervisor. Company management will share this concern, especially because your position as assistant office manager places you in line for promotion to office manager. Your limited experience has been considered, but of more importance is your evident weakness in accounting skills and your lack of ability to organize procedures. In addition, while discussing procedures with members of your staff, we found morale to be unduly low.

At present, you may consider yourself on probation. Your performance will be carefully monitored, and if, in our opinion, a definite improvement is not forthcoming, there is a possibility that steps will be taken to replace you. You have begun to correct some of the problems, but a review of your progress will be made in four months. We expect to determine your permanent status at that time.

Sincerely,

Dear Mrs. Deyo:

Although with regret, I feel it is necessary to inform you that the following items concerning your supervision of the Baywell House of our youth agency need your immediate attention:

1. The amount of gasoline consumed from Friday to Friday should not exceed $25. Special field trips are excluded. No trips are to be made in the agency vehicle that are not agency related.

2. Mileage forms should be turned in at the end of every month completely filled in. Trust receipts and allowance receipts must be turned in weekly.

3. The phone bill is not to exceed $70 for agency calls. This is separate from your personal calls, for which you pay. This means that all calls need to be monitored *before* the number is dialed, and a record should be kept for each boy stating whether or not his one long-distance, five minute call was made for that month. A log should be maintained for all calls.

4. The grocery list is to be filled in according to needs listed on the menu form ONLY. The grocery list should indicate the quantity needed. Food is ordered Friday through Thursday.

Improvement must be shown in these areas by March 9 or employment will be jeopardized. By this date, there should be enough improvement made that these issues will no longer be a problem.

I have read this and understand its contents.

Date: _____

_____
Francine Deyo

Classroom Performance

Dear Mr. Chaffee:

The school board has received several strongly voiced complaints regarding your practices in the classroom. Unless modifications of such procedures are undertaken, renewal of your contract cannot be a certainty.

In particular, your suspension of all homework assignments and the assignment of comic books as reading material in senior literature seminar have been cited. Parents also allege that numerous individual class sessions have become no more than verbal free-for-alls, with little direction by you.

Unannounced teacher evaluation will be utilized within the next two weeks in an effort to clear up this matter. I trust that you will make every effort to conform to the standard of education of this school.

Sincerely,

Borderline Work Effort

Dear Mr. Payn:

Your asking for a salary increase last week indicates an interest in continuing to work here. However, company policy requires an annual review of performance and potential for promotion before an increase in salary can be considered. The exception is for new employees who can receive an incentive salary increase after six months.

I'm sorry to say that you have not earned that exception. In fact, your work performance and attitude at this point is leading you toward unemployment. I believe you have the ability to advance, but you will have to work harder and cease complaining about situations you do not control. You are capable of changing. Let me see you do it.

Sincerely,

Tardiness

Dear Mr. Torr:

Promptness is important to the management and the customers at Rich Savings and Loan Association. Therefore, while we make allowances for occasional lateness, consistent lateness cannot be tolerated and offenders must be dismissed.

You have reported late to work for 17 out of the last 23 days. Unless this situation is remedied immediately, you will be asked to leave our organization.

Should there be extenuating circumstances, please come in and speak with me. If there is a problem, perhaps we can work it out together. Rich S & L never likes losing a good employee. I'm sure that the problem can be eliminated.

Sincerely,

Absentee Record

Dear Harvey:

Your work has been excellent, but your absentee record is about to overshadow your work record. I don't doubt that your health has been poor, but one requirement of a job is regular attendance. We have difficulty scheduling our operations when we cannot depend on your attendance.

This subject has been discussed several times before, and now your attendance must meet our requirements or termination will result.

Sincerely,

RESIGNATION

A letter of resignation must be fair to both parties involved. Show tact and consideration for the person or parties from whom you are resigning.

Regardless of the reason for resigning—you hate the boss, the work is too hard, the hours are too long, the work is boring, or you *did* get a better offer—tact is always required. A blatant statement of the facts may arouse the ire of the reader and preclude a good recommendation should you ask for one at a later date. The resigner should assume full responsibility and not blame the boss for causing the resignation.

A socially acceptable reason should be given for resigning. It may be because of poor health, someone in your family is being transferred, you wish to change directions, you want to spend more time with your family, or you have served for a number of years. The occasion may arise, however, when a one-sentence statement of resignation with no explanation or comment is all that is required. The recipient of the letter would already know the reason.

Avoid self-praise. It is well to mention the pleasant aspects of having worked for the organization, but do so by mentioning how your associates made work pleasant for you, not how you helped them.

Mention the specific date of resignation.

How to Do It

1. State the effective date of resignation.
2. State an acceptable reason for resignation.
3. Briefly mention the good points of having worked there.

New Position

Dear Mr. Larson:

With great reluctance I am submitting my resignation, effective July 31, _ _ _ _.

My association with Wiley Company has been a pleasant one, and I will miss the friendship here. However, as I mentioned in our brief discussion last week, the offer I have received cannot be ignored, considering the financial benefits to my family and the future potential of the position.

I appreciate your understanding of my decision to leave Wiley Company.

Sincerely,

Dear Mrs. Tansack:

I am resigning because I have been offered a position that includes a wider range of accounting tasks and different challenges. The new job also leads directly to a supervisory position.

My resignation will be effective October 31, _ _ _ _. Meanwhile, my best efforts will go into training a replacement.

Sincerely,

Seeking New Challenge

Dear Bill,

Harper Clean Air has grown rapidly during the past fifteen years. The problems of growth presented an intriguing challenge. The challenge was met, and I enjoyed my part in meeting it. The future promises more growth, but I have been at my desk handling the same problems over and over-for the past five years. I need a fresh challenge.

Thus, with mixed feelings of leaving an old friend and of needing my own "Clean Air," I am offering my resignation, to be effective November 30. I will join the new firm of Hoskins and Halloid. They manufacture air valves and plan to expand into related lines.

We have several people here who could take over my position with a minimum of training. Please accept my thanks for the opportunity you gave me to work with you in meeting the challenges of the past fifteen years.

With regards,

College Training

Dear Mr. Carlyle:

To make full use of my college training in business finance, I have accepted a position with the Norcross Development Company, builders of shopping centers. My resignation will be effective March 31, _ _ _ _. I will be glad to help in any way possible to train a replacement.

Over the past few years, I have given serious thought to making a change. I sincerely appreciate the opportunity you gave me here at Johnson's Hardware to learn about business and the importance of work, and especially the help this job provided in financing my college education.

I have enjoyed working here and will continue my personal friendship with you and your staff.

Sincerely,

Ill Health

Dear Ms. Willis:

Resigning was the furthest thing from my mind when I worked so vigorously to become director of the City Youth Program. However, I must leave the position at the end of December.

Ill health and growing burdens in other areas have drained me of the energy and enthusiasm needed to conduct such a program.

The young people and those with whom I've worked have added immense meaning to my life. I only wish I could continue to work with them.

Sincerely,

Heart Problem

County Planning Commission:

With much reluctance and regret I ask to be released from the position of County Planning Director.

Because of a heart condition I have developed, my doctor has instructed me to slow my pace of work.

As you may imagine, this is somewhat of a blow to me, but my doctor knows this condition better than I. During the past six years I've enjoyed working with the fine people of our county. It is difficult for me to resign, but I must do so effective August 15.

Let me extend my good wishes to all of you for success on the riverfront project.

Sincerely,

Personal Problems

Dear Mrs. Aldridge:

For nine months, I have enjoyed the pleasure and benefits of being president of the Milltown Businesswomen's Club. Thus, it is with great regret that I must resign.

Recent personal difficulties are creating more demands on my nonprofessional hours. As a result, I cannot give full attention to my responsibility as president, and I feel that I am shortchanging the Club.

Working with the other officers has provided pleasure as well as insight into the skills and competence of today's businesswoman. Please accept my regrets.

Sincerely,

Disagree with Goals

Dear Mr. Delhi:

Recent occurrences demand that I resign my position as vice president for public affairs, effective February 9, _ _ _ _.

Disagreement with the goals and philosophy of the company has hindered my performance and negated my ability to assist in furthering those goals.

I will miss the challenge and adventure my role offered, as well as the many people with whom I worked.

Sincerely,

Volunteer

Dear Mrs. Prejean:

Having been a library volunteer for six years, I feel I should devote more time to other activities. I will resign as of June 30. You should have no difficulty finding a replacement.

I have enjoyed the work (not really "work") and the association with the staff and other volunteers.

Best wishes,

Dear Mrs. Linton:

I wish to resign from driving the Red Cross van that takes nondrivers to medical and business appointments.

My nine years of volunteer driving has helped many less fortunate people, and I would like to continue. But my vision is deteriorating and may soon affect my driving ability.

I have enjoyed these years of helping people.

Warmest regards,

Reason Omitted

Board of Directors:

I hereby submit my resignation as chairman of the Credit Union Supervisory Committee effective March 1, _ _ _ _.

Sincerely,

Resignation Acceptance

The acceptance of a resignation should be with sincere regrets. Only ill will can be gained by implying that the resignation was anticipated or that it is eagerly accepted. Say something nice about the person resigning. If nothing else, say that he or she did a fine job. End with an expression of good wishes for the future.

How to Do It

1. Express sincere regrets.
2. Say something complimentary.
3. Express good wishes for the future.

Disagreement with Goals

Dear Mr. Simmons:

Although you have disagreed with the goals and philosophy of the Public Affairs Council and stated so in your resignation letter, it is with sincere regret that we accept your resignation as our vice president.

Your disagreements at times were a little harsh, but then upon reflection, we often found you had presented a point that gave us reason to consider your views, and we would end up agreeing with you.

We wish you well in your next endeavor.

Sincerely,

Declining a Transfer

Dear Will,

We accept your resignation in lieu of a transfer to Cleveland, but with deepest regrets. We understand your decision to remain here with your extended family.

Your contribution to the successful expansion of this plant cannot be overstated, and your expertise and cooperative spirit will be sorely missed at the Cleveland plant.

We wish you good luck in locating a new challenge to your many abilities.

Sincerely,

Accepting Resignation

Dear Jim,

All the Church School members and teachers will miss you very much. Your eleven years as Church School superintendent was an uplifting experience for all of us—in our faith and in our attendance.

No one can replace you, but we will find someone to carry on the work.

We wish you well in your retirement and your move "back to the old homestead," as you put it.

With God's blessing,

Dear Ben,

The Board of Directors regretfully accepts your resignation as the chairman of the Supervisory Committee of the Credit Union.

You worked many long, hard hours auditing the books and the operations of the other committees. We got many new insights through your willing efforts. Your judicious handling of the special meetings during our troubled times of changing managers will never be forgotten by the Board.

We want you to know of our deep appreciation of your work during the past five years, and although our acceptance of you resignation is reluctant, our best wishes go with you.

Sincerely,

Dear Bill:

We are sorry to see you leave and accept your resignation with regret.

You accomplished a great deal for us during your six years as our mechanical engineer. You deserve much of the credit for our smooth-running and profitable operation.

We do, however, understand your desire to be near your family. We know you will do as much for your new employer as you did for us. The best of luck to you.

Sincerely,

Dear Susan:

Mixed feelings well up in me when I accept a resignation. We never like seeing our associates leave, but at the same time we want you to know that our best wishes go with you.

We are proud that you received a promotion to Nursing Administrator at Wesley Medical Centre and know you are looking forward to your new surroundings and an interesting challenge.

Thank you for your valuable contributions and years of faithful service to our hospital. Our sincere good wishes to you, and if you are ever in this area again, please stop in for a visit.

Sincerely,

Acknowledgment of Separation Pay and Release

I (<u>Employee</u>), have received from (<u>Employer Company</u>) the net amount (after standard deductions) of (<u>write in the amount</u>) dollars ($\_\_\_\_\_$)—consisting of (<u>write in the amount</u>) dollars ($\_\_\_\_\_$) in severance pay and (<u>write in the amount</u>) dollars ($\_\_\_\_\_$) in vacation pay. In exchange for this payment, I will release (<u>Employer company</u>) as well as their directors, managers, staff members, program coordinators, supervisors, and other agents from any claim or causes of action that are connected in any way with my employment or the termination of my employment by (<u>Employer company</u>).

I have read this release and understand it. I also accept the payment described above as a final and complete settlement of all claims and causes of action that I have or may have against (Employer company).

Signed this _____ day of _____.

(<u>Signature of employee</u>)

_____
Witness

_____
Witness

(Reprinted from *"Wrongful Discharge" and the Derogation of the At-Will Employment Doctrine* by Andrew D. Hill, Wharton Industrial Research Unit, University of Pennsylvania, with permission)

CHAPTER 10

Sympathy and Condolence

The first essential of a letter of sympathy is a feeling of respect for the reader. He or she has lost a loved one or suffered an accident or succumbed to an illness. A respectful mood is called for. The sympathetic situations covered in this chapter are those in which a cheery greeting or humorous get-well card is not appropriate. The letter should be written from the heart and should be warm, human, and kind. The writer needs a feeling of empathy with and consideration for the reader. All of these feelings, however, need not be put into one letter. In fact, the second essential is brevity. Long eulogies and maudlinism are out. Do not burden the grief-stricken with more grief or long explanations of unrelated matters.

The third part of a letter of sympathy is an offer to help. This does not fit into all situations, but if the intent is sincere and follow-up certain, an offer to help at the end of the letter is a real comfort, especially at the time of the death of a loved one.

The use of the word *death*, along with *died* and *killed* in a letter of condolence is objectionable to some people, because these words seem unnecessarily strong. The word *deceased* is also used as a substitute for *dead*, but is hardly an improvement. References to sorrow, grief, tragedy, or loss can be used, and the meaning remains clear to the reader. Some of the examples that follow use the word *death* and some do not. The decision to use it or not will be based upon the writer's understanding of how the reader will react.

When the cause of death seems so traumatic the writer is uncomfortable stating it, a simple sentence such as, "May we express our sympathy," or "We are truly sorry," will reveal the writer's feelings. The cause need not be mentioned.

Some letters of sympathy include phrases similar to these: "There is nothing anyone can say at a time like this" or "Words cannot express our feelings" or "We don't know what to say at this time." Such phrases should be eliminated. They seem to be put in to lengthen a short statement of sorrow, and they express helplessness at a time when the reader needs help.

Sentences Expressing Sympathy

A list of sentences appropriate for letters of sympathy follows. In instances where they seem to fit, they can be added to the sample letters. These statements can also be substituted for statements in the sample letters in this chapter or can be the starting point for a self-composed letter.

We hope our caring will make your sorrow easier to bear.

We hope that time will ease the sorrow of your recent loss.

We know that memories will keep your lost one close to you.

May our sympathy help to comfort you.

May you find comfort in knowing that we care.

Our thoughts are with you in this time of sorrow.

We wish to express our deepest sympathy.

May the love you feel for the one you lost lessen your sorrow.

May the love that surrounds you be a source of comfort at this time.

May your memories be a source of comfort.

It may help to know that our thoughts are with you.

May the sympathy of those who care make the sorrow of your heart less difficult to bear.

Some things are hard to understand.

No one is ever ready for death.

We know death is certain, yet it remains hard to accept.

Those who have not experienced the death of a close one cannot comprehend the loneliness.

There is an emptiness that only those who have lost a close relative can understand.

Our sympathy and love go out to you, Mrs. (Mr.) Smith.

We shall miss her (his) smiling presence.

The loss of a son, (daughter, wife, husband) is giving up a part of one's self.

When one spouse leaves a loving partnership, it's always too soon.

Until you have suffered the loss of a loved one, you cannot fully understand the pain of separation.

Sentences Thanking the Reader for an Expression of Sympathy

Without you I wouldn't have known where to turn for the endless number of decisions one must make in a time of grief.

You were such a comfort to us following Edward's death.

Jon always thought of you as a real friend, and that you proved to be during my period of grief.

How much I appreciated your kindness and help when Alexander died.

I just couldn't have managed without your help.

The letter you sent at the time of Andy's death continues to be an inspiration to me.

Thank you for your kind words and your understanding heart.

Your kindness overcame the self-pity I was beginning to feel.

Your words of encouragement stayed with me during my bereavement.

Thank you for your understanding sympathy.

Your love and help during my recent difficulty have meant more than words can express.

We wish to thank you for your kind thoughts.

My husband and I wish to thank you for your kind thoughts.

We wish to thank you for your letter. The kind messages sent by friends have been a great comfort to us.

We appreciate your thoughts of us and your sympathetic note.

We appreciate your kindness in writing to us at this time.

We gratefully acknowledge your kind expression of sympathy.

We appreciated your sympathy in our bereavement.

We thank you for your kindness and sympathy.

Your note of sympathy helped me to accept Tom's death more courageously.

Your sharing of your recent sorrow helped me to bear my present bereavement. Thank you.

It is a comfort in a time of sadness to receive such a beautiful expression of sympathy.

Thank you for your kind expression of sympathy.

Your sympathetic note reminded us of the many kindnesses you have extended to our family through the years.

We are grateful to you for helping us bear our grief by your kind letter of sympathy.

I appreciate the kind thoughts that prompted you to send such lovely flowers.

The family of Joan Anderson accepts with sincere appreciation your kind expression of sympathy.

How to Do It

1. Mention the person about whom the sympathy is being expressed: for example, Henry, Dr. Miller, your boss, or your sister.
2. State your relationship with this person: for example, our friend at work, my acquaintance of many years, or all of us here.
3. Make a complimentary statement: for example, he was loved by all, he was a warm friend, she was always cheerful, she was helpful, or we spent many pleasant hours together.
4. If appropriate, offer to help the reader.

Lost Your Job

Dear Ellie,

I'm really sorry to hear that you lost your job, especially after so many years with the company. But try to look at it this way: You may have been handed an opportunity to do something you really like. After your anger subsides, go for something better.

I recall one clerk-typist I worked with who lost her job. After her tears cleared she joined a friend in the upholstery business. Soon the two of them were looking for a helper. Other interesting opportunities are out there.

Best wishes and good luck,

Failed the State Exam

Dear Andy,

Sorry to learn that you failed last month's State exam for your psychology license—and for the second time. From what I have heard, that is not unusual. So hang in there, keep studying those special textbooks, and try again.

With your educational background and experience, there is no way you will not pass after another try or two. It is possible that a certain number of applicants are passed over with each exam just to keep too many from flooding the market at one time, or perhaps to make sure you are serious about passing. I believe in your abilities.

Best regards,

Letters to Hospitalized People

When writing to a person in a hospital, be pleasant and optimistic while expressing an interest in the patient's welfare. Do not refer to the specific illness or injury—that is the doctor's job.

Hospitalized for Illness

Dear Will,

When I called at your office today, I was surprised to hear that you were in the hospital. Knowing your usual spunk, I can't see an illness holding you down very long. Take it easy and enjoy the rest while you can. I'll be looking for you to be back at work soon.

With regards,

Dear Scott,

Word of your illness just reached me, and I want to wish you a quick return to health.

Your many friends will be sorry to learn that you will be in the hospital for more than a week. But it helps to know you have a large group of well-wishers.

When you return home I'll be over to see you. In the meantime, please ask Mrs. Clines what I can do for her here. I'll be glad to help in any way possible.

Sincerely,

Dear Erma,

A black cloud hangs over the office since we received news of your sudden illness. We send our wishes for a speedy recovery: We need you here in the office. We hope the flowers will brighten your hospital room and cheer your spirits.

Sincerely,

Hospitalized for Accident or Injury

Dear Madolyn,

Your sister called me this morning to tell me of your accident Saturday and that you will be in the hospital three or four weeks. We will miss you, but don't concern yourself with your work here. We will take care of it for you. We all wish you a full recovery.

Sincerely,

Dear Mr. Allison:

I am sorry to learn of your injury. Please accept my best wishes for a quick recovery.

Since you will be confined for a few days, I believe you will enjoy this new book on your hobby of boating.

Cordially,

Other's Illness

Dear Ned,

Your friends at Speller and Associates are sorry to learn of your wife's serious illness. Please accept the flowers we sent with our sincere wishes that she will have a fast recovery.

Sincerely,

Death of Business Associate

Dear Mrs. Goel,

All of us here at Eltons Lumber are saddened by the death of your president, Wilbur Creighton. You have our most sincere sympathy.

Mr. Creighton was a true community leader and served as an example to all of us. His work with the Boy Scouts will long be remembered.

Sincerely,

Dear Linda,

It is with great sadness that we learned of the death of Thomas. I had worked with him in Denver and then in Atlanta until his transfer last August. We will all feel the loss.

Sincerely,

All Stockholders:

Arnold P. Stelly, our vice president of laser research and development, and a close personal friend of mine, died tragically this last year. He was an outstanding and personable young executive, on his way up after ten years with our corporation. He was well liked and respected by his many acquaintances both inside and outside the company. We extend our heartfelt sympathy to his family and many friends. He will be missed.

Sincerely,

Death of Business Friend

Dear Mrs. Jader,

It is difficult to tell you how deeply I feel about your husband's untimely death.

What started many years ago as a business relationship between Harold and me quickly became a warm friendship. It was a privilege to have known him so well, and I will never forget his thoughtfulness and kindness.

With great personal sorrow, I ask to share your loss and to extend my heartfelt sympathy.

Sincerely,

Dear Mrs. Huderson,

It was with heartfelt sadness that I learned of Charles' passing. Charlie and I worked so well together on the San Juan road project in the late seventies. We spent many pleasant hours together, both on and off the job. He was a great companion and a warm-hearted friend.

Sincerely,

Death of Spouse

Death of Husband

Dear Cecilia:

Losing one's husband can cause a loneliness unlike any other, but having your children near will help ease the difficulty of the days ahead.

Knowing your fortitude and courage, I am sure you will adjust to your new situation. I know you are grateful for the many happy years you shared with Tom.

Love,

Dear Margaret:

Your John made friends of everyone he met, even during his last days in the hospital. But this was only a part of his personality. We all will remember him for his generosity. He often involved himself in worthwhile civic projects. The community is richer for his having lived.

I wish we lived closer together so I could be with you at this time. I send my love.

Sincerely,

Dear Mrs. Nunan,

Please accept our heartfelt sympathy in your time of great sorrow. Only those who have lost a husband can know the depths of your feelings. We send you our love to give you strength to bear your sorrow.

Sincerely,

Dear Mrs. Hurtley:

Mr. Fried and I wish to express our deepest sympathy to you and your family.

I came to know Dr. Hurtley well these last few years. I had no friend whose wisdom and kindness meant more to me. We shall miss him.

Sincerely,

Dear Mrs. LaCosta,

We wish to express our sympathy on the untimely death of your husband. He was a great asset to our company for many years, and all of us old-timers will miss his steadfastness.

If I can be of any help at all please call me.

Sincerely,

Dear Mrs. Bascomb,

I was stunned yesterday to learn of Fred's untimely passing. I have known Fred since coming to work here nearly twenty years ago and have enjoyed these many years of friendship with him.

Fred was loved by all his co-workers, and his friendliness cheered us all. He will be greatly missed.

Mrs. Bascomb, our thoughts are with you, and we extend our deepest sympathy.

Sincerely,

Dear Mrs. Joyner:

We were both grieved to hear of your loss. Mr. Joyner was the one person we could always go to in time of trouble, however slight. He was so warm and wise and understanding.

If there is anything at all we can do to help you, please let us know.

Sincerely,

Dear Carla,

When there is love, any life is too short. Todd had a way of making the joys of life contagious. We remember especially his help with our storm windows. As a result of his helping us, we formed a lifelong friendship.

We know you are grateful for your life with Todd, and we feel fortunate to have known him.

With sympathy,

Death of Wife

Dear Bob,

Perhaps it will help to lessen the sorrow of Linda's death to realize that so many of her friends share your grief. We all appreciated the happiness she so willingly shared and inspired in her friends.

I know your courage will help you through this rough time. Our love is with you.

Sincerely,

Dear Mr. Gordon,

I wish to express my deepest sympathy. Mrs. Gordon was one of the loveliest women I have ever known. No one who knew her could ever forget her charm and warmth.

Sincerely,

Dear Mr. Sidman,

Bereavement is so personal that few of us, unless we have experienced it ourselves, can comprehend its grief. Jackie was loved by all of us who worked with her. Her pleasant vitality was a continuous inspiration. We hope that our caring will lessen the sorrow you bear.

Sincerely,

Dear Rick,

We were sorry to hear about Maryanne's death. We will always remember her for her fascinating interest in the environment and the people around her. She will be missed by many.

Cordially,

Dear Ismael,

My staff and I extend our heartfelt sympathy to you and your family upon the unexpected death of your wife. Your many years of happiness together will help you sustain your strength and calmness.

Perhaps we could help you and your business by rescheduling orders or extending payment terms. If we can do these or other things to make this period of grief easier, by all means let us know.

Cordially,

Death of Relative

Death of Mother

Dear Mr. Donaldson,

We extend our most sincere sympathy to you upon the loss of your mother. If there is anything at all that we can do to help, please call us.

Sincerely,

Dear Ms. Sootoo,

There is a lonesomeness after the death of one's mother, but I want you to know that your friends are thinking of you and sympathizing with you in this time of your great loss.

I will never forget the friendliness and kindness your mother extended to me. She was loved by all who knew her.

With sympathy,

Dear Robin,

My love for your mother will last as long as my memory of her. During the many years we were neighbors, she shared her smiles, her flowers, her recipes, and most of all her pleasing personality.

No one who knew her will ever forget her. I want to share my sympathy with you.

With love,

Death of Father

Dear Miss Elwood,

May I send you my deepest sympathy at this time and say that my thoughts have been with you since I heard of the death of your father. I admired him greatly. You must be even prouder of his devotion to you. I know you will be brave in your sorrow as he would have wanted you to be.

Sincerely,

Dear Mrs. Lansing

We were truly sorry to read of your father's death yesterday. We will be over tomorrow to help with whatever we can.

With sincere sympathy,

Dear Coleen,

I always admired your helpful and loving attitude toward your father during his extended illness. Home care after a period of time becomes a trial for the caregiver, but you never waivered in your show of love.

Your father was kind and generous to his vast number of friends. He will be sorely missed by all of them.

Love,

Death of Daughter

Dear Alice,

No person or experience will ever replace the happy days and love little Lana gave you.

We hope it will be of some comfort to know that you gave her all the love and care possible and that your many friends share your sorrow.

Love to you and Jim,

Dear Mr. Arronson:

It was with sincere regret that I heard this morning of the loss of your daughter. I know what a shock you have suffered. I wish to express my deepest sympathy and the hope that the kind thoughts of your many friends will make your grief a little easier to bear.

Sincerely,

Dear Kevin,

I was surprised and saddened to hear from Mrs. Tabor that your daughter succumbed to the injuries from her recent accident.

I want you to know how terrible we feel that you have lost a lovely and talented daughter at such an early age.

Please call me if there is anything I can do to help you.

Sincerely,

Death of Son

Dear Brad,

Please accept my sincere sympathy on the death of your son, Jerry.

Sincerely,

Dear Mr. Waechtler,

The loss of your son comes as a shock to us at the Boating Club. We all had the greatest respect for him and will miss his cheerfulness and lighthearted humor. We realize our loss is small compared to yours.

We offer our heartfelt sympathy in a time of sorrow.

Sincerely,

Dear Faye and Marvin,

We are very sorry that Jon did not survive his battle with cancer. He was so brave and optimistic. I found his attitude lifted my spirits. He did for me what I tried to do for him, and that I will long remember. He and you are in my thoughts and prayers.

With love,

Death of Sister

Dear Jane,

I have just learned with sorrow of the death of your sister. Because you and your sister were so close, I realize how deeply this loss will touch you. I know you will be able to adjust, and please accept my sincere sympathy.

Cordially,

Death of Brother

Dear Mr. Chickering,

The death of your brother brought profound sorrow to me as well as to his many friends. During the many years I knew him I often thought of him as my own brother.

May I extend my deep sympathy to you and your family.

Sincerely,

Miscarriage

Dear Andrea,

You have experienced a great disappointment when you were so excited about having your first child. We extend our sincere sympathy and know you will have the support of your many friends.

But all is not lost: the possibilities for motherhood are not over. Meanwhile let us know what we can do to help.

Lovingly,

Death of Others

Dear Dr. and Mrs. Inland,

We were shocked to learn of your recent loss. Louis had such promise and was so well liked that it seems hard to believe he is no longer with us. His passing will be mourned by those of us who loved him so much.

Most sincerely,

Dear Madolyn,

We wish to express our deepest sympathy upon the untimely death of Jim.

He was one of our great managers as well as a personal friend to so many of us who worked with him. The many years he devoted to community services will be long remembered by the people of Little Rock. May your memories be a source of comfort.

Sincerely,

Dear Benny,

I am deeply grieved when I think of your loss. Janice was a wonderful friend who always did more than was expected of her. She made this world a little better for me and for all the others who knew her.

Sincerely,

Dear Mrs. Solons,

It was a distressing shock to learn of Howard's death yesterday. We worked together here for many years. If there is anything I can do to help you, please don't hesitate to give me a call.

Sincerely,

Dear Jill,

I just learned in a letter from Tom about Al's accident and the misfortune you are experiencing. It's hard to face the loss of a long-time friend even from far away. If I were closer, I could be of more help to you at this time. But I do send my sincerest sympathy to you and your family.

With sympathy,

Belated Condolences

Dear Mabel,

I was deeply shocked and grieved to hear that Edward passed away last month. I will always remember his pleasant ways and how he made us feel so much at home whenever we visited with you folks.

I think it is great, and a great help to you these days, that you are spending so much time at the Convalescent Hospital as a volunteer helper.

Sincerely,

Dear Ellie,

I learned only yesterday of your father's death. I always admired the cheerful way he helped your neighbors and his willingness to get involved in the town's activities.

I will always think of him with fondness.

Sincerely,

Death by Suicide

Dear Alice,

Word has just reached us of Jerry's tragic death. As impossible as it must be to understand, Jerry must have felt in his own mind that this was the best alternative.

You have the courage, I know, that you will need to face the days ahead.

We send our love
and sympathy,

Dear Ron,

I am deeply moved by the news of Marie's shocking death. None of us understand it. I am sure she gave a great deal of thought to her decision to depart at a time of her own choosing.

It will require an untold amount of courage for you to carry on, but I have faith that you can surmount the tragedy.

Bless you,

Death—from a Business Firm

Gentlemen and Ladies:

I am sure the death of Allen Rogers is almost as great a shock to the entire accounting profession as it is to the members of your organization.

Few people have been held in as high esteem as he was for many years. No one deserved it more.

As a member of our profession, I share with others this tragic loss.

Sincerely,

Dear Mr. Johnson:

We at Basker Company were saddened to hear of Mr. Condon's death. We extend our deepest sympathy. Mr. Condon's leadership in our business community will be sorely missed by the community as well as by his numerous friends.

Sincerely,

My Dear Mr. Swayne,

We at Jordan's were very sorry to hear of the death of your daughter. Only one who has lost a lovely young daughter can know the tragedy of this loss.

All of us here wish to extend our heartfelt sympathy. Please let me know if there is anything we at Jordan's can do to be of help to you.

Sincerely,

My Dear Mrs. Sterling,

Everyone at our plant was surprised and saddened by the sudden death of your husband.

Although sympathy is only a small consolation, even from the hearts of us who share your sorrow, I want you to know how deeply Robert's loss is felt here. He was respected and admired by everyone who worked with him.

Each individual in our plant joins in this expression of sympathy.

Very sincerely,

Dear Mrs. Schulze,

No one can take the place of a devoted husband, and only one who has had a like sorrow can understand the grief that you are experiencing.

My words can bring only slight comfort when your grief is so great, but I did want you to know that we at Watson Corporation extend our deepest sympathy.

We share your personal grief, as we have lost a needed and valued member of our team.

Sincerely,

Dear Mr. Touchet,

We have just heard of the great personal loss suffered by you in the tragic tornado that brought death and destruction to your city.

Buildings and even cities can be restored, but the death of your son is an irreparable loss. We are willing to do what we can by shipping you anything you may need to rebuild your business. We'll gladly extend credit as long as necessary. Will you let us do that much for you?

To hear of a friend and customer losing his store and his son brings home to us the heartaches and sadness from which many people in your city are suffering. May you have the strength and courage to carry on.

Sincerely,

Birth Defect

Dear Anne,

A birth defect seems so terrible now, but since I also have a child with a birth defect, let me assure you that it won't be as bad later on as it seems now.

Some physical defects cannot be changed, but control of expressions, revealing a return of your love, can be learned. With your wisdom and patient understanding, your precious baby can develop so her personality shines right through the handicap.

I'll be glad to share my experiences and learning with you. I'll call you soon.

Cordially,

Divorce

Dear Annabelle,

We were surprised and deeply disturbed to hear that you and Jim are getting a divorce.

We don't know your intimate differences or the deep reasons for your decision, but as long as we have known both of you, we didn't realize there were any serious frictions or problems.

We have written a short note to Jim, also, to let you both know that we are ready to help in any way we can.

With love,

Dear Jim,

Your separation and pending divorce from Annabelle comes as a startling surprise. We hate to see this happen, but I know from my own experience that after the stages of denial, anger, acceptance and fear of the future, the adjustment to single status will be made.

We sent a note to Annabelle expressing our surprise and sorrow about this event. If we can help you while you make the transition, please let us know.

With best wishes,

Marriage Separation

Dear Janet,

As a lifelong friend of your mother—and of you, too—I am greatly concerned about your separation from George.

I know you are taking this step after serious consideration, but if it should be because of something that could be ironed out, please give the separation another thought or two. I am concerned that such a promising marriage should not endure. All marriages take a lot of work and compromise, but whatever your decision, I will always remain your close friend.

Love,

Misfortune

Dear Brother,

Misfortune hits each of us at some time or other. Hang in there, and don't let this drag you down. You have recovered before from setbacks by driving ahead with the next project. Although right now this may seem worse than before, I know your persistence and stamina will propel you to the top again soon.

We here are all rooting for you and know we can expect the best from you.

Regards,

Personal Reverses

Dear Peter,

Right now you probably feel like the phoenix bird that burned itself to ashes. But it rose from those ashes to live another long period of years.

I know your resolute courage will give you wings to fly out of the ashes and reach the success you achieved once before.

Your friend,

Unnamed Tragedy

Dear Mr. and Mrs. Alder,

I saw the report in the paper about Jim and want to tell you how sorry I am. Jim was three years younger than I, so we didn't play together often as kids. But when I met him at your daughter's wedding last month, I realized what a fine son you have and how proud you must be of him. You'll just have to take my word for how bad I feel.

Sincerely,

Thank You for Your Sympathy

Dear Mr. Cooly,

We appreciate and thank you for your expression of sympathy upon the death of Mr. Olson.

Sincerely,

Dear Beth,

It was heartwarming to receive your comforting letter of sympathy.

Sincerely,

Dear Mr. Nelson,

Thank you for your warm expression of sympathy upon the death of Hugh. The pain is lessened by your kind offer to help, which I may accept soon.

Sincerely,

Dear Mrs. Coulson,

Thank you for your thoughtfulness upon the death of my sister, Ellen.

Sincerely,

Dear Mrs. Eberly,

We were pleased to receive your letter of sympathy. It was a comfort to us. Eleanor always mentioned you with the greatest respect and admiration.

Sincerely,

Dear Mr. Franklin,

We appreciate your kind expression of sympathy.

Sincerely,

Dear Jane and Roy,

Thank you so much for the gift of your friendship. It is a great comfort to our family to know that Dad had such good friends at work. The spray of pink carnations you sent was just beautiful.

With appreciation,

Dear Joan,

Thank you so much for your thoughtfulness in sending me the beautiful dwarf pine. I appreciate your caring.

Sincerely,

The Sanford Office Group:

I wish to thank all of you for remembering me in my time of need. The plant you sent is beautiful.

Sincerely,

Ladies and Gentlemen:

On behalf of all of us at Morton, Martin, and Grove, I wish to thank you for your kind expression of sympathy upon the death of our Mr. Allen Rogers.

It is true that we have sustained a shock and a great loss by his sudden passing. We believe the greatest tribute to him will be maintaining the high professional standards he represented and so strongly encouraged.

Very sincerely,

CHAPTER 11

Apology

Writing a letter of apology is an ego-deflating task: You just hate to admit a mistake. Because the other party already knows of the error, the best approach is to take a deep breath and plunge in. To be effective, an apology must be genuine; the regret must be sincere but not overly emotional. To say "I am sorry," "I am truly sorry," or "I am sincerely sorry for my mistake" is a genuine expression of feeling. But to expound "I don't know what to say, but I ask your forgiveness for my terrible error of sending the wrong replacement parts. I know this has slowed your production startup and has probably cost you a lot of money. We are extremely sorry" is just too much for any reader.

In most instances make the statement of apology at the beginning of the letter. It is inconsiderate to the reader to hide the purpose in the middle or at the end. Use the middle of the letter for an explanation of the mistake—if an explanation is deemed necessary. Make the explanation as brief as possible while keeping it clear. Omit long, detailed, or technical explanations. The middle of the letter is also the place to relate what is being done to prevent a recurrence of the mistake, or to thank the reader for being tolerant while a confusing situation is straightened out. If an explanation isn't feasible, don't ramble on saying nothing. The whole letter can say, in effect, "We're sorry; we'll work to avoid repeating the error."

Close a letter of apology on a forward-looking and positive note. If something has been delayed, state the new delivery, completion, or approval date. Make a promise of future promptness and fewer errors. Relay to the reader your confidence that relations will improve.

Sentences of Apology

Here are some statements that will prove helpful when composing a letter of apology:

> We appreciate your patience in allowing us time to research the information and respond to your complaints.

> We are sorry that this is one of the few instances in which we cannot make a refund.

We are sorry for any inconvenience we caused you.

We are proud of our excellent service, and you should expect it at all times. We apologize for our failure and will try not to let this happen again.

We try our best, but occasionally errors do slip by. We will try even harder to prevent future errors.

This is one of a very few areas of loss that Forward Insurance Company does not cover, and we are sorry we are unable to help you in this time of need. We suggest you contact Hanford Insurance of Brooklyn for this type of coverage.

Thank you for your patience while we straightened out the confusion about your order. We are sorry for the inconvenience.

Thanks for staying with us while we contacted all parties involved in this confused situation. Your understanding has helped us clear the many tangled ends.

Again, we are sorry for the inconvenience we caused you.

We appreciate the amount of work you put into your bid, and we are sorry we could not offer you the contract.

For an efficient operation, we have found that our policies must be followed in detail. We are sorry we cannot make an exception for you.

Please accept our apology.

Reasons for an Apology

The following are acceptable reasons for making an apology:

I am sorry I missed our scheduled dinner meeting yesterday in Kansas City. Because of stormy weather there, the plane did not stop over but went directly to Chicago.

I am sorry to hear about the poor printing on your last order. The printer acknowledges the faded-out appearance and will credit you for the full amount.

There was a delay in shipping because the demand exceeded our expectations, and we had to order a second printing.

The delay in shipping was due to a local trucker's strike, and alternate carriers were busy beyond their capacity.

The delay was due to our error, for which we have no excuses, if you cannot use the belts sent, please return them for a full refund.

Please accept our apology. We have no explanation for our obvious error.

Mr. Johnson has been ill for the past week.

An unexpected field trip kept me away from the office.

The Chicago trip required two days more than I anticipated.

Unfortunately, due to my oversight this notice did not go out sooner, and I must apologize.

Mr. Sanders is away for two weeks, but Ms. Lawson will do the report and have it for you as soon as possible, probably by next Wednesday.

We regret the delay in getting copies to you, but our copying machine broke and we had to send your work to another printer.

We are sorry we omitted the samples when we sent your package yesterday. We made the mistake, but the samples are on the way now.

Unexpected developments prevented my being there.

How to Do It

The following sequence is suggested for a genuine, goodwill-retaining letter of apology:

1. Apologize at the beginning of the letter.
2. Explain the error and the determination to prevent further errors.
3. Close on a forward-looking, positive note.

Bad Behavior

Dear Mr. Caronna:

I am sincerely sorry for what happened Wednesday, and especially for my actions. I hope you will accept my apology. Please rest assured that nothing similar will occur again.

Regretfully,

Dear Nadine:

I feel I must make a double apology for the fiasco yesterday at our group's luncheon meeting. I should not have brought hyper little Randy, and I could not control his behavior.

My baby-sitter canceled at the last minute, and I was unable to get another. Then my eagerness to visit all of you overcame my judgment, which told me to phone and apologize for not being able to attend.

I'm sorry for the disturbance I caused and will think more clearly next time. I ask for your forgiveness.

Sincerely,

Dear Angela,

If I seemed to slink away from your delightful cocktail party Friday night rather than thanking you, it was because I was mortified—and still am. I am the one who ripped the back of your new sofa.

I will be out of town until the middle of next week, but will call you as soon as I return. Arrangements can be made for an upholsterer to pick up and repair the damage, and I will pay for it.

I'm terribly sorry for what I did and for your inconvenience. Will talk to you next week.

With regrets,

Dear Ms. Tran:

This is a letter I never expected to write. It is an honest effort to apologize for what I find hard to believe I said to you last evening at the company office party. I've been told what I said, and it makes me so ashamed I'm sick.

I apparently find it hard to adjust to the modern concept of women either having to or choosing to work outside the home. All through my growing-up years, my mother was always there when I needed or wanted her—perhaps she spoiled me a little. I have assumed that her way of taking care of the household and her children was the ideal way. But times have changed, and I haven't kept up.

I admit I consumed too much delicious punch and lost control, but rest assured it will not happen again. I realize that at home or at the office, it is women who keep us men on the right track. Please accept my humble apology.

Sincerely,

Billing Error

Dear Mr. Rodgers:

You are right and we are wrong. We apologize for the error and thank you for calling this to our attention. A corrected bill is enclosed.

Sincerely,

Sorry for the error . . .

We're enclosing for you, Mr. Silva, one invoice not included with your February statement. We are sorry this invoice was omitted. The total of the invoices will now equal the statement amount of $150.65.

We appreciate your being a customer since 1957.

Customer Service Division

Company Policy

Dear Ms. Arthur:

I am sorry we cannot write you a check from our local plant for your past-due freight bill No. 278-089789 as you requested.

We received the copy of the bill on Wednesday, November 21. We have matched it with our purchase order and will mail it today to our headquarters in Detroit for payment.

Although the bill is overdue, because we have not received the original bill, our corporate procedure requires that our headquarters office pay the bill. This procedure speeds payment in practically all instances and includes an audit of all paid freight bills.

You should have your money in less than a week.

Sincerely,

Dear Mr. Melton:

You have excellent qualifications for the supervisory opening in our billing department. However, company policy requires that positions at this level be filled from our existing staff. It is part of our company training program.

I will send your résumé to our human relations department. They may have a staff opening that would interest you. I wish you success in finding a position.

Sincerely,

Dear Mrs. Everidge:

We received your letter about your problem with our portable baking oven/broiler. We are sorry that we cannot refund the purchase price. You have had the oven over two years and the warranty is for only one year, although most of these ovens last ten years.

Repairing this appliance is as costly as buying a new one. If you wish to purchase a new model, you can use the enclosed coupon for a 25 percent discount. We hope this will be satisfactory.

Sincerely,

Confusing Word Usage

Dear Mr. Dunbar:

I want to apologize for not helping to sponsor the TV program on containers and the environment that we discussed last Wednesday. We were favorably inclined until we realized that the word *containers* as you used it meant beer cans, pop bottles, and plastic bottles used to contain thousands of varied products.

In the paper and forest-products industry, the word *containers* means corrugated boxes (often called cardboard boxes).

I hope you understand our confusion and appreciate that we do not wish to help sponsor a program not related to this association's industry.

Sincerely,

Declining Dinner Invitation

Dear Mr. Hamilton:

Julie and I appreciated your invitation to dinner on July 10, and it is with regret that we find we have another engagement on that date.

Thank you for thinking of us.

Sincerely,

Dear Mr. Jones:

Since accepting your kind invitation to dinner and the theater on March 2, I have learned of the serious illness of my mother and I will be leaving for Chicago tomorrow.

I am sorry to have to forgo a delightful evening with you.

Sincerely,

Dear Mr. Parrott:

We are sorry we can't accept your invitation for dinner and the Snappers show on May 3. I have a budget meeting scheduled for that night and there is no way I can skip that meeting.

With regret,

Postponed Appointment

Dear Sonja,

Hope you received my call on your answering machine in time to get another couple for bridge Wednesday afternoon. We had counted on being there, but my sister called from Los Angeles to say Mother is getting worse. We left right away. Perhaps we can get together in a couple weeks. I'll call you when I get home.

Love,

Postponed Dinner

Dear April and Edwin,

I am sorry that the dinner we had planned for May 29 must be postponed. We are still looking forward to helping you celebrate your twenty-fifth wedding anniversary. I will write soon to see what we can arrange in June.

My sister is not expected to survive much longer, and we have been asked to join the family in Cleveland.

Cordially,

Dear Mr. and Mrs. Rulless:

Mr. Webb and I regret that due to the illness of our daughter, the dinner arranged for Friday, September 28 must be postponed.

Regretfully,

Missed Lunch Appointment

Dear Mr. Mobley:

Please accept my apology for not meeting you for lunch Tuesday. At 11:30 our press had a breakdown, and I had to be there to help locate the problem.

Could you have lunch with me on Friday? I don't anticipate any maintenance problems then, and we should be able to enjoy a leisurely lunch.

Sincerely,

Delayed Answer

Dear Ms. Ralston:

Please excuse my delay in answering your letter of February 13, but this has been one of those busy, hectic periods beset with all kinds of deadlines.

I am glad you found some of my survey data useful and look forward to seeing your report on condominium growth in San Diego.

Sincerely,

Dear Mr. Markowitz:

I hope you will forgive the long delay in answering your letter of June 9. We are temporarily understaffed, but we *are* getting inquires answered—although admittedly somewhat slowly.

The information you requested will be mailed early next week. We are happy to send you records of our experience with the Anhold starch maker, which we find exceptionally efficient.

Thank you for your patience.

Sincerely,

Dear Ms. Herlock:

I apologize for not writing sooner about the letter you objected to receiving, which pertains to an unpaid bill for $239.79.

I was away from the office for almost two weeks with a severe cold and have just returned. I checked your account with our bookkeeper, and I am happy to say that you are correct: You don't owe us any money.

The error was caused because we have another customer whose name is Jan Herlock. We are correcting our records.

We apologize for any unpleasantness and concern this may have caused you. We value your goodwill.

Sincerely,

Delayed Credit

Dear Mrs. Sanders:

I am sorry you had to wait so long for your credit of $51.20. We had some difficulty tracing the sale and return of part of the merchandise. The refund check to you is now in the mail. Again, please excuse the delay.

Sincerely,

Dear Ms. Mejia:

Thank you for your recent request for a charge account at Oliver's Department Store. Your confidence in our store is appreciated.

Although we are not in a position to open an account for you just now, we should be able to when your residency has been established for six months.

Meanwhile, please visit us and enjoy the many conveniences of shopping at Oliver's. Remember, too, that cash purchases have no monthly finance charge. Please contact us again in March.

Sincerely,

Delayed Order

Dear Bill:

I don't have any excuse for the delay, and I am truly sorry.

The booklets you ordered are being mailed today, and I'm sure you will find them worth waiting for. I enjoyed working on them for you, but they did take a little more time than I had anticipated.

I would appreciate hearing how well they are received by your clients.

Sincerely,

Dear Mrs. Wiseman:

We regret that the items you ordered on April 12 were not shipped promptly. Because of floods this winter, several products had been moved to a warehouse above the flood waters. Your order will be filled on May 4.

Your patience is greatly appreciated.

Sincerely,

Delayed Paperwork

Dear Ms. Sampson:

Thank you for reminding us of the credit due you. We ran into unexpected delays, but the accounting department has notified me that your check for $51.20 will be in the mail today.

Thank you for your understanding.

Sincerely,

Dear Mr. Harnick:

My apologies to you for not getting the Ward Company freight-claim information to you earlier. I was sent to Chicago to work on a machine installation for six weeks and got back just yesterday.

I called Ward Company this morning, and Mr. Andrews said he had a detailed listing of the expenses for your claim. He will mail a copy to you. If you don't get it by Tuesday of next week, call me and I will follow up with Mr. Andrews.

Again, sorry for the delay.

Sincerely,

Delayed Return of Borrowed Item

Dear Ms. Sanders:

Let me apologize for not returning your folder and two pamphlets on the collection of delinquent accounts.

I have found the information of great benefit but was slower in getting through it than I had promised.

It is really helpful when two credit unions can exchange information.

I hope you haven't been inconvenienced by my delayed return of the data. I thank you so much for you generosity.

Sincerely,

Dear Mrs. Stone:

I'm really sorry I didn't return your book sooner. I put it in the bookcase when I returned home from the hospital and completely forgot about it. The book was just lively enough to keep me in good spirits while spending so much time flat on my back.

I appreciate your lending me this interesting book, and I apologize for keeping it so long.

Sincerely,

Dear Mr. Parker:

Last year's issues of *Business* magazine that you lent me are being returned. I owe you a thank-you as well as an apology for not returning them sooner, as intended.

I found the articles I was looking for and got much useful information from them.

It was kind of you to lend me these magazines, and I hope the delay has not been an inconvenience to you.

Sincerely,

Delayed Thank-You

Dear Mr. Radosta:

Please excuse my delay in thanking you for the interesting visit with you and your staff on July 20 and 21.

I found our contract discussions helpful: We now have a better understanding of your needs. We are on schedule and will have the proposed contract ready for your approval by the end of next week.

Again, thank you for the informational tour.

Sincerely,

Dear Mr. Simon:

Please let me apologize for not writing sooner to thank you for your assistance with the Bradford Associates account while I was in Phoenix. Your previous experience with them proved a great help in putting across my proposal.

Don't hesitate to call me when I can be of some help to you. As they say, I owe you one.

Sincerely,

Indiscretion

Dear Ms. Stamm:

Please forgive us for the indiscreet inquiries we made. After I explain the reasons for the questions we asked, I hope you will accept our apologies.

For open credit of $100,000 that you requested, we investigate our customer's credit potential thoroughly, often following seemingly insignificant leads. Our forty-seven years of experience have proven this to be beneficial to both us and our customers. A customer suffers as much as we do from overextended credit.

We apologize for any inconvenience and hurt we have caused you. You will be glad to learn that your open credit line for $100,000 has been approved.

Sincerely,

Dear Mr. Gonzalez:

I am sorry that we seemed indiscreet in making inquiries about you. Let me explain the reasons and then I hope you will forgive us.

For a life-insurance policy as large as $250,000 we investigate our clients rather closely. Issuing such a policy is a risk to us. To lessen our risk and to ensure our financial stability, we sometimes check references two or three people removed from the references given by you. We have found this to be a sound business policy, and we are sorry for the concern we unintentionally caused you.

You will be pleased to learn that your policy has been approved.

Sincerely,

Ignoring a Customer

Dear Mr. Avery:

I was surprised when I heard that you feel you haven't been getting the same attention you received when we were a smaller company. I was wondering why we hadn't seen you lately.

I am truly sorry if anyone in our organization has been giving you less service than you deserve, since you have been one of our most loyal customers for many years. If this is the case, I offer my personal apology and trust you will give us another chance.

I look forward to seeing you personally the next time you stop in. I would enjoy discussing our business relationship, and I will see to it that you are taken care of to your satisfaction—and incidentally to mine as well. Our relationship has been very pleasant and profitable for both of us, and I would feel hurt—less for business than for personal reasons—if through some fault of ours that relationship were changed in any way. See you soon.

Sincerely,

Incomplete Instructions

Dear Mrs. Wordsworth:

We agree that the blouse you returned shrunk in your washing machine. This particular blouse is not washable although some blouses of similar appearance are. Our sales staff has been instructed to make each customer aware of how each blouse must be cleaned. Sometimes a clerk will forget.

Whether or not this was the case, we are sorry, Mrs. Wordsworth, for the disappointment and inconvenience to you.

Please let me know if you wish a replacement of the blouse or a credit to your account. Above all we want our customers happy.

Sincerely,

Incomplete Project

Dear Mr. McGuire:

We have just discovered that it will be impossible to complete the project for you as we promised.

My colleagues and I spent many hours collecting the data you requested. Most of it was in a car that was stolen, and to date the local police haven't recovered it.

Please accept our sincerest apologies for any inconvenience to you. Enclosed is a refund of your $100 retainer fee.

If our property is recovered soon, we will send the data to you without charge.

Sincerely,

Late Report

Dear Opal:

You're absolutely right; my project report is due this Wednesday, the 7th. I'm embarrassed to say I haven't finished it. In error, I had noted on my calendar that it was due next Wednesday, the 14th. I just confused the dates.

I'll start working on the rest of the report today, and it will be on your desk Monday. In the meantime, is there something I could do to alleviate any problems my lateness may have caused you?

I appreciate your patience.

Sincerely,

Missed Meeting

Dear Mr. Iavell:

Mr. Anderson was called to Houston unexpectedly and asked me to express his regret at not being able to attend your demonstration of the Hasting-Allison process. He was looking forward to an interesting afternoon.

Sincerely,

Dear Mr. Radican:

There is no excuse for my not meeting you for lunch yesterday, or at least getting word to you. I had the appointment written on my calendar, and I was looking forward to the occasion, but somehow I thought our date was for next Thursday. It was just one of those days.

Please forgive me. I am anxious to talk with you and will phone you Tuesday to see if we can arrange a meeting before you leave town. I won't let you down this time.

Cordially,

Dear Miss Pappleton:

This is an apology I feel embarrassed at having to make. I have no excuse for not checking my appointments calendar before dashing off to Denver—even if it was an emergency call.

After looking forward for six weeks to meeting you and discussing your latest research results of the Matson project over lunch. I feel bad about forgetting to even notify you of my absence.

I will call you next week when I return and perhaps we can get together in San Francisco at your convenience.

Please accept my apology.

Sincerely,

Missing a Caller

Dear Ms. Englund:

I am sorry I was out of the office when you called Tuesday. I had told you I would be available any time during the week, but a labor problem at the Northside plant required my presence Tuesday afternoon.

Please phone and let me know when you will be in town again. I'll try to forestall any emergencies that day.

Sincerely,

Project Failure

Dear Mr. Payeras:

I had never before experienced a failure like the Madison project. I assure you it will not occur again. All our people feel bad about it and have reviewed in detail with me the reasons for failure, and, more important, ways of preventing mistakes in the future.

My apology at this time will not undo the past damage, but my regret is sincere, and my efforts in the future will be guided by this experience.

Sincerely,

Quote Error

Hello Mr. and Mrs. Watson:

I am sorry to report this, but I made a mistake on your homeowner's policy. The policy will cost you $428 per year rather than the $379 I told you.

I confused the policies issued by two of the several insurance carriers we write for.

I am sorry for the mistake. You have the option of canceling the policy if you wish, or having us rewrite the policy for coverage that will cost you only $379 per year. Please let me know which you decide.

Kindest regards,

Shipping Error

Dear Mr. Tittensor:

Will you accept our apology? We made an error in putting your shipment of May 22 together. Thank you for calling this to our attention. We work very hard to please our customers, but obviously we must work even harder.

The chair you ordered is being shipped today. You may return the other chair, collect, at your convenience.

Sincerely,

Dear Mrs. Montez:

You are certainly justified in being angry about our blunder in returning the unordered merchandise you had returned to us. Please let me apologize. The error was ours, but it would help us when you return merchandise if you would enclose a note to me or our sales representative stating why it is being returned. This will ensure proper credit to you.

You will receive immediate credit for this returned merchandise and all shipping charges.

Again, I am sorry for the inconvenience to you. We do value your business and your friendship.

Cordially,

Slow Payment

Dear Mr. Allison:

We are sorry to have caused you a financial inconvenience by not paying a group of your invoices sooner. We have had internal problems, but these are resolved now. We will start paying your invoices tomorrow.

You could ensure quicker payment in the future by extending us terms of 1 percent, 10 days. Invoices marked this way are paid as soon as received. Invoices with no payment terms are paid in 30 days.

Again, we are sorry for the past inconvenience, and future payments will be on time.

Very truly yours,

Small Reward

Dear Frank:

It was an exciting year, struggling to overcome our many difficulties. You are given much of the credit for the turnaround toward profitability.

I realize a thank-you is small reward for your diligent work, but next year we expect to make our thank-you more tangible. Meanwhile it's great having you on our team. We are running strong and in the right direction.

Sincerely,

Statement Error

Dear Mr. Wendell:

A corrected statement of your account is enclosed. We are sorry about the error and hope that it didn't cause any great inconvenience. We check every step in our processing of accounts, but even then clerical errors occur at times. Please accept our apologies. And we do appreciate your giving us the opportunity to be of service to you.

Sincerely,

Our Apologies . . .

The finance charge information for the year _ _ _ _ is not printed on this statement, but will appear on your statement next month.

Please use your February, _ _ _ _, statement for income-tax preparation.

Thank you for being our customer.

Sincerely,

Dear Customer:

Hello! Here we are again. We recently mailed you the Statement of Account for your mortgage loan for the year _ _ _ _.

Our face is red because that Statement of Account appeared to have had some errors.

The Revised Statement of Mortgage Account, enclosed, is current and the errors are eliminated. Please review the amounts under Taxes and Interest.

Again, we wish to apologize for any inconvenience our error may have caused you.

Sincerely yours,

Wrong Information

Dear Customer:

OOPS! WE GOOFED!

Our order blank states: "All offers expire April 30, _____." It should read: ALL OFFERS EXPIRE JULY 31, _ _ _ _.

Sincerely,

Sharing the Blame

Dear Bill,

Computers are a technological advance in processing information in a hurry. But even after being debugged the installers won't issue a 100 percent guarantee of no errors.

And that is why you were underpaid for the goods you delivered in March. This is extremely embarrassing, and I sincerely apologize. My computer technicians have been informed that this will *not* happen again.

The money we owe you is enclosed.

To show my sincerity, I'll pay double for any similar errors that occur in the future. You have my word.

Best regards,

CHAPTER 12

Congratulations

We enjoy sharing our enthusiasm and delight with friends who have won awards or have been recognized for outstanding work. This special accomplishment is an occasion for a letter of congratulations, a time to send good wishes. Your friend will appreciate a little boost to his or her ego. If you are writing to a business acquaintance or associate, a letter of congratulations can do much to stimulate cooperation between the two of you or to strengthen an existing good relationship. Goodwill should be nurtured at every opportunity

Many occasions are appropriate for a letter of congratulation: winning a hole-in-one golf tournament, winning a skating championship, receiving a superior rating in a music contest, earning an appointment to an office, doing the best selling job last month, receiving a job promotion, or winning a bride.

Write a letter of congratulation as soon as possible after the event. Six months later, your friend may feel let down that it took you so long to recognize his or her promotion.

Along with your bubbling enthusiasm, sincerity must come through to the reader. Use expressions that would be natural in a conversation with the reader; don't overblow the occasion or smother it with flowery phrases. The tone of the letter, however, will depend on your relationship with the reader. To a staid business acquaintance, straightforward and conservative statements may be appropriate, while to a sorority sister or fraternity brother, jocular informality may be just the thing.

Now for the easy part: Make the congratulatory letter brief; from three to six sentences is sufficient.

How to Do It

1. State the occasion for the congratulation in the first sentence.
2. Make a comment that links the person and the occasion.
3. Write or imply your expectation of continued success.

Sales Volume

Dear Bob,

Your successful sales efforts have secured an annual sales volume of $1 million from Amsterdam, Inc.

My congratulations to you for this fine job. As you know, business conditions being what they are, the Amsterdam account is doubly important. Keep up the good work!

With best regards,

Dear Tanya,

Congratulations on establishing a new sales-volume record in the month of March. I recognize that this is the result of work done during the past year by your sales staff, but it looks great on our financial records, and I know you played a big part by inspiring your sales staff.

Sincerely,

New Customer

Congratulations, Jim—

on securing this new account!

I know you worked hard on this one, and it is great that you were able to close the deal before being transferred out of the territory.

Again, let me say, "A job well done."

Regards,

Author Appreciation

Dear Miss Garland,

Your new book, *Dinners from the Deep South*, has a well-deserved place on the current best-seller list. I was delighted with your choices of recipes and am recommending the book to all my friends. How about more on the cooking secrets of various regions?

Sincerely,

Job Well Done

Dear Rick:

GREAT!

Sincerely,

(Rick, a salesman, knew this referred to his obtaining a new account following three years of hard work.)

Dear Mr. Navratil:

I would like to congratulate you and your people for the fine job you did reducing our raw-materials inventory in the past three months.

This result, so effectively presented by the graphs Vic Jones prepared, turned out to be the high point during the recent manager's meeting.

I would appreciate receiving these graphs each month.

Sincerely,

Dear Joe:

Please note the attached copy of Mr. Robinson's letter of congratulation.

To it I wish to add my own congratulations for the outstanding achievement in inventory reduction.

Keep up the good work.

Sincerely,

Top Salesperson

Dear Janet,

Congratulations on being the #1 salesperson in the Northwest sales group last month. Your volume and the gross-margin dollars were the highest for any November in the company's history.

Good luck in December,

Dear Fern,

A general announcement was made today by Maloney Ford that you received the much-sought-after award of Salesperson of the Year. Congratulations! It is a well-deserved honor, and I am happy for you. I'm also proud to be a co-worker and close friend.

When our schedules permit, let's get together for a personal celebration. I'll bet you win this award again.

Regards,

Exceeding Goal

Dear Joe,

My congratulations to you and the sales force for having surpassed our goal for the year _ _ _ _ on scrap recovered from our customers. During the month of October we collected 485 tons, which amounts to 5,800 tons on an annualized basis. This is well in excess of our 4,000 ton goal.

Regards,

College Acceptance

Dear Flo,

I am exceedingly pleased that you were accepted by Harvard University. Only a small number of applicants can boast of that honor.

Even Harvard will be thankful to have you, considering that the University of Southern California offered you a full four-year tuition and living-expense scholarship.

Congratulations!

All the best,

Graduation

Dear Jack,

Congratulations! and an extra hurrah for making the top ten! Our family is proud of you.

We regret, Jack, that earlier commitments prevent our attending your graduation ceremonies.

Best wishes for continued success as you start your new career.

Sincerely,

Dear Mrs. Takarli,

We just heard that Patricia graduated from the University of California at Berkeley with honors. You must be extremely proud of her accomplishments, and I am happy right along with you.

Please give Patricia our best wishes for continued success as she enters law school (. . . pursues her career.)

Sincerely,

Dear Lynn,

I was delighted to receive the announcement of your graduation from Stanford. Congratulations on your well-earned degree.

My blessings go with you as you face a new career and new challenges.

Cordially,

College Degree

Dear Howard,

Your long years of study, practice, playing, and teaching have finally won you a coveted Master of Arts degree in music from Mills College. My hearty congratulations on an honor that does not come easily. The degree will certainly enhance your opportunities for teaching; you are already widely recognized as one of the best.

Keep up the good work; we are all proud of you.

Best regards,

Dear Wally,

Congratulations on your graduation from Arizona State University's School of Fine Arts with a major in advertising design.

It was a long, hard pull going to school while working for your bread and butter. But you made it with honors and have already found a job in your field.

We are proud of your accomplishments. Again, congratulations.

Best of luck,

Specialized Teacher

Dear Jean,

Congratulations on your graduation! I understand you already have a position teaching sight-impaired children. It is most encouraging to you, I am sure, having the opportunity to apply your specialized training so soon. With your interest in children, you and they will surely have a pleasant learning experience.

I am confident you are equal to the unusual challenge.

With best wishes,

Handicapped

Dear Kathy,

You'd be the last one to want special recognition for graduating from college, but with your disability you deserve the highest praise for your accomplishment.

Your hard work and courage will carry you far in this world. You are a heartening example to many others.

Sincerely,

New Position

Dear Mike:

Congratulations on your new position as an aeronautical design engineer. You must be glad to get back to a familiar line of work. Around here, we will miss your cheerful personality and most sorely miss your willingness to help in any problem areas.

Please stop by any time you are in town: we don't want to forget you.

Again, congratulations,

Promotion

Dear Otto:

Congratulations on your first promotion. Now you know your hard work has been recognized and accepted by the company. This is a positive sign that you are on your way up, and it couldn't happen to a more deserving person. I look forward to congratulating you on your next promotion.

Best regards,

(See also Chapter 8, Employment: Congratulations on Promotion.)

Service Award

Dear Marge,

I quite agreed with the members of the Golden Years Club when they honored you with this year's Special Service Award.

You have made many contributions to the club—and to this community with your long hours of dedicated work—a beautiful example of unselfish love.

We are all proud of you.

Sincerely,

Five Years

Dear Andy Colfax:

Five years of service with Jacobs Company deserves recognition. The continued success of our company depends on loyal employees who pull together. Your work and loyalty are appreciated.

Your five-year pin will be presented at the general-office meeting on February 26 when several others will join you in receiving service awards.

In another five years, I hope to see you receive your ten-year pin.

Sincerely,

Twenty Years

Dear Eleanor,

Congratulations on your twentieth anniversary with Fibre Containers.

Your steady progress is a result of your many accomplishments, but the one that stands out is your success in getting cooperation from co-workers as well as subordinates.

We would find it difficult, Eleanor, to get along without you. Best wishes for many more rewarding years with us.

Sincerely,

Golf Tournament

Dear Tony,

Congratulations on winning the company golf tournament. A champion manager can also be a champion golfer. Keep up the good work.

Sincerely,

Industry Award

Dear Mr. Miles:

Let me congratulate you on winning the Hartford Award! Your leadership in our industry has long been known to many of us, and I am happy to see you receive the nationwide recognition you have earned by your years of diligent work.

Best regards,

Retirement

Dear Kevin,

The good news: Congratulations on a well-earned retirement after 42 years on the job. You can snooze on the patio, lob a few tennis balls, walk in the park, and sleep in every morning.

The bad news: After a month or two of this you will be bored almost to tears. Fear not: There is an unlimited variety of volunteer activities in schools, playgrounds, retirement centers, hospitals, day-care centers, and on and on to keep you healthy and alert for many years. Enjoy!

Best regards,

(See also Chapter 8, Employment: Congratulations on Retirement.)

President of Rotary

Dear Mr. Briney:

It was a pleasure to read in last night's *City Ledger* of your election as president of Rotary.

Let me offer my sincere congratulations upon your receiving this honor. I wish you success in your new office.

Sincerely,

Anniversary

Dear Mary and Joe,

Congratulations on your anniversary!

May the past happy memories be a prelude to future memories.

Happy Anniversary,

Dear Marilyn and Andrew,

Congratulations on 50 years of a loving relationship. They say all it takes for a long life is good genes. And I'll bet you say it takes attention to your health and consideration for your spouse. We are happy for you.

With love,

Honorary Sorority

Dear Joan,

So you made the Honorary Sorority! Congratulations to a hard working (as well as bright) young woman. I know your pleasing personality played a large part, too.

Best wishes for the continuing scholastic achievements I know you will earn.

Cordially,

President of Association

Dear Mr. Ramsey:

My hearty congratulations to you on your election to the presidency of the Western Management Association. Your election is earned tribute from your colleagues and is recognition of the outstanding work you have done for the Association and for your profession.

The Association chose the right man in my opinion. Best wishes for success in your new position.

Sincerely,

Store Opening

Dear Steve,

Congratulations on opening your own auto-repair and -parts store. I found you the best mechanic, as well as the most pleasant and accommodating, at your previous location. I know you will soon have a large following for both your repair service and your parts department.

I'm glad you decided to set out on your own.

Best wishes for success,

Dear Andy,

Congratulations on the opening of your own hardware store! I know it has been a dream of yours for many years. With your know-how and willingness to work, there is no reason why you shouldn't have a booming business in a short time.

We are happy to see you make the big step.

Good luck,

Dear Mr. Sanders:

You are invited to the opening of Ballad Books, the new store at Fourth and Ballad, on July 10, _ _ _ _ , from 9 A.M. to 9 P.M.

The overwhelming collection of books in all categories—from children's stories to chemical research—will be introduced with entertainment: balloons and candy for the children, hot dogs and pop for teenagers, coffee and sweet rolls for adults, and clowns and three live bands for everyone.

We will feature sizable discounts on all books purchased opening day.

Please join us.

Your new friends at Ballad Books,

City Councilperson

Dear Rona,

Congratulations on your election to Concord City Council. I am pleased that we now have a financial expert in our city government. We can look forward to a closer scrutiny of fiscal matters, something we have needed for a long time.

Sincerely,

Loan Paid

Dear Mr. Crown:

Congratulations!

We are pleased to notify you that you have fully paid the enclosed loan.

Now, why not continue making regular payments into one of our savings accounts? You have already discovered a convenient, safe place to save money—and be paid for saving it—and a friendly place to borrow money at a low interest rate.

Sincerely,

Engagement

Dear Dawn,

It's wonderful that you and Tony are engaged.

Congratulations! A more compatible couple would be hard to find. I am sure your marriage will be even happier than your engagement—and much longer lasting. The best to both of you.

With love,

Marriage

Dear Andrew,

Congratulations on your marriage.

Let me wish you and your bride your full share of happiness as the years go on.

Sincerely,

Dear Alice,

It is somehow hard to believe you are no longer the pretty little girl down the street, but have already grown up to become a happy bride.

Please congratulate your husband for me and tell him I think he is most lucky.

You both have my best wishes for a long and happy life together.

Affectionately,

Adoption

Dear Mavis and Milton,

At long last, through miles of red tape and years of waiting, you and Barbara are a family. Congratulations. She will add so much meaning and love to your already strong relationship. I am happy for all three of you.

The best for the future,

New Home

Dear Alice and Ed,

Congratulations on the purchase of your new home. Your family activities will be more comfortable in this larger house, and I understand you now have four bedrooms. I'm sure you will be happier, and that makes me happy.

Our best wishes,

Happy Birthday

Dear Bob,

Congratulations, new driver, on having arrived at that long-awaited age: 16. Now you can be on your own and free as the birds—except for that mass of other cars clogging the roads.

Take care and enjoy the new driving experience.

Your Buddy,

CHAPTER 13

Thank-You and Appreciation

A thank-you letter should be sincere, expressing appreciation without excessive flattery. The tone should be pleasant. Clearly state what the thank-you is for and, if appropriate, offer something in return.

Business people appreciate receiving a thank-you letter because it adds a touch of warmth to the cold world of business. The letter reveals consideration and appreciation. Large manufacturers often receive letters from students asking about products, processes, or procedures. These are usually answered with pamphlets, brochures, and letters from production managers or administrative executives. One corporate executive complained that after sending large quantities of printed material and innumerable letters, no thank-you letters were received. He lamented that even a postcard saying, "Thank-you for the materials," would have shown consideration for his company's efforts. The goodwill of your company, and also of yourself, can be enhanced by a letter of thanks.

A thank-you letter should be short. The sincerity of the thank-you is emphasized by brevity. Basically, all that need be said is, "Thank-you for this," or "Thank-you for that." A long thank-you letter may be a sales letter in disguise, or it may be loaded with unnecessary flattery, lowering the reader's opinion of the party sending the letter.

Pleasantness is another requirement of a good thank-you letter. One way to accomplish this is with an informal opening, for instance:

Enjoyed meeting with you and appreciate the time given to Don and me.

Just a "thank-you" for being a customer this past year.

Any harsh thoughts or words should be eliminated, because their inclusion will completely destroy the purpose of the letter, which is to show gratitude for help that has been given.

While thanking a person for something he or she has done, it is often possible to return more than just words of thanks. This will emphasize the writer's gratitude. When a person has spent time showing you his or her company's operation or the sights of the city, offer to do the same when that person visits your company or city. When giving thanks for information received, it would be appropriate to relay how the information is being used; for example:

The sketch fits so well in our den.

I would never have heard of the exhibit otherwise.

Your suggestion led to this fabulous job.

Your recent payment clears your longstanding debt.

Your work made it possible for us to catch up.

The information is exactly what I need for my report.

Your suggestions enabled us to increase our machine speed 20 percent.

When an organization has helped your group in some way, volunteer your group's help as a return favor.

Thanking someone for a favor indicates polite manners and is good business practice. But thanking in advance is considered, by some authorities in the use of the English language, an objectionable habit. For example, it is common to write:

Send the completed project to Mr. A. B. Andrews at Headquarters by September 15.

Thank you.

This seems to imply to the reader that the project was of so little importance that a thank-you for an excellent and timely submission will not be worth the effort of writing again. To overcome this possible adverse reaction by the reader, start the letter with, "Will you please" or "I would appreciate your sending . . ." or "Please." An alternative is to open the letter with a paragraph stating appreciation, for example:

Your sending this project to Headquarters by the 15th of September will be greatly appreciated.

Your sending this freight bill to Friedman, Inc., is greatly appreciated.

Sending me the samples will be truly appreciated.

Your cooperation and hard work on this project is really appreciated by us.

When a letter expressing thankfulness is appropriate, a prompt answer will make the reader aware of your thoughtfulness. Three months later, the reader shouldn't be reminded that he or she had been piqued by not having received a deserved note of thanks.

While writing the letter, assume an attitude of polite sincerity.

How to Do It

1. State what the thank-you is for.
2. Mention the appropriateness of what was received.
3. Be sincere, brief, and pleasant.
4. When appropriate, offer something in return.

Gift

Dear Friends in Albany,

My heartfelt thanks (no pun intended) for the beautiful terrarium you sent while I was in the hospital for heart bypass surgery. It will remind me for years how nice friends can be.

Sincerely,

An alternate last sentence might be:

It will remind me for years of my many friends in Albany.

Dear Mrs. Orland,

Thank you for the wedding gift. I have the black ceramic vase on my mantel. It is always nice to receive an item unique to a certain part of the country. It has a history of its own, and we love it.

Cordially,

Dear Al,

The little brass travel alarm clock is exactly what we needed. Now Peter won't have to phone the hotel desk—which he often forgets to do—when he is on the road. He likes the way the alarm starts softly then keeps on getting louder. Thanks again; it's a wonderful gift.

Cordially,

Pamphlet

Ladies/Gentlemen:

Thank you for the illustrated pamphlet on personnel forms. We are considering changes in our personnel reporting and will find the samples useful.

Sincerely,

Information

Dear Marge,

Thank you for your letter and the announcement of an antiques dealers' convention in New England. I would not have learned of the meeting otherwise. It was nice of you to take the time to send it when you knew I would be interested.

I'll see you there.

Cordially,

Materials Received

Dear Mr. Latter:

Thank you for the brochure *Trees Are Forever*. It contains exactly what I need for a speech I am preparing.

Sincerely,

Thank you . . .

For your interest in our Plain English Multicover Policy. I am pleased to enclose an information kit for your review.

Cordially,

Advice

Dear Mr. Manning:

You helped me a great deal with my future plans only six years ago as we sat in your office working to eliminate my frustrating uncertainty.

I took your advice—probably the best thing I ever did. Since then I have advanced several times with this company. The cooperation of the people here is better than I should really expect. I am sure my future is here.

I want to express my sincere gratitude for your consultation and help and to wish you and your family a happy holiday season.

Cordially,

Personal Support

Dear Vivian,

How can I possibly thank you enough for your constant support during my traumatic separation and divorce. You suggested trips to take, you suggested groups to join, you invited me to accompany you and your friends in various activities, you had faith in me, and you listened while I talked out my tensions.

You helped me when I needed help.

Faithfully,

Recommendation

Dear Ellis:

Just a short thank-you for the recommendation you gave me yesterday. Your well-chosen words were a big boost in getting me the transfer I wanted.

I sincerely appreciate your help.

Regards,

Dinner Invitation

Dear Tim,

It was certainly a privilege to be with you and your friends at the excellent Service Club dinner last night. Tom Powers had a message to give, and he gave it superbly.

Thanks ever so much for inviting me!

Sincerely,

Recognition

Dear Jan,

Thank you for mentioning my Music Teacher's Conference award. It is a great feeling to receive recognition for work covering a period of years, and I appreciate your mentioning it in your daily column.

Sincerely,

Dear Jeff,

Thank you for mentioning my Music Teacher's award in your column. The award means a great deal to teachers and I appreciate your giving it public recognition.

Sincerely,

Going-Away Party

Dear Lois,

Frank and I are most appreciative of the dinner party given for us last Saturday. We really enjoyed your efforts, the good drinks, the good food, the friendly chats—and the bridge cards.

Leaving a group of such good neighbors and friends after 15 years fills us with a puzzling mixture of nostalgia and appreciation.

We will try to get back from time to time, but meanwhile, our phone number is 000-000-0000.

Sincerely,

Hospitality

Dear Yvette,

I wish to thank you and Alan for your kind hospitality during my three days in Tucson. I thoroughly enjoyed the short trips to the city's points of interest and the evening meal at your beautiful home.

Perhaps we can get together for another visit at next year's sales meeting in Las Vegas.

Again, thank you.

Cordially,

Dear Annabelle,

Spending a whole weekend beside your pool with your friends, the Worthingtons, was most interesting, as you suggested it would be. The Worthingtons' stories of their trips to South Africa were so stimulating that I have been reviewing an old history book about the settlement of that area. Again, thanks for a wonderful time.

Love,

Dear Carl and Ellen,

It was wonderful of you to invite a "new couple on the block" to your party last Saturday. Ted and I were made to feel welcome and not at all like strangers. We appreciate your introducing us to your friends and our new neighbors.

You are gracious hosts, and we hope to reciprocate before long. It was a delightful evening.

Cordially,

Companionship

Dear Katy,

This gift is only a token of how much your friendly companionship this summer has meant to me.

There will always be love in my thoughts of you.

With affection,

Friendship

Dear Don,

This gift is just a small thank-you for the friendship you showed me this summer.

I will always think of you as a kind friend who took a real interest in both my work and play.

Sincerely,

Dear Sandy,

You have that rare knack of making strangers feel right at home. Sharing your friends with me yesterday certainly made a newcomer feel like a comfortable old-timer. I know I will like this friendly city, and I hope Ron and I will be here for a long time.

Thank you so much for all you have done for us.

Sincerely,

Book Loan

Dear Lorraine,

I'm glad you nearly insisted I read the new book you got for your birthday. I had never read a story of such an exciting but probably illegal medical procedure.

It was a real page turner; thanks again.

Cordially,

Dear Brad,

Thank you for letting me use your Mechanical Drawing textbook during my course at the Byron Technical School. Your book made several procedures clear that were not covered by other texts.

I mailed the book back to you yesterday.

Regards,

Appreciation

Dear Tommy,

It was thoughtful of you to write me and let me know how much you enjoy working at Exxon. It really doesn't surprise me, because I well remember your enthusiasm as well as your record here at the University—and also your popularity among the students. I was glad to be of help in setting your career course.

Kindest regards and best wishes for your continued success.

Cordially,

Dear Mr. Takemoto:

Your letter of appreciation for my work on the recent project was warmly received. It was a time of struggle for both of us. If you need any data from me during my short absence, please call and leave a message. I will be able to pick it up in the evenings.

See you in November.

Sincerely,

Dear Dave,

Thank you for your letter of appreciation for my work during the past year. It was generous of you to give me so much credit for the company's operating improvements.

Our struggles and difficulties certainly added interest to the year's activities. I do enjoy working with and for you and am sure next year will be economically better for the company.

Sincerely,

Fond Memories

Dear Aunt Ella,

Thank you so much for sending me the Brownsville, Oregon, newspaper of March 1, 1997, with the headline article about the restoration of Shedd's 103-year-old United Presbyterian Church. The building, because of its declining congregation, was sold in the 1960s and turned into an antiques shop. In 1997 it was rededicated as the Valley Rose Chapel and is available for weddings, reunions, and meetings.

The article brought back fond memories of my attending that church in my teens and becoming a member. Mother told me she was married, and I was baptized in the original building.

With love,

Dear Mrs. Alvarez,

We had always wanted to see Daffodil Hill in the spring—the whole hillside of yellow blossoms was beautiful. We fully enjoyed our visit and thank you again for your invitation to join you and for the lovely brunch at your home.

Cordially,

Illness

Dear Fred:

Thank you for the letter you wrote to me while I was in the hospital. It really helped to brighten my days.

I am now back to work on a half-day schedule, but will be working full time next week. The operation went well and the recovery period gave me a chance to relax. I was a little disappointed though that the office got along so well without me.

When you are in Los Angeles again, please stop by and we can share a couple of hours over lunch.

Sincerely,

Dear Nadine,

No one but you would have thought of having a comic card delivered each Sunday during my convalescence. What a terrific morale booster. You are so thoughtful.

With love,

Dear Church Members,

I wish to express my deep appreciation to the members of the Congregation for their cards, phone calls, flowers, and personal visits during my recent hospital stay.

Cordially,

Dear Church Members,

My sincere thanks to the members of Riverside Church for their prayers, visits, and support during my recent surgery. Your friendship is overwhelming but comforting.

Thank you all,

Dear Temple Members,

My special thanks to Rabbis Sidney and Frank for their visits and prayers during Fran's extended home confinement.

Also, the many visits by friends and their gifts of food, flowers, books, and cards helped to lighten her daily burdens. There seems to be no end to the heartfelt warmth of this Congregation. Both Fran and I are sincerely appreciative.

Bless you,

Caregiver

Dear Gallen,

Thank you for the frequent and loving help you give Dad. He enjoys your visits a great deal because they get his mind off his aches and pains and disability. Your visits also give me a respite from the constant attention he needs. I am delighted to have a little time for myself now and then to relax my emotions and recharge my spirits.

Many thanks,

Family Crisis

Dear Cynthia and George,

I find it hard to believe all you have done for us since Alan was so badly injured.

You have assumed the family chores and duties: getting the children fed, sending them to school, bringing them home from after-school activities, putting them to bed, cooking our meals, and doing the household chores. It has been a wonderful relief for me.

Your help has left me time to concentrate on the myriad details of hospital care, rehab care, police reports, insurance reports, and attorney contacts.

I hope I will some day be able to repay all your help.

Affectionately,

Job Well Done

Dear Andy,

Just a note to let you know that your hard work during the past year has been sincerely appreciated.

I hope that you and Theresa enjoy a happy holiday season and vacation in the West. You both deserve a good rest, and I trust the weatherman will cooperate to make your stay in Phoenix truly relaxing.

Cordially,

Dear Jim,

We know you will be pleased to hear that your June sales broke all previous records. It's great to have you on our team.

Sincerely,

Dear Mr. Ludwig:

Your decision to retire as director of Ableson Corporation has been received with deep regret by the directors and officers of the Corporation.

Leaving after nearly half a century is not easy, but during your tenure you played an important part in doubling our market coverage. Your annual market-survey trips endeared you to many throughout the corporation.

I look upon your retirement as a real personal loss. Your example and counsel has been most beneficial to my work as officer and director. For that I thank you.

I sincerely hope that your retirement from many years of cares and tensions will be a pleasant experience for you.

Cordially,

Dear Mr. and Mrs. Washington:

Your daughter, Shamira, has worked for us for six months now. I thought that you would like to know that she is doing a remarkable job, and we are extremely pleased with her work attitude.

Shamira is a credit to you, her parents. We are proud of her, and we know you are too.

Sincerely,

Dear Frank:

It was an exciting year, struggling to overcome our many difficulties. You are given much of the credit for the turnaround toward profitability.

I realize that a thank-you is small reward for your diligent work, but next year we expect to make our thank-you more tangible. Meanwhile, it's great having you on our team. We are running strong and in the right direction.

Sincerely,

Being Our Customer

Dear Mr. Smith:

Just a thank-you for being a customer this past year.

We want you to know we appreciate the business you have given us, and we hope to continue serving you during the coming year.

With regards from

Hamilton's Heavy Hardware,

Dear Mr. Choo:

Thank you for your confidence shown by placing your first large order for lumber with us. Building your own home can be a frustrating experience, but we are prepared to help you by supplying first-grade building materials, reasonably priced hardware, and the necessary credit.

We can also provide help in design, time-saving installation techniques, and a selection of specialists for jobs that are beyond your experience.

Call us for any home-building suggestions you need.

Best regards,

Thank you—

I want to let you know how much we value your business. The prompt manner in which you maintain your account makes it a pleasure to do business with you.

I hope Ralph's can continue to serve your motoring needs for many years to come.

Sincerely,

Charge-Account Convenience

Dear Mrs. Shapiro:

Thank you for the opportunity to add you to the growing number of satisfied charge account customers of Long's Department Store.

The privileges of a charge account are many. You have 25 days to enjoy your purchases before paying for them. You are notified of special sales before a general announcement is made: and often, by presenting the mailed announcement, you may purchase sale items a day or two before the sale officially begins. Special delivery and layaway services are open to charge-account customers. When you wish to place an order by phone, or want a special favor, please mention your charge card and just ask. We are always pleased to do a little extra for the convenience of Long's customers.

Sincerely,

Dear Mrs. Mouritsen:

Thank you for requesting a charge account at Ansell's. Your credit has been approved, and you may use the enclosed charge card at any time. It will add convenience and enjoyment to your shopping.

You will be pleased with the fine-quality merchandise and pleasant service always available at Ansell's.

Sincerely,

Loan

Dear Preston,

I appreciate beyond my ability to thank you for your loan last year. It got me out of a rough personal jam and thereby probably saved my new business venture.

The first payment on the loan is enclosed, and I'll make monthly payments until the loan and interest are cleared.

Your thankful pal,

Dear Rachel,

Thank you for your final loan payment. I know you benefited from having the money when you desperately needed it, and I appreciate receiving your prompt and steady repayment checks. I was glad to help a good friend.

Cordially,

Sales Presentation

Dear Mr. Wyley:

The "shoe-box size" package you lost and inquired about in your letter of June 7 was found behind a chair in the lobby.

We are happy to return it to you via United Parcel and wish to thank you again for your informative presentation of your computer line.

Sincerely,

Accounting Help

Dear John:

Thank you for coming to San Jose Wednesday to help us straighten out our accounts with you. We have been shorthanded for several months and just couldn't seem to get our payables accounts right. Your help in reconciling the differences got us on top of the work, and I beieve we can keep our records in agreement with yours from now on.

Again, thank you for your help.

Sincerely,

Payment

Dear Mr. Evers:

Thank you for your payment of $327.80. This clears your delinquent account.

We appreciate your cooperation and look forward to serving you again.

Sincerely,

Dear Mr. Jones:

Thank you for your partial payment of $200. This leaves only $92.40, which will be due in 30 days. By making this payment on time, your account will be open again.

We look forward to having you as an open-account customer again.

Sincerely,

Referral

Dear Mrs. Mayer:

Thank you for referring Peter Seller to me for an eye examination. I certainly appreciate your thoughtfulness and want to assure you that your confidence in me will be justified.

If at any time in the future I may again be of service to you, please feel free to call me.

Once again, thank you for referring Mr. Seller.

Sincerely,

Attending

Dear Mr. Ronald:

Thank you for attending our meeting last Thursday and for sharing your suggestions based on your long years of experience. Being new, our group found your suggestions and recommendations extremely helpful.

We hope we can return the favor by doing something for your group. Please call when we can assist in any way.

Sincerely,

Dear Mr. Alberts:

The Business Elders group wishes to thank you for your inspiring remarks at our dinner last Wednesday. You gave us some good ideas that we will discuss at our next regular meeting, and I believe we can successfully act on some of them.

We will let you know the outcome of your ideas. The dinner committee is already planning to ask you to speak again.

Cordially,

Visiting

Dear Mr. and Mrs. Lyons:

Thank you for visiting Highland Estates.

If I may be of any help, please call me.

My home phone is 000-0000, and my office phone is 000-0000.

Sincerely,

Dear Bill:

Enjoyed meeting with you and appreciate the time given to Don Allen and me on such short notice.

As we discussed, we are going to pursue the problems you are encountering with various materials you purchased from us. We anticipate that when you visit our mill in the near future, our technical people will have some answers.

Thanks again for the time and courtesies shown Don and me.

Sincerely,

Dear Mr. Gundersen:

I really enjoyed my visit with you during my recent trip west. You were more than considerate to rearrange your schedule on such short notice and to spend the afternoon with me.

When you come to Chicago next time be sure to call me, and we can have another pleasant visit.

With regards,

CHAPTER 14

Other Business Letters

Only the imagination of the reader can limit the number of categories for business and personal letters. It is hoped that the variety this books presents and suggests is enough to fulfill your needs. Many letters fit neatly into more than one category; a little thumbing through related areas may turn up just what you need. Perhaps parts of different letters can be combined to provide one better suited to your need.

Regardless of how the letter is classified, remember that it is the reader who must play the starring role. Forget I and me and we: think *you*. Give full consideration to the feelings of the reader. Be pleasant and sincere. Revealing an attitude of sincerity is the art of writing a letter that accomplishes its purpose. Along with attitude, correct technical aspects of word usage will help the reader respond positively to your letter.

GOODWILL

A letter of goodwill is basically a low-pressure sales letter—low pressure because no particular product or service is being pushed, only a friendly relationship. The letter can also be thought of as a public-relations gesture—something that is often neglected with good, steady customers—or as a reaching out for a kindly feeling of approval and support. If we express kindly thoughts toward our customers and friends, we hope to receive consideration (and increased business) in return. The expressions or impressions of goodwill may be combined with a thank-you, appreciation, request, apology, regrets, or just pleasant thoughts.

The letter can vary in length from a short statement of appreciation to the several paragraphs appropriate for a year-end holiday-season letter. A combination of the occasion and the mood of the letter writer will determine the length, but don't overburden the reader.

Goodwill is not a one-time thing, but a continuing relationship. With this in mind, do not make the letter a conclusive statement, but indicate a desire to continue the friendship. For example, the model letter headed

Sales Agreement Ended expresses regrets that a customer has ended a sales agreement, but the writer is not ready to admit that this is a lasting decision. He ends the letter with the upbeat, "I know our paths will continue to cross in the future."

How to Do It

1. Begin with a complimentary or pleasant statement.
2. Make a comment that relates to or expands upon the first statement.
3. Express anticipation of continued good relations or of a future meeting.

Seasons Greetings

Dear Mr. Anderson:

Do you recall some of your childhood fantasies? A high tree stump would be your throne; you were king or queen of all you surveyed, and everyone obeyed your wishes no matter how whimsical. The rays of a sunset would glisten from the walls of your make-believe castle. The snow-covered ground was your peaceful paradise, completely void of screaming kids and demanding parents.

These imagined experiences are a part of growing up, and the rewards of their success seem real.

The display of lights, the warmth of fireplaces, the trimming of the tree, the preparation for Santa's descent down the chimney, or the glow of Hanukkah candles all become a part of our children's fantasies. But the gathering of families to celebrate love and being together is no fantasy.

My wish for you this year is that as your children's imagination—and yours— dances freely this holiday season, you will appreciate the reality of your family's love.

Cordially,

Good Work

Dear Frank:

It was an exciting year, struggling to overcome our many difficulties. You are given much of the credit for the turnaround toward profitability.

I realize that a thank-you is a small reward for your diligent work, but next year we expect to make our thank-you more tangible. Meanwhile, it's great having you on our team. We are running strong and in the right direction.

Sincerely,

Free Bulletin

Dear Miss Conrad:

Here's a copy of our latest news bulletin. I think this one will keep you completely informed about our industry. Other publications lack many of the special features that we include.

If you'd like to receive it monthly, just drop me a note and I'll put your name on our mailing list—no charge to you.

Sincerely,

Golf Invitation

Dear Bart,

We enjoyed having you with us Saturday.

Since I know you will forgive the photography, I am enclosing some pictures of you and Ray at the Yacht Club.

If you happen to be in the Bay Area and have time for a game of golf, please let me know and maybe we can get together at the Westlake Course.

Sincerely,

To a Salesperson's Spouse

Dear Mrs. Wentling:

Welcome to the Sun Ray Distributors family.

As the wife of one of our new salespersons, you become a part of our growing family. We are pleased to welcome you.

We are a new company, but the selling and installation of solar heating systems is expanding rapidly, making the potential for growth almost unlimited.

We know Ted Wentling will play a large part in our growth. He was carefully selected as one who will dig in now to get us going and continue his enthusiasm as he participates in our growth.

We have a quality product to sell; our engineering consultants made sure of that, and our growing list of satisfied customers points to the truth of their findings.

As will all salespersons in a new position, Ted will find a few tough spots and discouragements at first, but we have found that wives are a real source of understanding, encouragement, and cheer during the initial period of adjustment to a new job.

Ted will also find you a help in entertaining an occasional customer and in recognizing that selling is not a straight 8-to-5 job. Some late hours will be required as well as a small amount of traveling.

We are sure that these few inconveniences will be worked into your time schedule and you will derive pride and satisfaction from contributing to Ted's success with Sun Ray.

Sincerely,

Sales Agreement Ended

Dear Ben:

We are sorry to learn of your desire to terminate our sales agreement, which has been in effect for nine years. We can understand your position and appreciate the reasons.

Although nothing was said in your letter, I assume you wish this agreement to terminate as of October 22, _ _ _ _, without the ninety-day cancellation notice mentioned in the contract.

It has been a pleasure to work with you, Ben, and although our formal arrangement is terminated, I know our paths will continue to cross in the future.

Sincerely,

Enjoyed Meeting You

A candidate for an elective office made a personal visit. The candidate follows up with a goodwill note.

Dear John:

I enjoyed meeting you this past weekend.

Sincerely,

Real-Estate Service

Dear Mr. Trebes:

Just a note to thank you for inquiring about our real-estate service in Detroit. We have both residential and commercial departments there. We can help you find a location for your business and for your home.

Please give us a call at 000-0000 when you make your final decision about the move. We are always glad to make suggestions and show you the area.

Sincerely,

Requested Information

Dear Dan:

It was a pleasure meeting you on my recent visit to San Diego. My wife and I always enjoy ourselves on a return visit. The changes in the city leave us in awe as we remember the "old home town" of the 1940s.

I will look forward to receiving your mailings on scuba-diving trips to Mexico. It is a certainty that some members of our household will be participating in this activity.

My family anticipates spending two weeks in San Diego during Easter. If you are about, I will be happy to share a pitcher of Margaritas.

Best regards,

Sending Information

Dear Donna,

I meant to send the enclosed brochure sooner, but my travels and my secretary's vacation put us behind in our correspondence.

The brochure examines some of the latest changes in adhesive making. Most of the ideas won't be refined for sometime yet, but these new chemical approaches sound interesting. Perhaps some day we can get our raw material costs low enough to make a decent profit.

Best regards,

Making Contribution

Dear Mr. Haggard:

I have provided medical treatment for many of the disabled children since my arrival in City two years ago. I have found them to be very courteous and responsible. It has been a pleasure serving them.

Enclosed is a contribution. I wish you and all of them happy holidays!

Sincerely,

Dear Mrs. Vochim:

After reading Mr. Trufant's letter describing the facilities and the leadership at the Bay Youth Recreation Center, I have been persuaded to make a contribution each year. A project of this importance needs ongoing financial support.

Also, it needs continuing leadership support. I will provide some publicity through newspaper articles describing the activities at the Center and the opportunities for sports leaders to help their community.

Best wishes,

Favorable Adjustment

Dear Mr. Parnado:

There will be no charge for rewiring your water heater. Our service technician checked the electrical circuits thoroughly and discovered a manufacturing flaw.

Thank you for bringing this problem to our attention.

We will phone you on Monday, July 23, to arrange a time for our service representative to do the work at your house.

Sincerely,

Dear Mrs. O'Loughlin:

A replacement for the broken connecting cord for your recently purchased compact disc player was shipped this afternoon via Federal Express one-day service. It may arrive before this letter.

We apparently did not thoroughly inspect the cord before packaging it with the disc player. This rare occurrence should not have happened, and we apologize for the inconvenience it caused you.

Sincerely,

INTRODUCTIONS

The purpose of an introductory letter is solely to introduce one person to another. It is not a reference letter, which can be used to sell the qualifications of one person to another, so get right to the point with a letter that is brief.

The tone of the letter will depend on the relationship between the writer and the reader, and the anticipated relationship between the person being introduced and the reader. This will usually be a friendly and informal relationship, requiring a letter with a touch of warmth.

Provide at least the first and last names of the person being introduced, and, when possible, background, or at least some interest common to both parties. An explanation that is reasonable to the reader should be given for the introduction. This is often really asking for a favor; therefore give full consideration to the feelings and probable reaction of the reader.

In commenting about the person being introduced, make the reader *want* to meet him or her. Without overdoing a good thing, make the person sound interesting.

How to Do It

1. Provide the full name of the person being introduced.

2. Give a reasonable explanation for what is really a request for a favor.

3. Make the reader *want* to meet the other person.

New Sales Representative

Dear Jack:

Our new sales representative, Sulaman Sharif, will be calling on you soon.

Sulaman has a wealth of background in bag-making machinery, including manufacturing, assembling, and repairing, as well as supervising machine operators and scheduling orders—and even sales. Not many people have such thoroughgoing experience with a machine they are selling and servicing.

You will find Sulaman as pleasant and helpful as he is knowledgeable. We are proud to have him represent us, and I know you will soon think as highly of him as we do.

Sincerely,

Friend for Sales Position

Dear Mr. Sonist:

Jack Zimmer has been a successful salesman for over twelve years in the field of industrial equipment. I have known him a long time and believe he would fit well into your organization, based on the needs you described to me last month.

Please give him your consideration. You will find him worth it.

Best regards,

A Friend

Dear Ms. Blackman,

Marvin Melville is a good friend of ours. He will be in Minneapolis about the middle of next month for a few days, and I would like him to meet you. You both have a strong interest in juvenile runaways. Marv is doing research in San Francisco now, and I told him about the study you did on juveniles in Chicago last year. I'm sure you both would have a lot to talk over. You'll find Marv extremely pleasant.

May I give him your phone number? Please write and let me know.

Best regards,

Dear Charlie,

My good friend Jim Hoskins will be in Atlanta the week of February 10. Jim is director of marketing for a large folding-carton manufacturer. I told him you are doing research for a textbook on the use of graphics designs in advertising. Jim was more than a little interested in your project and how it might apply to the sales of folding cartons, which his company makes and prints.

If you have time, give him a call at 000-0000, room 000. I told Jim you might be tied up that week, so he will understand if he doesn't hear from you.

I know you would enjoy each other's company.

Regards,

Dear Mrs. Leipzig:

This will introduce Linda Grayson, who is leaving us to be with her husband who was transferred to Cambridge.

Mrs. Grayson has been our assistant librarian for the past ten years, specializing in reference works, and has often substituted in other departments. She has a Masters Degree in Library Science, is a willing worker, a fast learner, and is personable. Any visit with her is a pleasant experience.

Sincerely,

Dear Sara,

This will introduce one of our dear friends, John Anson. I could not let him go to the Great Southwest without at least the promise of visiting you. He will be there only a few days—you may regret the shortness of his visit when you meet him. I envy his having the chance to visit you and the beauty of the desert in the spring.

Love,

Academic Assistance

Dear Professor Tufts:

I would like to introduce Mike Urby. He has been a straight-A student here at Ohio State and shows great promise in the area of graphic arts. I know your university has a much better graphic-arts program than we have. It would be to Mike's benefit to take advantage of your school's teachers and well-rounded program.

Could you please give Mike whatever guidance you can to get him started in the right direction. I will appreciate it—and so will Mike.

Sincerely,

New Employee

Dear Mr. Spanol:

It's our great pleasure to introduce to you Georgia Nelson, our new senior vice president, who came to us in January and is in charge of sales, acquisitions, and finance. Ms. Nelson comes to us with a wealth of experience in the acquisition and operation of syndication properties. We are delighted with Georgia's immediate and expert command of our remarkably complex organization.

Sincerely,

ACKNOWLEDGMENT

Send a letter of acknowledgment as soon as practical. Special or unusual business transactions should be acknowledged. A thankful acknowledgment of the receipt of money or information you have repeatedly sought (rather than saying, "It's about time") improves business and personal relations.

How to Do It

1. State what you are acknowledging.
2. Describe any action you are taking.
3. Be clear and precise.

Late Payment Received

Dear Mr. Witzler:

Thank you for your payment dated April 3, _ _ _ _. Although long overdue, we appreciate your effort to make this payment in spite of your recent decline in sales volume.

Your account is now cleared, and we will be able to resume credit sales to you, but on a reduced and closely monitored basis. We do appreciate your business and will help you maintain a required inventory level.

Sincerely,

Large Order

Dear Mr. Wong:

Thank you for your large order dated October 10, _ _ _ _ . You have been a regular customer, and this order seems to indicate your business is expanding. We are happy for you.

You will receive your complete order by October 20. We will continue to do our best to supply all your needs.

Sincerely,

Cannot Meet Deadline

Dear Mr. Wainright:

We have thoroughly checked your drawings and specifications for a special truck body for transporting empty milk cartons. Because this is a light cargo, you will need all the inside van space possible.

We are required, however, to build the body to meet highway department limits. The inside height you request can be met only if the truck chassis is lowered. This may require smaller wheels or a reduction of inside space by adding wheel wells.

Please have your design engineers contact our manufacturing vice president, Orson Andrews. I am sure some agreement can be reached.

Sincerely,

Report Received

Dear Ms. Ames:

Thank you for your report on proposed changes in our Boston office. We will review your recommendations next week. We may also send representatives from the Caldwell Corporation, which specializes in office reorganization, to

Boston for an outsider's viewpoint. Please cooperate with them and rest assured their suggestions will carry no more weight than your recommendations.

You should have our final decision on changes within two months.

Sincerely,

INVITATIONS

A letter of invitation is one of goodwill. It is a friendly letter (even if solely for a business purpose) because you wish to retain the reader's good thoughts about you. It is also a personal letter because you are writing to one person who will feel pleased to be singled out. To attain this good feeling, the letter must be warm and express an honest wish for acceptance, as in these sentences:

We will be waiting to hear from you.

Please let us hear from you soon.

We are anxious to get together with you again.

Please confirm by May 4 that you can attend.

It will be so good to see you again.

The degree of formality to use in the writing depends on the relationship between the writer and the reader. It can vary from "old-buddy" jocularity to third-person formality, from "Hi Skip, I hear you'll be back in town next week. How about pouring a few with Don and me at Morland's," to "The Onward Civic Club cordially invites you to attend . . ."

As well as being specific about when and where you will meet the recipient of the invitation, it may be appropriate to mention why you have invited the reader. This is primarily true in business invitations: You wish to discuss a specific aspect of your business relationship, or you have a particular reason for inviting this person to speak or to join an organization.

How to Do It

1. Mention the purpose of the invitation.
2. State when and where and, if appropriate, why.
3. Request confirmation or express anticipated acceptance.

To Do Advertising

Dear Mr. Callby:

We have a new line of coated stainless-steel cookware ready to market. Would you be interested in discussing the product and the possibility of advertising it for us?

Please phone me before Friday to arrange a date for further discussion. I will be waiting for your call.

Sincerely,

Use Company Hotel Room

Dear Ms. May:

When you come to Minneapolis for your sales meeting next month, perhaps you would enjoy staying at our company hotel room. I can reserve it for you for March 17, 18, and 19.

I think you would enjoy the location (as well as the room) because it is only three blocks from your meeting place.

It will be a pleasure to reserve the room for you. I must have your decision by the 15th of this month.

Please let me hear from you.

Most sincerely,

Dinner Guest

Dear Jim,

The East Bay Accounting Society is having an exciting guest at its dinner meeting next Thursday. The guest is Ben Stoddard, who has won fame as a tax-avoidance authority—not tax *evasion*, he will point out.

I thought you would be interested in attending as my guest. The meeting is at 7:00 P.M., Thursday, the 24th, and will be over by 10:30 P.M.

Please let me hear from you. I can pick you up on my way there, and I know you will enjoy the evening.

Best regards,

Accepting Invitations

A letter accepting an invitation should emphasize warm gratitude and anticipated enjoyment. It was really nice of the person to invite *you*, and in return you should say you are grateful by writing:

> I shall be happy to accept . . .
>
> It was thoughtful of you to invite me to . . .
>
> Thank you so much for thinking of me.
>
> Thank you for your invitation to . . .

An invitation is written only to those who are expected to enjoy the occasion, and it is appropriate for the accepter to concur with the writer's statement or impression that a good time will be had by all. For example:

> We look forward to seeing you again.
>
> We always enjoy the Michigan State games.
>
> It will be a pleasure to meet your club members.
>
> You can count on my being there.

The degree of formality or informality in the acceptance letter would normally follow closely the tone of the invitation.

How to Do It

1. Express thanks for the invitation.
2. State acceptance.
3. Confirm time and place.
4. Express pleasant anticipation.

To Speak

> Dear Ms. Lawson:
>
> Thank you for the invitation to speak at your fund-raising committee meeting. You suggested reviewing last year's successful campaign. I think that is a great

idea. I plan to emphasize the positive aspects and suggest how you can build upon the successful techniques to strengthen this coming year's campaign.

I will be at your meeting place a little before 7:00 P.M. on Friday, May 17.

I am happy to do what I can to help your campaign.

Sincerely,

Football Celebration

Dear Dave,

Thank you for the invitation to celebrate the A's victory at your home.

Doris and I will be there about 4:00 P.M., Saturday, the 24th. We always enjoy visiting with you, and it seems like a long time since our last get-together.

See you Saturday,

Retirement Dinner

Dear Sharon,

Thank you for inviting Cheryl and me to attend the retirement dinner at the Aztec Restaurant on May 4 at 7:30 P.M.

We will be there.

I think it is nice of you to add something special to our standard retirement activities.

Cordially,

Dinner Invitation

Dear Mr. Sheridan:

In reply to your faxed invitation of May 24, I would be pleased to meet with you and Mr. Hanson on Wednesday, June 6th at 7:00 P.M. at the Marboro Hotel dining room.

Sincerely,

Dinner, Company President

Dear Esther and Eric,

Gordon and I wish to invite you to an informal dinner on January 8 at seven o'clock at our home. The occasion is to welcome Joan and Alex Wilhem to our company and to the area, which is quite a change from the green hills of Idaho.

We are inviting the four other corporate officers and their spouses.

If you have any questions or cannot come, please call me at 000-0000.

Cordially,

Join a Group

Dear Alice,

Thank you for inviting me to join the Women's Hospital Auxiliary. I do have many years of enjoyable experience in this line of work and am sure I can be of much help to your organization as well as to the patients we serve.

I will be able to attend your meeting on August 4 at 4:00 P.M.

Sincerely,

Declining Invitations

See Chapter Two, Declining Requests.

ACCEPTING A POSITION

When accepting an office or position with a social organization, the acceptance letter will probably be the only written record of either the offer or acceptance.

The first sentence should include an acknowledgment of the acceptance and an expression of appreciation; having accepted the position, you should have no trouble feeling appreciative. Here are some examples:

I am happy to accept your offer to join Lending Hands charity.

I am pleased to accept the position of program manager.

Your acceptance of my bid for the position of committee chairman is greatly appreciated.

An expression of thanks for being considered can enhance the employer's confidence in you and in his or her judgment in selecting you.

Your confidence in selecting me will be well founded.

I appreciate your selecting me from the large number who applied.

I am happy that you found a way to utilize my varied experience.

In some acceptances of a position, you may be able to include what you hope to accomplish. This lets the group know you are looking ahead, but be general and cautious; many unknowns await the new volunteer. You may, however, be able to include statements similar to these:

Your decision to grant me full control will enable me to give first priority to improving the annual fund raiser.

I have some procedures in mind for improving control of the accounting data.

There are effective promotion programs that can be implemented with a minimum of change in your current procedures.

I am aware that long hours will be required to accomplish your immediate goals.

Although this is a part-time activity, I will involve myself fully.

How to Do It

1. State with enthusiasm what is being accepted.
2. Express thanks for being considered.
3. Indicate what you hope to accomplish.

Committee Chairperson

Dear Mrs. Brown:

Your eagerly awaited letter stating that I have been selected for the position of chairperson of the Fund Raising Committee arrived today. Your confidence in me is appreciated and I heartily accept your offer.

As soon as it is appropriate, I would appreciate discussing the function and duties of the position with the outgoing chairman, Jim Smyth.

Please let me know when I can start.

Sincerely,

Lions Club

Dear Mr. Samuelson:

Thanks for passing on the word that I've been selected as the next president of the Lions. With so many good men in the running, I hardly expected to make it to the top five, let alone the presidency itself.

A training period will be necessary, however, to familiarize myself not only with the official duties but also with the ceremonial aspects of the position.

My efforts are aimed toward making this a most successful presidency by promoting unity as well as service among members.

Sincerely,

COVER LETTER

The purpose of a cover letter is to help the recipient save time and effort. Rather than having to read the first part of a written document or a group of papers, then having to decide what they are and what they are for, the reader can read a cover letter and know immediately what is enclosed.

A cover letter should be brief. For example:

Four copies of the May 1 revision of the _ _ _ _ budget are enclosed.

That statement tells what is enclosed and how many. In this case the reader was expecting the budget revisions, but some cover letters must include a little more information. If several different items are enclosed, a listing is helpful. It may be appropriate to mention who requested the enclosures or who instructed the sender to mail them. If the receiver is not expecting the item, an explanation of its purpose may be required.

A job résumé cover letter should also be brief, but long enough to mention what job you are applying for and one or two of your strongest selling points.

People given the task of reading résumés usually do this infrequently; it is an added-on task. They are still busy with their regular work. The cover letter, therefore, should be brief, to the point, include an applicable selling point, and, of absolute importance, make the reader anxious to turn to the résumé itself.

How to Do It

1. State what is enclosed or attached; if in answer to a request, name the person who made the request.
2. If applicable, mention the quantity enclosed or make a brief listing.
3. The purpose of the enclosure may be mentioned.

Expenditures Request

Dear Mr. Wade:

Attached for your consideration is our Capital Expenditure Request No. 400-32, covering installation of cooling units in front of the roof ventilators. At present, the ventilating air picks up a large amount of heat from the tar-covered roof.

Regards,

Lists

Dear Mr. Holmes:

Enclosed are three (3) copies of lists showing miscellaneous items in Warehouse Inventories.

These lists have been revised to October 31, _ _ _ _.

Sincerely,

Agreement for Signature

Dear Mr. and Mrs. Custom:

Enclosed is the Modification Agreement as proposed in our letter of April 30, _ _ _ _.

If you agree to the change, please sign the agreement, have your signatures notarized, and return the document to this office.

Sincerely,

Warehouse Report

Dear Ms. Anwan:

Enclosed is Ashton Warehouse Co. Commodity Report covering the inventory for Ren Bearing Co.

Will you please reconcile this report to your records.

Sincerely yours,

Statement Requested

Dear Ken:

Attached is the signed Compliance Statement requested in your letter of December 14.

Sincerely,

Savings Statement

Dear Miss Donner:

Enclosed are sealed envelopes containing individual Savings Account statements as of December 31, _ _ _ _, for:

C. O. Sanders
B. B. Wankel
A. T. Younts

Please mail the statements to these individuals.

Sincerely,

Insurance Renewal

Dear Mr. Matson:

Your insurance renewal is enclosed, continuing this important protection for you over the coming months. This renewal protects you against lapse of coverage and is in force from the expiration date of your present policy. After looking over the coverage, should you have any question or if any corrections are necessary, please call or write our office promptly.

Our sincerest appreciation for your continuance of this business. Do not hesitate to contact our office if there is any way we can be of further service.

Once again, thank you,

Price Increase

Dear Ms. Waterford:

The Abel Company has announced a price increase of approximately 6 percent effective July 1, _ _ _ _. Attached is their National Account Price List No. 17.

Two account changes have been made in this latest price list:

1. Chemical Coatings have been added.
2. All products are now listed alphabetically by name, making them easier to find in the list.

Sincerely,

Dear Customer:

We have maintained a stable price level for the past five years. Now, however, we find that constant increases in many of our costs require this new price list. Most prices will go up only 5 percent starting March 1, _ _ _ _.

We appreciate the loyalty of our customers and hope this increase will not be a burden. Our well-accepted service policy will not change.

Sincerely,

Valuable Document

Dear Mr. and Mrs. Frame:

We are pleased to enclose your Policy of Title Insurance. This important document should be placed for safekeeping with your other valuable papers.

Sincerely,

Follow-Up

A follow-up letter can be a reminder, a progress report, a request for an explanation, or even a sales letter. Examples of each of these are in this section.

Start right off with a statement of the event or situation you are writing about. State the topic in the first sentence. This is followed by facts, figures, or a description of what has occurred between now and your prior contact with the reader. End with a statement of what action you will take or what specifically you are now requesting.

If the time interval between contacts is short, the facts and descriptions in the second step may be omitted, assuming there is no doubt in the reader's mind about what has occurred, as in this introductory sentence:

> Is my face red! I just read your letter of January 17. How we could make a mistake like that I don't know, but we did, and here's what we are going to do about it.

How to Do It

1. State the situation or event that is being followed up.
2. Describe what has been learned or what has happened since prior contact with the reader.
3. Stipulate what action you will take or what you are requesting.

Correct an Error

> Dear Ed:
>
> As a follow up, I am attaching copies of two letters dated April 19 and May 27, to which we had no reply.
>
> The letters relate to incorrect shipments to our Charleston and Richmond offices.
>
> We would appreciate your looking into this and letting us know what you find.
>
> If you require copies of the backup material sent with the letters, or any other information, please let me know.
>
> Sincerely,

Additional Information Requested

Dear Mr. Naughton:

Stanley Company's quote on the cost of relocating two presses appears to be more general than specific. Working with our local engineers, you will have to take the information supplied by Stanley, get what information you can from sources within our company, and come up with some hard-dollar figures on the cost of this project.

I think it's important that we give this our immediate attention.

Sincerely,

Inactive Charge Account

Dear Mrs. Walters:

Have we disappointed you?

We hope not, but we are disappointed . . . that you have not been using your open credit account recently. When an account is active, we know you are pleased with our merchandise, our service, and the convenience of charging your purchases.

If there is something in particular we can do to make your shopping more convenient, please let us know on the postage-paid card enclosed.

Our goal is to have happy customers.

Sincerely,

Dear Mr. Zaha:

You asked me in your letter of May 12 why my Anzo Oil Co. credit card has been inactive for so long. The reason is this:

The local Anzo full-service station personnel do not take the time to check the little things that make a motorist pleased with their service. The windshield is not washed, the oil level is not checked, the tire pressure is not checked, the water level is not checked. Their "full service" consists of holding the hose while the tank is filling and writing out the credit card slip. That's it.

Sincerely,

Power Lawn-Mower Purchase

Dear Mr. Morton:

Your Huston Power Lawn-Mower dealer, J & J Warner Bros. of St. Louis, has written us of your recent purchase of a Huston mower. We at Huston head-quarters, as well as J & J Warner, appreciate your decision to buy a Huston. We are sure you will become a satisfied owner.

We are proud of our dealers: They are responsible business people, they oper-ate sound businesses, and they participate in community activities. They help make your city a better place in which to live and grow.

Your Huston dealer is trained and qualified to assist you with any mainte-nance problems or operating questions. J & J Warner stands ready to help you.

We are enclosing three Western prints for your enjoyment. Every three months for a year we will send you a small gift to show our appreciation and contin-ued interest in you, our customer.

Sincerely,

Magazine Subscription

Dear Ms. Ng:

Three months ago, August 14, _ _ _ _, we sent our check for $67 for a year's subscription to Western Outdoor Adventures. We received our canceled check but no magazines.

Please investigate the reason for our receiving no copies and let us know as soon as possible when we can expect the magazine.

Sincerely,

QUERY LETTERS SEEKING PUBLICATION

A query letter is designed to convince an editor that your article or book is worthy of serious consideration. It is primarily a sales letter that, for nonfic-tion writers, helps sell your composition before it is written. The piece can then be written to meet the requirements of that publication.

The query letter is the editor's first impression of *you* as well as of your writing ability. Do it carefully. Concentrate on the following when writing a query letter.

- Study the publication for which you are writing.
- Do enough research to convince the editor you know what you are writing about.
- Address the letter to a person, not a title.
- Arouse the editor's interest in the first sentence
- Keep the length of the query to one page.
- Mention the title in the query letter.
- Include samples of your work. If you have none, make no mention of them.
- Proofread: Errors in your query letter will imply errors in your manuscript.
- Include a self-addressed, stamped envelope.
- Ask yourself, "Would I be favorably impressed if I received this letter?"

How to Do It

1. State what the article or story is about.
2. Describe who the intended audience will be.
3. Present your qualifications for writing this particular piece.

Book

Dear Mr. Wilson:

Improve Your Business Letters is designed as a textbook for the college-level business student or the serious business person interested in improving communications. It is not intended to be a complete book on Business English but rather a supplemental text specifically to teach effective written communication.

There is a difference between *Improve Your Business Letters* and other business-letter books. This book not only provides examples of effective and ineffective letters but in addition

- analyzes the examples.
- lists reasons for the letters being winners or losers.
- lists techniques for improving the letters.
- illustrates the improvement by rewriting the letters.

The following parts of my book are enclosed:

Preface
Contents
Chapter I, The Chaos of Words
Chapter II, Brevity
Chapter III, Straight-Arrow Information

I taught Freshman English at the University of New Mexico for ten years and conducted evening seminars for business people for five years in Albuquerque.

I will be pleased to submit a detailed outline.

Sincerely,

Magazine Article

Dear Ms. Duston:

How do you handle the rapid turnover of low-wage employees? Often after the three-day training period and a couple of days on the job, your new employees quit and your staff has to work overtime to fill in for them and train replacements. How can you arrest this debilitating cycle?

Sandra Olinger, head of a direct-response phone agency named Call Central, answered that dilemma with a double punch. By combining efforts with the Oklahoma State Corrections Administration, she arranged for female inmates on good behavior to work as Call Central operators in an innovative program that was recently awarded the "Best New Program for Business" honors by the Rockefeller Business Institute.

It's a winning situation, benefiting inmates, companies, and taxpayers. The inmates learn marketable skills, the companies stabilize entry-level jobs, and the taxpayers save because participating inmates pay the institution one third of their wages for room and board. This solution could mean the difference between fortune and failure for businesses caught in today's vicious wage-employment conflict.

Would *Business Solutions* readers like to know more about how Olinger and her team are bringing former Appelate Court Judge Ian Strauss's dream of "factories without fences" alive in "Cons Are Entry-Level Pros"? The story would run 1,500 to 2,000 words. A sidebar about the Call Central management team, which turned a one-horse service into a full-steam contender in their field, could run 750 to 800 words. Interviews would include participants Fred Boscoe, CEO of the state agency monitoring the program, and Justice Strauss. Photos are available.

My more than 150 published credits include contributions to *Saturday Review*, *The Wall Street Journal*, and *Tulsa Living*. I also have a business degree and am ready to begin working on the article.

Looking forward to hearing from you,

(With thanks to Mary Westheimer, author and former Executive Director of the Arizona Authors' Association, with permission.)

PROCEDURAL PROPOSAL

Paying Invoices

Memo to: Mr. Upchurch
     from: Jon Alderwood

You requested a proposed procedure we should follow to alleviate the problem of consistently paying our printing die vendor invoices 60 to 90 days late. Here is my suggested procedure:

The corrugated box sales person works with the customer on the design of the box printing and obtains a pattern from the customer.

The die pattern is taken to the sales-service clerk, who coordinates the sales and the production (manufacturing) departments. The sales-service clerk enters the factory order number on the die pattern and sends it to the die-order clerk. The die-order clerk writes a purchase order for the die and sends it to the die vendor.

When the die is received, the plant receiving clerk writes a receiving record and forwards a copy to the die-order clerk along with the die. The die clerk checks the die against the order. He or she attaches the receiving record to the die order, then notifies the production department so they can schedule the manufacturing process.

Vendor invoices received are sent directly to the die-order clerk, who checks the invoice against the die order. The die-order clerk sends the invoice, receiving record, and die order to the sales-service clerk, who checks them against the original order for boxes. The sales-service clerk initials the vendor invoice, indicating approval for payment. The invoice and attachments are sent to the accounts-payable clerk.

The accounts-payable clerk verifies any computations on the invoice, prepares an accounts-payable voucher, and sends all the papers to the office manager for a final review of the paperwork. The office manager then forwards the vendor invoice and the accounts-payable voucher to the headquarters office, where the actual check to the vendor is written. The receiving record and purchase order are retained at the local plant.

If each step is handled expeditiously, vendor invoices will be paid on time while putting accuracy first.

(signed)

Going over Another's Head

Dear Mr. Tully:

This is to notify you that Abbott Paint Company may send a salesperson directly to you in their efforts to sell us paint for our vehicles. You are aware that they have been attempting to become our sole paint supplier for several years. I recommend that you do not talk to Abbott's salesperson.

Abbott seems to believe we are stalling just to be contrary. The real reason is that their paint doesn't meet the quality standards of Johnson Bros. paint, which we have used successfully for many years. This fact has been demonstrated many times by trials our own purchasing department has made of Abbott's paint bought randomly from various dealers.

Sincerely,

Dear Mr. Cassels:

I am sorry to have gone over your head to request timely and legible weekly chemical-test reports of our manufactured paper.

The results you report are sent to our corporate chemists. They demand that information reach them at certain intervals so they can evaluate the products for our marketing department.

My job depends on legible and on-time reports from you. I have mentioned and discussed this with you many times, but with no tangible improvements. However, recent reports have come in on time: Your supervisor accomplished what I could not.

Sincerely,

CHAPTER 15

Other Personal Letters

Because they contain elements of both, some letters are hard to classify as personal or business. A business letter should have a touch of personal friendliness. Even a letter containing only straightforward facts can be presented in a way that is more friendly and warm than cool. See Chapter 6, Information—Providing and Requesting, for suggestions. Going further, even a business letter of criticism or reprimand must show personal consideration for the reader, or the reader will become disturbed, with the result that the letter does not accomplish its purpose. Should the person to whom you are writing a business letter be a personal friend, both your personal and business relationships can be enhanced with a sentence or two referring to some mutual personal interest such as, "Give my regards to Alice," "How do you like your new city by now?" or "I'll call you next week about the Bowling Club dance."

On the other hand, a personal letter has some aspects of a business letter. When you wish to give information to a personal acquaintance, the same techniques of organizing and presenting facts will be used as in business letters. Again, the introductory remarks in Chapter 6 will help. If you are writing a get-well note to a co-worker, it may be a personal expression, but the fact that you work together keeps your business relationship from being completely excluded.

Whether you believe you are writing a business or personal letter, keep the reader uppermost in your mind. Write about what will interest the reader, what you want the reader to know and believe, what will appeal to the reader, and foremost, what will get the reader to react the way you want him or her to. A letter, even a friendly note, is written to accomplish a purpose, and the key to this accomplishment is to think the way the reader does. Put yourself in his or her place and ask, "How would I react to this letter if I were the reader?"

WELCOME

"Glad to have you here! You will find us friendly." This is the congenial mood that a letter of welcome should reveal to the reader. It is a gesture of courtesy and consideration.

Since a welcome letter is also a second cousin to a sales letter, you can mention something nice about your organization, place of work, or group. Let the reader know that you are proud to belong, hoping that he or she will be too.

Include some suggestion as to how the person can fit into your group, or how he or she can learn what is available, or what you will do to help orient the reader.

End the letter with a note of encouragement or a suggestion of how the reader can take the initial step.

How to Do It

1. Express pleasure at making the welcome.
2. Make complimentary remarks about your organization or place.
3. Draw a relationship between the person and the organization.
4. End with an encouraging comment.

To New Resident

Dear Mr. and Mrs. Webster:

Welcome to Seattle, the heart of the Evergreen State!

Coming from the East, you will especially enjoy our temperate climate, but you will not be leaving behind the thrill of the changing seasons. Most of all, you will enjoy the friendly, down-to-earth people here.

To help you get acquainted, please phone the New Residents Club at 000-0000. We will be happy to answer any questions you have, and we will suggest that someone call on you for a more personal discussion of how you can find your niche in this wonderful city.

Sincerely,

Dear Mr. and Mrs. Sweig:

Welcome to Phoenix and the Valley of the Sun.

We have sun practically all year, and when the heat rises, the air conditioners come on. The economy is booming and new homes are rising fast to keep up with the population. Sports activities are increasing but haven't replaced the symphony and opera.

We work closely with the Chamber of Commerce, and when you visit our office, we can suggest contacts to help you become acquainted with all this Valley has to offer.

Sincerely,

To New Member

Dear Ms. Wallace,

As president of the East Side Bridge Club, I want to extend a warm welcome to you.

I am sure you will be a great help to us in our annual friendly competition with the West Side Bridge Club.

I also want to explain that our Club is involved in social activities as well as in playing bridge. We attend stage shows, enjoy late pizza parties, and organize picnics for our families and their friends. It's all great fellowship.

Welcome to our group. I'm sure you'll enjoy the friendship.

Sincerely,

ANNOUNCEMENT

Engagement

Dear Uncle Tony,

It has happened at last, although perhaps it's no surprise. I'm ENGAGED. Yesterday Ed asked me to marry him—but he waited until he was sure of my answer.

We haven't set a wedding date, but probably next March, maybe April. You'll know in plenty of time to arrange a trip to Philadelphia. There is so much to plan for, but I'm too excited to start now.

Love you,

Broken Engagement

Dear Aunt Sue,

I don't know if this is bad or good news, but after postponing our wedding several times, Derek and I decided to give up the idea. I'm not sure what started our change of feelings for each other because it has evolved slowly over the past several months. It was a mutual agreement with no harsh thoughts, and we both seem relieved.

Love,

Death of Father

Dear Ted,

Sorry to tell you this, Ted, but my father died last Wednesday, June 14. He had been ill for the past six months. We were not surprised at his going, but still the trauma is there.

He thought of you as one of his great friends and talked of you often.

Funeral and memorial arrangements are pending.

Cordially,

Birth of Daughter

Dear Mr. and Mrs. Ursin,

We are so happy to announce the birth of Joan Karla Tullis on May 4, _ _ _ _. She weighed seven pounds, eight ounces. Joan has the dark hair of her mother and the loud voice of her father.

Cordially,

Adoption

Dear Mr. and Mrs. Yeager,

We are happy and proud to announce the adoption of Jon Marvin Carls, an eighteen-month old Asian boy.

Cordially,

GOOD WISHES

A letter of good wishes is appropriate for a business friend who is also a personal friend, one to whom you can express your feelings in a friendly and natural way. It is a letter of sincerity combined with informality.

One special occasion for a letter of good wishes is the year-end holiday season. You can use this annual time of goodwill and good feeling to thank a customer for being *your* customer, to wish him or her well in the coming year, and to express pleasant thoughts to acquaintances and cheerful thoughts to friends.

Another occasion for sending good wishes is the convalescence of someone who has been ill or in an accident. A cheerful thought is great therapy, and all it takes is a short letter.

Whatever the occasion—even if there is no occasion—being remembered is always appreciated.

How to Do It

1. Mention the occasion for the good wishes.
2. Describe briefly some common topic or feeling or idea that is appropriate for the occasion.

Season's Greetings

Dear Mr. Allen:

As the magic of the holiday season approaches, our thoughts turn to those who have made our progress possible. We wish to express our appreciation for your goodwill—the very foundation of business success. In the spirit of friendship, we send you our hope for a continuing business relationship and best wishes for a pleasant holiday season.

Sincerely,

Dear Mr. Artz:

At this time of the year, many of us like to reminisce, and that led me back to that especially pleasant visit when you were here in September.

In the future, I hope we can have more of these interesting and stimulating meetings.

Have a relaxing holiday season—you have earned it—and we'll plan another get-together early next year.

Cordially,

Dear Mr. Woodard:

You have been a good customer all year, and we are glad to pause a moment to thank you for that. We also want to wish you a happy holiday season and a pleasant new year.

Best wishes,

Dear Mr. Wyatt,

With the New Year approachng it is time to wish both personal and business friends bountiful success in the coming year.

You are both a personal and business friend, so perhaps wishing you a doubly great year ahead is appropriate.

Your friend,

Convalescing

Dear Ethel,

How good it is to send a note to your home for a change. You must feel by now that you own the South Wing of the hospital.

I'm glad to hear that you are better and will be back to work soon.

Sincerely,

Dear Don,

Since you are now out of the hospital and convalescing at home, you have made a big step toward recovery; congratulations.

To help you along the recovery road (waterway) I am sending you a book about boating on the Sacramento-San Joaquin Delta. Some refer to it as the California Delta. I'm sure you will find the book intriguing.

Regards,

Dear Alex,

Looking out your hospital window on a sunny day sure beats looking into dark rain clouds, but it will be even more pleasant when you are outside in the warming sun yourself.

Your confinement is only temporary, and you have the opportunity to think ahead about the big picture of your life, what's ahead, when and how, maybe even why.

I'll visit you soon.

Your pal,

Dear Jean,

It's been a long, hard pull, but you made it! Your husband tells me you're now on the way to recovery. All your friends are cheering for you. Believe me, we are full of admiration for your spirited determination to get well.

Sincerely,

ACKNOWLEDGMENT

Send a letter of acknowledgment as soon as you can. The person who sent you something or did you a favor will be pleased. Your promptness is an expression of goodwill.

How to Do It

1. Mention what you are acknowledging.
2. Describe any action you are taking.
3. Be clear; do not ramble.

Gift Received

Dear Aleata,

Thank you for the computer disc version of the book *Lifetime Encyclopedia of Letters*. It arrived yesterday. I'm anxious to set it up in my computer because it will make finding the letters I need much easier. I greatly appreciate your thinking of me.

Cordially,

Dear Mrs. Alto,

I wish to acknowledge your generous gift to the Amanda Warner Fund, collected by the Concord Savings Bank. Amanda is smiling again.

We did receive enough money to replace Amanda's motorized wheelchair that was destroyed last month in that unfortunate car accident. It's comforting to know that so many people respond to an appeal to help the less fortunate.

Thank you so very much.

Cordially,

Dinner Postponement

Dear Anne,

We appreciate very much your invitation to dinner on December 3. Eric will be in Chicago on business that day, and I will be visiting our daughter in San Antonio on December 2. But we can get together another time. Perhaps you could come to our home in late January. We can discuss it when I return in mid January.

Cordially,

Help Received

Dear Al,

I really appreciated your suggestion for how to research the address of a charity organization. I found it in one day after only seven phone calls to charity associations. The charity I sought had moved. A similar investigation last year required twelve letters over a two-month period.

Thanks again for your time-saving know-how.

Regards,

Dear Jeanne,

It was considerate of you to send me a copy of the advertisement you designed and wrote, which you hoped would increase sales of your new chocolate candy. I am happy that you found my advertising copy suggestions useful. And I was especially pleased that your sales immediately increased. Keep up the good work.

Sincerely,

Invitation

Dear Ms. Eakes:

Thank you for your invitation to Mr. Gerald Comstock to introduce the speakers at the Independence Day celebration.

Mr. Comstock is now in Europe on business but will return on March 29. When he returns, I will alert him to your invitation.

Cordially,

Dear Mr. James:

Thank you for your invitation to speak to your students. I will be happy to talk to them.

To verify our discussion on April 2, I will present the current thinking on long-term investments in foreign countries to your class at 1:00 P.M. on May 4 in room A402, Business Building on the Plymouth campus.

I have enclosed a brochure that presents our company's impression on global investments. It will give your students a specific viewpoint on the subject, if you wish to discuss it before my talk, which will provide a broader view.

I look forward to seeing you on May 4.

Regards,

ENCOURAGEMENT

Baseball players are not alone with their batting slumps. The rest of us have "batting slumps" too. That is when we need encouragement to try harder, to take a deep breath and hold on, to blink our eyes and take a new look.

When you see a person feeling low or in a state of depression, a letter of encouragement may be just the needed stimulant.

Whatever (or whoever) the cause, admit that an adverse condition exists. Trying to offer help while avoiding mention of the problem that necessitates the help requires the type of thinking best left to politicians. If, however, a problem does not exist, and you wish to make your letter more of a compliment than an encouragement, please refer to the section on Compliments in this chapter.

Admit that a problem exists and mention what it is so you and your reader are thinking together, but don't dwell on the problem.

If you are offering encouragement, you must be convinced that the adverse condition can be overcome. With this conviction in your mind, it will almost automatically show in the words and phrases you use.

The really helpful part of an encouragement letter is your suggestion of *how* an improvement can be made. Strong, forceful language or ideas are likely to create resistance or even discouragement. A more successful way is to make a clear and simple statement. For example:

> Encourage your staff to be more aggressive.
>
> Please reconsider, then I would appreciate discussing your decision.
>
> Consult your adviser about reorganizing your format.
>
> We will rework the equipment to provide you with better working conditions.
>
> You love challenges and have met them before.
>
> Abe Lincoln found himself a defeated candidate for eight offices before being elected President.
>
> When you feel your rope is nearly played out, tie a big knot at the end; it will help you hold on.

How to Do It

1. Admit that an adverse condition exists.
2. Name the condition or problem.
3. Indicate your conviction that the condition can be overcome.
4. Suggest how to overcome the condition.

Low Productivity

Dear Mr. Zach:

Here is an idea for improving productivity in your bottlenecked, small-but-essential polishing section. This proposal is based on time studies done in the late 1800s. The technique is to make the employees *different* from the other production workers. They will receive *special* treatment.

> Each employee will wear a white shop coat; waist length is long enough. Pants or slacks will be dark; black is preferred. A back pocket will be available to hold a red wiping cloth; this will contrast with the gray or dark-blue cloths used elsewhere in the plant. Working hours and coffee or rest breaks might be staggered.

This technique of treating one group as SPECIAL has proved to be a morale-boosting stimulus to production efficiency. It is worth a try.

Sincerely,

Dear Mr. Waterman:

Recent reports indicate that productivity has dropped to an all-time low in your department. It appears that the new computer system is slowing the output of your daily reports.

Our estimate that installation of the system would result in improved efficiency was inaccurate. We will, therefore, remove the computer and make a study of alternate computer systems.

Your operation has been hampered for a time, but I am certain that, in light of past performance, your department will not only resume normal promptness but get even more reports in ahead of the deadlines.

Sincerely,

Sales Contest

Dear Harry,

Just a personal note to follow up last week's announcement of our Resort Vacation sales contest.

You were among the top five in our last contest. With our two top salesmen, Young and Godeaux, almost sure to top you again this year, why should you exert yourself?

There is a very specific reason. You have increased your sales dramatically in the last two years, and you are being considered for a base salary increase. Don't let us—and yourself—down at this point in your career.

Best regards,

Dear Ed,

You were second in our sales contest last year, and you had Sam working so hard to stay ahead that he was glad retirement came before this year's contest. I'm rooting for you to win this year.

Right now, you are neck and neck with Don. To keep ahead, it may take just a little more push on your part. I am sure you can make the special effort to become number one this year.

Sincerely,

Promotion

Dear Ms. Phillips:

The main office empowered me to offer you the position of CEO of its Wagner facility, with all of the accompanying difficulties the position entails. As you know, several recent strikes have literally crippled the plant and the Board has several times suggested shutting down the facility entirely.

Your continued strong growth with the company and the abilities you have exhibited here in the last two years recommend you as the ideal person to return the plant to a profitable operation.

Please consider the offer and let me know as soon as you have reached your decision.

Sincerely,

Research Paper

Dear Mr. Roback:

The committee did not approve your dissertation on Fulani mating habits. The manuscript was somewhat carelessly written and researched, and the approach echoes Powder's view of the subject too closely.

Stop in and discuss the problem with me. Let's see where we can tighten up some of the writing and pull in a few more sources on the subject. It might be good for you to review both the style manual and the handbook of research before coming to see me.

With all the research you've already done and the recent papers you've presented, the corrections should pose no real problems. The committee should approve your efforts at their next review.

Sincerely,

Fund Drive

Dear Miss St. George:

Time is closing in on us and, with the end of the fund drive only two weeks away, the goal seems awfully hard to reach.

The early mix-ups in planning and scheduling delayed our moving ahead with much of the publicity and soliciting, but we still haven't picked up the proper momentum for getting people interested. A little more publicity in the area and some strong staff support should do it. But, we have to really begin moving to meet that goal.

The past few fund drives have been pulled through by your special talents, and we hope that this one will be the same. You just have to get your people moving.

Sincerely,

Dear Tommy,

When I talked to you last week about giving our church men's club a visit or two, you were reluctant to say yes. I'm sure you would enjoy it: coffee and donuts and good speakers and discussions about pancake breakfasts and Christmas cards with a picture of our church on the front and lots of friendly men to talk to.

Unless you call to decline, I'll pick you up at your house at 8:15 A.M. this coming Wednesday.

See you,

Teaching

Dear Mr. Skiles:

Word has reached me that you are ready to hand in your resignation and to leave P.S. 24 at the end of the school year. I can't say that I blame you. A teacher can take only so much of the testing and of disciplining instead of teaching before throwing in the towel. P.S. 24 is the ultimate test.

Maybe, though, you're being a little hasty. The past months have been rough, but this was what you wanted. You always spoke of the challenge of teaching in the inner city. Your face would glow as you anticipated giving children the thrill that you've found in learning.

The school was difficult to face, but you've really brought out the talents of several students whose previous teachers had never given them a chance. These children may be difficult, often trying human beings, but they are also very grateful to you. You're a fine teacher and they've truly learned something from you.

Sincerely,

LETTERS TO THE EDITOR

One newspaper suggests that letters to the editor be limited to 200 words, another suggests 250 words. However, both publish some that are three times that length. The longer letters are usually written by people who are experienced authorities on the subject they are writing about.

Most newspapers and magazines publish letters covering both sides of current issues. Published letters present strong arguments or feelings. Not many middle-of-the-road views get published. Observations of many printed letters to the editor suggest that arguments against an action, proposed action, or an idea are preferred to arguments in favor of past or future actions.

Operations Are Bloody

Dear Editor:

In the proposed legislation to criminalize late-term dilation-and-extraction abortion, Senator Michael Folmer says he is fighting for this bill only because he finds the procedure "grisly."

He undoubtedly would find removing organs to save the lives of others "grisly." Would Folmer also object to a heart, liver, or kidney transplant to save his own life?

(Signed)

Photo Radar

Dear Editor:

Does photo radar on our city streets infringe upon our freedom? Is speeding through busy streets and red lights one of our freedoms? Is endangering lives and property one of our freedom rights? Perhaps photo radar takes away our right to break the law.

(Signed)

Cult Suicides

Dear Editor:

Why does your paper, along with so much other media, cover in detail and at length mass cult suicides and not even mention the larger number of suicide hotline personnel who prevent such tragedies?

(Signed)

(Editor's note: It seems that good news is no news.)

Children Smoking

Dear Editor:

Your article on June 29 by Elden Rock about the government's responsibility to keep children from smoking never touched on parental control. Where are the parents? Who raises (or doesn't raise) our children? City, county, and state governments can tax and try to regulate sales of tobacco to underage youth, but those government efforts haven't been effective. Parents, why have you neglected *your* responsibility?

(Signed)

Lying Approved?

Dear Editor:

There seems to be a continuing chain of publicity-seeking liars who successfully fool themselves and are accepted by the public, for instance, Jim Jones,
David Koresh, Marshall Applewhite, and the people in the White House.

(Signed)

Computer Research

Dear Editor:

Your editorial of March 30 fails to mention one of the important reasons for
Samuel Dumas's losing his party's nomination for governor: He admitted that
he lied when explaining that the "special" one-cent gasoline tax would cease
as soon as the Seventh Avenue Bridge was opened.

This fact was found in a clipping from your newspaper. Clippings are sometimes easier to retrieve than electronic data.

(Signed)

Teach Children to Write

Dear Editor:

A recent article in your paper reported that it would cost $100 billion over the
next ten years to get our schools on top of the problem that high-school graduates just can't write. This amount was an "educated guess" by an educator. In
spite of all his talk about improving the educational level of school children,
President _____ and his advisers have not given any serious consideration
to the cost, the cost of educating and training leaders to reach the goal of teaching high-school graduates to write in a reasonably intelligent and clear manner.

Schools often follow the current emphasis on technology. One example of the
technological advances we have achieved stated that middle-school students
had retrieved National Aeronautics and Space Administration (NASA) satellite
images that show the Gulf Stream's movements. This is Disney-like entertainment that reveals the preference for easy visual information over thought. It
would require thinking to write about this event. Whatever the national cost,
how to write is what students must be taught.

(Signed)

Automobile Air Bags

Dear Editor:

Your article of July 12 emphasized that walking is actually more hazardous than traveling by plane, train, or ship. I long suspected that.

Rather than being placed on the dashboard area of autos, endangering small children (several have been killed) and older people, air bags should be installed on the *outside* of vehicles. This would provide padded protection for pedestrians and cyclists from the carelessness of comfortable drivers, snug in their two-ton automobiles.

(Signed)

Sirens and Lights Save Lives?

Dear Editor:

The article you printed on September 6 reported another too-frequent death resulting from an overzealous "emergency" trip by an ambulance driver. A 70-year-old woman from North Beach was hit by the ambulance hurrying "to assist a person with a mental problem."

Police officers usually handle this type of case, making unnecessary the need for a speeding vehicle with red lights flashing and sirens howling.

Although the number of deaths resulting from emergency vehicles speeding unnecessarily has apparently been diminishing, nearly every month another death is reported. Local and state regulations require that even vehicles using lights and sirens stop at red traffic lights.

The time saved by using lights and sirens is usually less than a minute according to traffic studies. Only in rare cases does this one minute save lives. More frequently the speeding loses lives.

(Signed)

COMPLIMENTS

What is nicer to receive than a compliment? Not too many things, because everyone appreciates praise. A pat on the back can make new friends, cement old relationships, win admiration, and furthermore, can be a powerful influence in making day-to-day relationships more pleasant and rewarding.

Sincerity must be at the heart of every compliment to make it acceptable to the other person as truth. Beware of flattery that can destroy an intended congratulatory remark and lower the esteem of the writer.

Above all, a compliment is an effective stimulant to those who are recognized for a job well done.

How to Do It

1. State what the compliment is for.
2. Comment on the action that led to the compliment.
3. Encourage continuance of that action.

Staff Help

Dear Allen:

Efficiency accompanied by courtesy is a rare combination in today's work world. The courtesy extended to me by your staff during the recent week of meetings and planning sessions was impressive because of its rarity.

Both office personnel and executive planners provided detailed explanations and personal assistance when needed.

Such concern is refreshing and should become more widespread.

Sincerely,

Orientation Help

Dear Ellen:

You've got quite an operation going, and your people are even more to rave about. They seem to love their work and carry out their duties both competently and enthusiastically. Certainly, productivity is high as the monthly report shows. Morale appears to be equally high.

During that round of meetings and brainstorming sessions last week, your people worked to fill me in on unfamiliar material. Without being asked, they pulled files, reports, and memos to justify items and to increase my knowledge of vagaries. They even supplied me with advice regarding several good restaurants and entertainment in town.

With your production rates and the quality of your people, you must be doing something right. Keep it up.

Sincerely,

Unusual Help

Dear Jerome,

Many thanks for the long hours, weekends away from home, and all the other inconveniences you've endured during the past months. The help you gave is much appreciated.

I have a fishing trip out of San Francisco scheduled for May 27. I'd like to invite you to join us if you can. Please let me know.

Best of everything to you in the future.

Sincerely,

Finding Error

Dear Mr. McAbee:

Tim Andrews, during his routine posting of energy usage for the month of July, noted an unusual increase and questioned me about this increased cost.

I investigated the procedure for recording electric power usage and found that an error in calculating the kilowatt hours used during July raised our costs by more than $4,000. An adjustment will be given to us next month.

I would like to compliment Tim for his alertness and thank him for the added $4,000 bottom-line profit.

Sincerely,

Construction Bid

Dear Tom.

Your proposal passed with flying colors, and Fairfield has given us the Municipal Plaza job. Construction should start next fall, but we'll be needing your talents in the meantime for a few other bids we're working on.

Our specifications needed that extra polish that your way with words gave them. The Council looked at the proposals of a half-dozen other firms and accepted our offer faster than we'd anticipated.

Don't get too tied up in other work for a while. We'll be in touch in a week or two. Once again, we appreciate the great job.

Sincerely,

Good Salesman

Dear Torry,

The order from Easton arrived today, and it alone raised our sales volume for the month by several points. Allen managed not only to sell a new account, but one that eluded us for several years despite serious work by several of our best people.

Allen's perseverance paid off. He spent several days trying to see Easton's president and finally caught him in the evening. Thanks to Allen's refusal to limit his working hours, the biggest account on the West Coast is ours.

You've got an eye for talent, and Allen is one man who is going to go far in this company.

Sincerely,

Sales Increase

Dear Kashina,

John Harvey from our headquarters office reports that your sales volume for August was more than double July's volume.

We offer a good product to consumers, and equally important are the aggressive and competent employees like you who take our product before the public.

Continue the good work.

Sincerely,

Dear Dave,

The latest issue of ACE had a circulation of over one million, a figure that no one thought we'd reach after the setbacks of the last three years.

A large part of the credit goes to you and the people you've chosen to rework what was once a dying publication. It looks as if you've chosen a new format. Eliminating the "cute" departments and mindless quizzes has had its beneficial effect. You, Tom, Jean, and Dale have something to really gloat about in the industry. And ACE can look forward to increased profits in the months to come.

Please pass my appreciation on to your staff. Continue the good work.

Sincerely,

Improved Grades

Dear Andy,

You make your parents proud. Your grades had been sputtering along below college-entrance requirements. Then you suddenly realized that a college education would be helpful to your future, whatever your goal. You also realized that you were capable of attaining college-entrance grades.

Your decision to spend more time and effort with your studies was lauded by your mother and me.

You made the "grade." Congratulations on making your parents proud.

Lovingly,

Vote Getter

Dear Wendell:

Rarely has a city experienced so high a percentage of voter turnout as in this last election. Well-planned publicity and careful scheduling brought out 72 percent of the registered voters who made their voices heard and their choice known.

Although the opposition often echoed the platform presented by our candidate, your work behind the scenes in managing the campaign made a major difference in voter reaction.

Local politics needs more dedicated workers like you.

Sincerely,

Ministerial Evaluation

Board of Directors
Riverside Community Church

We understand there is disagreement among some church members about the
way our Community Church minister, Dr. Raymond Bartanski, is carrying out
his duties.

Our view is that Dr. Bartanski is committed to each individual member and
church friend. He is loving and sincere, with a smile and cheery word for each
one.

The cooperation among our three ministers has improved since Dr. Bartanski
became our leader. They don't voice this, but their actions reveal a feeling of
consideration and cooperation with each other. Their morale is noticeably
higher than ever before.

The cooperative spirit among the ministers has spread to the numerous groups
within the Church. With the exception of a few members retreating into dark
corners, the love of Jesus is shining upon our congregation.

With God's love,

RECOMMENDATIONS

In a letter recommending one person to another, mention two or three
points of strength. The person you are recommending should have more
than one good quality, but if too many are listed, the authority of the letter
is diminished.

Statements should be specific. Rather than saying, "Joan has a good
attendance record," say, "Joan was absent only four days during the three
years she worked here." Rather than saying, "Kathy is a good worker," say,
"Kathy turns in her reports on time."

Assume a pleasant state of mind when writing the letter, because a cool
or standoffish attitude will only harm the person you are trying to help. A
feeling of warmth and enthusiasm should be felt by the reader.

Of course, mention the full name of the person you are recommending. Also state your relationship: employer, teacher, friend, and how long
you have known him or her.

Usually the last sentence can be an affirmation that the person of your letter will fulfill the needs of the reader.

I recommend her highly as a statistical clerk.

I wish I had her back.

She will rise to the top, whatever she tries.

Tom was always a great help to me.

He is one I can recommend with complete confidence.

I know he will measure up to your expectations.

He did so much to increase our sales, and I know he can do the same for you.

She earned the confidence of all her customers.

His enthusiastic hard work will be sorely missed here.

Her efficiency may surprise you.

How to Do It

1. Mention the person's name and his or her most favorable trait.
2. State your association with the person—use specifics, not generalizations.
3. Reaffirm your recommendation.

Customer

Gentlemen:

This is to inform you that we have done business with our customer, Seymour Port Company, for more than five years. We are pleased to report that all business has been conducted by Mr. Seymour and his company in a highly satisfactory manner.

Mr. Seymour and his staff have always been most helpful in providing information and advice about both domestic and overseas packaging and packaging materials. In the specialized field of overseas shipments, we have found that he has a broad range of information that has been helpful to us.

If you wish further information, please write or phone.

Sincerely,

Domestic Service

Dear Mrs. Watson:

Annette Winton has worked for me two days a week for almost twelve years. She is punctual and a hard worker. In my opinion, her work is better than average. I have found her steady and cooperative—two qualities I appreciate.

I am sorry she is leaving, and I sincerely feel that whoever is fortunate enough to have her will be rewarded with work well done.

I have found Annette loyal to those she serves. My best wishes go with her.

Sincerely,

High-School Graduate

Dear Ms. Wilson:

The best I can say may not be a sufficiently good recommendation for Joanne Grebner. She will be an excellent administrative-assistant trainee. She had the highest rating in my senior computer class during the five years I have taught here. Joanne is punctual, accurate, most willing, and quick to grasp new ideas.

In whatever she tries, she will rise to the top.

Sincerely,

DISCREET LETTERS

Keep in mind two important factors when writing discreet letters. First, you must not hurt the feelings of the reader. Use all the diplomatic tact of which you are capable. Do not anger the reader.

Second, anything that is written can lose its confidentiality. Numerous ways exist for the writing to be seen by someone else, for a copy to be made, or a word to be unintentionally voiced. Do not let what you write cause future anxiety.

Reacqaintance

Dear Irene,

It has been years, so many, since we last visited. We used to enjoy each other's company, just to talk and wile away the afternoons. Could we try that again? Let me hear from you.

With fond memories,

Dear Carl,

I thought I'd write just to see how you are doing. We haven't talked or written for close to a year. Since then I've joined a tennis club, and many of them want me to join their dance group. We used to do both, remember?

How about getting together again. I'd like that.

Hopefully,

Respect My Privacy

Dear Karla,

Please Karla, will you wean yourself from your every second- or third-day phone calls. You know I don't want to talk to you anymore; I've made that clear. Hanging up on you has had no effect, and even changing my phone number worked for only a short time.

I admit you are a sincere and attractive woman—but not for me. I don't want to have to take stronger measures, so please free me from your life.

Goodbye,

Dear Winston,

Your annoying attentions are still unwanted. You phone me at work, you write me notes, you find me during my lunch hour, you follow me home. I can't stand this treatment any more.

I have written a letter to the attorney general and will mail it Monday if you haven't left me alone by then.

Mean it,

REPRIMAND

A reprimand should include constructive criticism, and constructive criticism starts with a compliment. Show appreciation for some part of the other person's work that has been good or for some event he or she has participated in. A phrase such as, "We appreciate your willing attitude" or "You have been with us a good many years" lets the person know that he or she is being treated with consideration. The complimentary attitude should not be overdone, however, or the turnabout to a reprimand will seem contradictory.

Make a letter of reprimand short: There is no reason to prolong the agony. Shortness will also prevent a tendency to ramble around the fringes of the subject. Make the fact of a reprimand direct, but in a tactful and considerate way, To keep criticism easy to take, criticize indirectly. Rather than saying, "Don't smoke in the lunchroom," say, "Please smoke outside." Replace, "You are late all the time," with "Please try to be more prompt."

The Eastern concept of saving face is applicable to a letter of criticism. Let the reader keep his or her ego; let the reader know that you too are not without fault—that you are human. A word or two of praise now and then in the letter will let the person retain his or her good image. This leads to a cooperative attitude on the part of both parties. Then, corrective action can be suggested. Tell the reader how errors can be corrected, what action needs to be taken, and how you will help.

Set goals that can be reached, not grand goals of improved self or a happier life ahead, but specific goals, such as only four errors next month, or a chore completed by 4:00 P.M. each day. In a work environment, one person's accomplishing suggested goals can boost the morale of co-workers. In a personal situation, reaching goals makes one feel good. End your reprimand with encouragement.

How to Do It

1. Start with a compliment.

2. Use indirect criticism.

3. Set definite goals for improvement.

4. Offer encouragement.

Outside Activities at Work

Dear George:

Your work record in the past has been excellent, but now it has come to my attention that you have been spending a lot of working hours campaigning for new officers. I haven't been there to observe, but reports have come to me from several sources. Since this interferes with the amount of work you are doing, I would suggest you devote less time to campaigning and more to company work.

Sincerely,

Lack of Cleanliness

Dear Betty,

You have a lot of good friends here. We all like your smile and your cheery greeting in the mornings. There is one area, however, in which we feel there is room for improvement. We would like to suggest a stronger deodorant and perhaps more frequent washing of your blouses. You no doubt have been unaware of this need, but your co-workers would appreciate your considering the problem.

Keep smiling and please hold on to your cheerful ways.

Sincerely,

Bad Behavior

Dear Employees:

We had a minor fender-bender accident in the parking lot yesterday at quitting time between an employee and one of our customers. Our employee disregarded the directional arrows in his rush to leave.

Our customer was astounded that so many employees were dashing out against the arrows. He was more than unhappy, and threatened to take his business elsewhere.

Not only because of loss of business, but also for your own physical safety, DIRECTIONAL ARROWS IN THE PARKING LOT MUST BE OBEYED. If you cannot correct this type of behavior, strong measures will be taken to ensure that you do.

Safety requires not only care, but also courtesy and consideration for others.

Sincerely,

College Washout

Dear Son,

Let me commend you on your decision to attend college to better equip yourself for the career in retailing you have started and enjoy.

However, going away to college or the work of studying or the influence of your friends or your old habit of trying to drift through school have all caught up with and passed you.

You won't show me your grades, and I had great difficulty getting them from the college. They intend to refuse you enrollment next year, and I will no longer pay for any more of your schooling. Sorry, Son, but that's the way it is.

I might suggest a trade school that teaches a specific vocation. That type of learning would probably suit you better. Call this tough love, but . . .

With love,

Travel Expense

Dear Ms. Rundell:

The executive committee has reviewed your travel-expense account for the past year. Your overall expenses seem reasonable, and although we have not established a budget for each salesperson, we plan to have one developed for use next year.

One facet of your travel strikes us as probably uneconomical. You appear to be covering the western states in a disorganized way. For example, in May you made calls in cities in this order: Portland, San Francisco, Oakland, San Diego, Los Angeles, Boise, Denver, Portland, Seattle, Salt Lake City, Sacramento, and Oakland.

Looking at a map of the western states, this schedule involves a lot of skipping and backtracking. The committee believes that money and travel time could be saved if you traveled in a roughly circular route to prevent backtracking. Is this thought correct, or is there a good reason for not following a more direct route from city to city?

Please let me have your comments on this by April 30.

Regards,

Lack of Cooperation

Dear Mr. Bell:

Reports on the attractiveness of your displays in our midwestern stores and favorable comments by customers indicate you are doing an excellent job of displaying our merchandise.

These reports come to me from our department buyers who also bring up a situation that needs correcting. They report that you often appear on the selling floor during busy periods and request too much help from the salespeople. There is no reason why you should need help from the sales staff. Disruptions in the sales area could be minimized by organizing all your materials and tools in the work areas before bringing anything onto the selling floor. This will also lessen your time on the floor. You should be able to schedule your work on the sales floor so that most of it is done before customers arrive and after the store is closed.

Please give this some thought and let me know by March 20 your plans for closer cooperation with the department buyers. I know they tend to be difficult at times—but they do have a point.

Sincerely,

Unsafe Conditions

Dear Ms. Benjay:

I commend you for never having had a fire, but the January 31 report from our fire insurance company states that the fire insurance on the Belson plant will increase 30 percent next year. The reason stated is unsafe conditions, supported by two citations from the fire marshall for the *same* violation within four months.

This is poor management. You are risking the lives of the Belson employees.

By February 27, I want to have on my desk a compliance certification from the Belson County Fire Inspector.

Regards,

Trespassing

Dear Al:

A situation has recently come to my attention that must be corrected. Evidently some employees' families and friends are coming in to the plant, particularly on the second and third shifts.

As you know, this is strictly against company policy, because of the liability we could incur if someone were hurt. Any tours of the plant must be arranged through the Human Relations Department.

Effective immediately, please take whatever steps are necessary to secure the manufacturing area from unauthorized persons.

Sincerely,

Bullying Child

Dear Mrs. Yeates,

Your Betty is a strong, healthy child, but sometimes she takes undue advantage of those attributes. She and my Cheryl walk home from school together because they are in the same grade. But Betty is much larger and stronger, and she uses those advantages to beat on Cheryl, knock her down, and even rip the buttons off her coats.

We found the buttons along the street last week, and I sewed them back on, but this is far from proper behavior for your daughter.

I will no longer let Cheryl play with Betty, and if Betty's behavior continues at school, I will notify the principal and follow up on her recommendations to correct Betty's physical abuse of Cheryl.

Sincerely,

Child's Coach

Dear Ms. Yua,

My wife and I have encouraged our daughter, Carol, to become involved in elementary-school sports, both in and out of the school curriculum. Your Thursday afternoon Hitters softball team seemed ideal for her.

We have attended all your games and saw Carol at bat only once. She struck out and didn't seem to have much control of the bat.

Why, as coach of preteen girls, do you not show them how to hit and run and catch? Obviously you are interested *only* in winning games. The players who already know how to do these things do all the playing while those wishing to learn, learn nothing. All children need encouragement and training (coaching?).

Sincerely,

Dear Mrs. Neihardt,

Our son, Peter, is a member of our homeowners association's junior-high-school swim team. I participate as a timing judge. Peter attends all practice sessions and works on his own at other times. This part is going well.

The problem is at the swim meets. Every member of this youth swim team should be allowed to swim at the meets, primarily to build character and self-confidence.

One meet was nearly over when my wife asked you why Peter had not been in any of the races. You said, "Oh." Peter was later placed in a backstroke race, a stroke for which he had not trained. Is this a lack of organization or a matter of placing winning above character building?

Sincerely,

Presenting Gifts

The purpose of sending a letter with a gift is to indicate that the giver is really a part of the gift; it is a way of giving oneself. Use individuality of expression as much as possible because it will put your own personality into the message. The letter should be short and friendly and reveal pleasure in the giving.

How to Do It

1. Mention the occasion for the gift.
2. Express pleasure in the giving.

Companionship

Dear Kathy,

This gift is only a token of how much your friendly companionship this summer has meant to me.

There will always be love in my thoughts of you.

With affection,

Friendship

Dear Don,

This gift is just a small thank-you for the friendship you showed me this summer.

I will always think of you as a kind friend who took a real interest in both my work and play.

Sincerely,

Advice

Dear David:

I am sending you a Chinese puzzle. It is a small thank-you for the consultation and advice you offered Tuesday. I felt much better about approaching the problem after discussing it with you. Your interest is appreciated.

Sincerely,

Funeral Officiating

Dear Reverend Thomas:

Please accept the enclosed check for conducting the funeral service for my father. We deeply appreciate the extra time and effort you devoted to making this a memorable service.

Sincerely,

Baptismal Officiating

Dear Reverend Thomas:

Thank you for the beautiful baptismal service for our daughter, Becky. Please accept the enclosed check as a personal gift for the thought and work you put into making the service so beautiful and meaningful.

Sincerely,

Hospital Patient

Dear Jo Ann,

Please accept this robe as a gift to someone special. I am sure that you will find use for the robe now that you are doing a little walking each day. I hope it buoys up your spirits enough for you to leave the hospital soon.

Sincerely,

Dear Joe,

Here is a book from your old friend Jack Hoskins. It should help to wile away the long daytime hours as you recuperate in the hospital. I'll drop by to see you next time I'm in town, and I hope that by then you will be home. If not, I'll stop by the hospital.

Regards,

Eightieth Birthday

Dear Mr. Winslow,

For your eightieth birthday, the bunch at the Neighborhood Center thought we would give you a reason to relax a little—about time.

The reclining chair you will receive this Thursday is a gift to show our appreciation for all the little things you do at the Center to make life more pleasant for your many friends.

Please enjoy the chair for many years to come.

Your friends,

Illness

Dear Ron,

Your friends at Elton Corporation are sorry to learn of your wife's serious illness. Please accept the flowers we have sent as sincere wishes that she will have a fast and complete recovery.

Sincerely,

Dear Amy:

Please accept this book from the office group. We hope it is not too exciting while you are recovering from your operation. If the book is too exciting, it is good enough to keep until your stitches heal over.

Sincerely,

Retirement

Dear Doug:

The company, we are sure, will present you with a watch upon your retirement. If you are going to watch the time go by, we thought you might appreciate a place to relax while doing so. That is why we in the Production Department are sending to your home a high-back reclining chair. Lean back and enjoy your retirement in comfort.

We have all benefited from working with you, and your presence will be sorely missed.

Congratulations,

ACCEPTING GIFTS

Accepting a gift graciously can be disquieting at times. The receiver may feel an obligation to reply while being unable to think of an appropriate expression of thanks for a gift that is really not wanted.

In spite of this seeming difficulty, one can write an appropriate gift-acceptance letter by starting with a statement of what the thank-you is for:

We wish to thank you for the book . . .

Your box of goodies arrived yesterday . . .

Your recent contribution of $ . . .

The watercolor chosen by you for my office arrived today.

After the opening statement, make some comment about the gift; try to do a little better than merely saying, "It is just what I always wanted." Try to be original with a few words about the gift's desirability, beauty, usefulness, appropriateness, or some distinctive phase of the gift. For example:

The refrigerator you gave us has upgraded the cooler department to the point where I may have to trade in the boat for a larger one.

Your care in selecting a gift that coordinates so well with my office decor serves to further increase my enthusiasm.

Your gift of the finely crafted glass unicorn, so fragile in appearance yet strongly made, is distinctive.

We shall treasure the gift for its beauty and craftsmanship, but even more as a constant reminder of your friendship.

The gift-acceptance letter should express gratitude and pleasant expectancy in a courteous and tactful way.

How to Do It

1. Mention the gift received.
2. Make an original comment about the usefulness, desirability, beauty, or other distinctive phase of the gift.

Chess Set

Dear Mr. Danforth,

Your gift was waiting for us when we returned home. It reminded us of your gracious and pleasant hospitality.

We shall treasure the chess set for its beauty and craftsmanship, but even more as a constant reminder of your friendship.

Sincerely,

Food Snacks

Dear Len:

Your letter and box of goodies arrived yesterday, and I have to return the thanks. It was nice of you to send along the snacks and everyone here at Albany will partake of the treats.

We are glad you enjoyed the golf game with Brenner; he is a very personable young man.

Since I know you will forgive the photography, I am enclosing some photographs of you, Brenner, and the gang that played golf together.

Please let me know if you have a day while in San Francisco, and maybe you and I can play golf at the Olympic Course.

Sincerely,

Book

Dear Ms. Vaughn,

The arrival of your gift was a pleasant beginning for my day, especially since the book was so unexpected. I admire greatly the works of Victorian authors but have never anticipated actually owning a signed first edition.

The volume will remain among my treasured displays to bring me pleasure and to remind me of your consideration.

Sincerely,

Money

Dear Mr. Dodson:

Your recent contribution of $12,000 to the fund for aid to battered wives was a long-needed boost to our program. The money will be put to use in providing temporary shelter and protection to abused wives and their children and in generating further contributions.

Your gift is an affirmation of the kindness and humanity that still exists in this world.

Sincerely,

Dear Mr. Gough:

Your gift to the battered wives' fund is a real start for us. A few months ago, none of us knew whether the project could even get off the ground, let alone survive all the red tape and expense.

Now, thanks to you, things will begin moving. We can do a lot with $25,000 to make people aware of the problem and to set up facilities.

Once the program has a real home, don't be surprised if we name it after you. Many women are in your debt.

A big thank you from them—and from me.

Sincerely,

Oil Painting

Dear Mr. Cowden:

While admiring your fine work last Wednesday, I never anticipated actually owning an original oil painting for my personal collection. You have an eye for color and proportion, and the work fits in beautifully with the decor of my office.

Stop by the office and see just how good a choice you made.

You can expect that whoever enters the office will notice the work and leave familiar with your name.

Thank you for your kindness.

Sincerely,

Watercolor Painting

Dear Ms. Meadows:

The watercolor that you chose for my office arrived today. The quality of your work, of which the gift is an excellent example, has long been familiar to me.

Your care in selecting the gift, which coordinates so well with my personal work surroundings, serves to further increase my enthusiasm.

Thank you once again.

Sincerely,

Art Object

Dear Mrs. Skeen:

Although Annie is still too weak to thank you herself, I wanted you to know immediately how much your concern and your generous gift is appreciated.

Seriously ill children often receive many gifts from kind yet impersonal well-wishers. Your gift of the finely crafted glass unicorn, so fragile in appearance yet strongly made, was different. The care and love that you took in selecting the gift for Annie are visible, just as your concern for her well-being can be felt. It may be only our imagination, but we can see her gain strength daily as she gazes upon the tiny creature, knowing that many people love her.

Thank you for caring.

Sincerely,

Free Product

Dear Mr. Bauer:

The shipment of cartons with a "No Charge" invoice and your best wishes arrived today. Rarely does one business provide anything, even merchandise that it doesn't need, to another fledgling company free of charge.

Your effort and the merchandise are both greatly appreciated.

Sincerely,

Cooler

Dear Don:

The food cooler for our boat arrived here in Sausalito yesterday, and I can't thank you enough for the wonderful gift. You have actually upgraded the cooler department to the point where I may have to trade the boat for something larger and more appropriate.

We are glad you enjoyed your day with us and hope you will return to San Francisco for some more sailing. Should Betty and I get to New Orleans, we will take you up on your offer to do some lake sailing.

Sincerely,

DECLINING GIFTS

Declining a gift is a delicate task, but at times a refusal may be necessary. Company policy may forbid gifts that could be valued at more than a very few dollars; a gift from a near stranger may be expensive; a gift may be a duplicate and of no use to you, but of value to the giver; you may feel your position could be compromised; or public opinion may be opposed to your accepting gifts.

Whether accepted or declined, a gift should always be acknowledged. However much you dislike the gift or the giver, never criticize either. You received the gift because of a kind thought, and there is no reason to indirectly criticize the thought by directly criticizing either the gift or the giver.

Make the letter brief to avoid drawing out the disappointment of a refusal.

How to Do It

1. Agree on some points with the giver, or apologize, or offer thanks for the thought.
2. State the refusal.
3. Offer an explanation.

Company Policy

Dear Ms. Sylvan:

I am sorry I cannot accept the case of champagne you sent me. Although the thought is gratefully accepted, company policy prevents me from accepting a gift of this value.

The gift has been returned, but not my appreciation of your thoughtfulness.

Sincerely,

Dear Ms. Carrell:

The company appreciates your offer to provide free service and supplies for the copying equipment in return for an agreement to deal exclusively with Aabco.

Regrettably, the offer must be refused. Our long-standing policy is that no one company may be dealt with on an exclusive basis. While the reputation of Aabco and the quality of your product are well known, company policy must be followed.

Sincerely,

Must Maintain Image

Dear Mr. Tso:

Your recent gift of appreciation as a result of the court decision last Tuesday was a kind gesture.

However, I must decline your offer, although I know it was well meant.

As a civil-court judge, I take great pains to maintain my image of impartiality. Acceptance of gifts in this manner could compromise that image. Nonetheless, your kindness is appreciated.

Sincerely,

Duplicate Gift

Dear Grandpa:

Thank you for so thoughtful a gift. You are right. Every writer should have a computer of such quality.

I am sorry that I must return the computer, because, you see, Mom and Dad have the identical belief and good taste, and they bought a similar computer for my last birthday. Once again, thank you so much for caring.

Love,

Gift Too Valuable

Dear Mr. Ault:

Once again you show that your taste in gifts is impeccable. Thank you so much for the lovely, and valuable, antique silver vase.

I regret that I must return it; a sincere regret because of its great beauty.

It is unfortunate but my frequent business trips make my home vulnerable, and several area homes have recently suffered burglaries. Although insurance would provide financial reimbursement, the irreplaceable nature of the vase would leave me forever guilty. Please allow me to return it.

Sincerely,

Expensive Gift

Dear Mrs. Byers:

The painting you sent is well suited to the decor and mood of the office.

I regret, however, that it must be returned.

It is my policy not to accept expensive gifts from clients, and an original painting by Picasso certainly fits the category of "expensive."

Sincerely,

TRIBUTE

Tribute to a Wife

Dear Pastor Jim,

You knew Peggy only during the time she was fighting for her life against cancer. Let me fill you in on our fifty-one years of marriage: 1949-1999.

We were married during the year following WWII. Only her careful management of my meager salary kept us going. I quit smoking even though my two packs a day cost only a quarter. We both made sacrifices.

Our three sons, born in 1952, 1955, and 1959, are all responsible, successful men because they were taught to be polite and respectful by their mother. I like to think I helped a little.

Peggy was known as "Mrs. Presbyterian" in our church in Dearborn, Michigan. She was a dedicated choir member for thirty years, taught Sunday School, held almost every church office, and took part in all aspects of church life.

Our move to Sun City West, Arizona, didn't stop her activities. Of course choir was first; she was one of the first Elders and helped organize the women s association.

Even with all the problems we had after moving here: the loss of everything we owned in a moving-van fire, her first bout with cancer and surgery, her two broken elbows—at the same time—and the recurrence of cancer in spite of chemotherapy and radiation, Peggy was as cheerful and gracious as she could be. She was a wonderful manager, mother, and mate and she was loved by all who knew her. I was fortunate to have been a part of her life and love.

We all miss her.

Kindest regards to you and Betty,

Tribute to a Husband

Dear Joanne,

I am writing early this year. This note is going to a very divergent group of Al's and my friends. Some of you already know and to others it will be "news"— of a sort.

Al died July 31st in Quito, Ecuador, at age 75. He was on his way to the Galapagos Islands on a nature safari with a small group of 14. He never got to his goal, to which he had aimed for many years, but he was doing what he loved—traveling. And, most important, he died without a long, lingering illness, which had been a real worry to him for several years. I am most thankful for that. It was a heart attack, and I am convinced that the over-9,000-foot elevation at Quito was his undoing. I had a memorial service, and his ashes were scattered at sea outside the Golden Gate Bridge. (His many years in the Navy prompted that.)

The write-ups in the two San Francisco papers were well done, I thought. I am very proud of Al's many accomplishments in a broad spectrum of local, state, national, and international organizations and endeavors. He was still in practice after 42 years, and not too many doctors can say they have delivered more than 12,000 babies in their careers!

The past two months have been and continue to be hectic. Those who "have traveled this path" know only too well what I mean. But the outpouring of love and concern from hundreds of friends, and especially patients, has been most heartwarming to me.

To those dear friends of Al's I wish a happy holiday season, its many blessings and good health. To my special friends I can only wish the same, and to all our mutual friends—"God bless us everyone."

Please keep in touch. I truly value the memories of all our past contacts and the friendships that ensued and have endured even though we may not have seen each other often or for many years.

My best wishes and love,

(With permission from Eleanor E. Long, wife of Dr. Albert E. Long, San Francisco.)

TESTIMONIALS

A testimonial is (or should be) authoritative. A basketball professional may endorse basketball shoes, a housewife may praise a vacuum cleaner, but probably neither is an authority on English grammar. For that you want a professor of English or a recognized professional writer.

Many testimonials state how *good* something is, such as, "This book is a page turner," or "Zig Zag is the best cold cereal." This is fine, but a better testimonial tells how the letter writer has benefited from the item mentioned.

The following examples of the "heart" or essence of testimonials illustrate this point. The letter can begin with a thank-you or show of appreciation for having been asked to present your opinion. Your professional position, occupation, or personal status as an expert should be stated. For example:

> I am happy to confirm that Bouncer basketball shoes are the best ever made. All basketball players, whether in elementary school or in the National Basketball Association (NBA) in which I have played professionally for eleven years, should wear Bouncer shoes. They are soft, comfortable and have a helpful spring that other shoes lack. Bouncer shoes truly improved my playing.

Letter Book

- The range of topics is exceptional, and I have used many of the letters in my business correspondence. I wish I had found this book sooner.
- I find the book especially helpful as a teaching tool in my business communication courses.

Vacuum Cleaner

- My Benson vacuum cleaner with its efficient micro filtration system cleans the rugs better than any I have used before, and it keeps the dust and pollen out of the air.
- The self-propelled Barger vacuum makes rug cleaning easier than ever before.

Automobile

- My long-time auto mechanic is disappointed because my Smoother auto requires so little maintenance. He says his next car will be a Smoother.

- My Smoother auto is the easiest handling and best riding car I ever owned. My wife loves it.

Tires

- Seventy thousand miles on one set of Ellison tires may seem impossible, but I have the mileage and dealer records to prove it.

Blender

- The word *dependability* is defined by my Workall blender. I have used it daily for thirty-two years.
- The 10-speed Olsen blender with its 48-oz. jar and food-processor attachment does most of my food preparation chores.

Index